INTERMEDIATE RUSSIAN

INTERMEDIATE RUSSIAN GRAMMAR

William Harrison and **Stephen le Fleming**

UNIVERSITY OF WALES PRESS
CARDIFF
2000

British Library Cataloguing-in-Publication Data.
A catalogue record for this book is available from the British Library.

ISBN 0–7083–1576–3 (paperback)
0–7083–1577–1 (hardback)

Typeset at University of Wales Press
Printed in Great Britain by Gwasg Dinefwr, Llandybïe

CONTENTS

PREFACE

This grammar takes you through the second stage of Russian. It builds on what you learnt during your A-level course or in your ab initio year and aims to take you through to undergraduate finals. It revises and consolidates some of the things you were introduced to on those courses and extends your range into some new areas. Since courses vary we cannot identify precisely which parts will be completely new to you, but there will be some, while others look like old friends, albeit with a few new twists.

Grammar is vital for anyone learning Russian after early childhood and wishing to progress towards proficiency rather than a few set phrases or the simplified Russian of GCSE: the grammar systematizes the large number of endings employed in this highly inflected language, and without mastering this system a serious student will find the language virtually impenetrable.

The first ten sections are primarily for reference − for checking up on the endings of the declensions and conjugations and their sub-divisions. Others are more concerned with usage and are intended to develop your ability to say or write things in Russian with the degree of accuracy required at university level and beyond. We have included examples from a broad range of sources from nineteenth-century literature to contemporary media, corresponding to those that you may expect to encounter.

Translations are provided for the examples, but use of a dictionary is recommended to get the full benefit of the exercises; looking up words in a dictionary is in itself a grammar exercise since the form encountered in a context is rarely the form under which the word is listed in the dictionary.

There may be some imbalance in the treatment of individual topics. We aim to concentrate on those topics which have caused problems for students. The final section is specifically designed to clarify what we have found students need at this stage. In this sense we have adopted a 'practical', rather than an idealistic, approach to what should be included. We have not aimed to provide a complete, comprehensive compilation of all the exceptions and irregularities that lurk in obscure corners of the language − only those that you have a fair chance of encountering.

ACKNOWLEDGEMENTS

We would like to record our thanks to many students and to colleagues who have assisted us in conceiving and defining the scope of this book. In particular we would wish to mention the assistance of Russian teachers who have had temporary appointments in our department in checking different sections of the typescript: Elena Osetrova of Krasnoyarsk State University, Galina Asafova and Galina Bukharova of Ulyanovsk State Technical University, Natalya Rozhnovskaya of the St Petersburg Railway Engineering University and Svetlana le Fleming of the University of Northumbria at Newcastle. For the 'Pearls of Popular Wisdom' used to illustrate some grammatical points we are indebted to *Russkie poslovitsy i pogovorki*, edited by V. K. Sokolov (Nauka: Moscow, 1969), *Russkie poslovitsy i pogovorki*, edited by V. P. Anikin (Khudozhestvennaya literatura: Moscow, 1988) and the late Mrs Serafima Turkina of Novosibirsk.

Some further recommended reading:

Larissa Ryazanova-Clarke and Terence Wade, *The Russian Language Today*. Routledge: London, 1999.

Derek Offord, *Modern Russian: An Advanced Grammar Course*. Bristol Classical Press, Duckworth: London, 1993.

Derek Offord, *Using Russian: A Guide to Contemporary Usage*. Cambridge University Press: Cambridge, 1996.

V.V. Vingradov et al., *Грамматика русского языка*. АН СССР: Moscow, 1960.

Terence Wade, *Comprehensive Russian Grammar*. Blackwell: Oxford, 1992.

Terence Wade, *Prepositions in Modern Russian*. Durham Modern Language Series: Durham, 1983.

BASIC GRAMMATICAL TERMINOLOGY

A word designating a phenomenon – a *thing, person, feeling, idea*, etc., is a NOUN.

If the phenomenon is tangible – an *object, person, place*, etc., – it is a **concrete noun**.

If the phenomenon is intangible – a *feeling, idea, process*, etc., – it is an **abstract noun**.

If the phenomenon is an animal, or a human being – an *elephant, bug, doctor, Anna*, etc., – it is an **animate noun**.

If the phenomenon is a particular person or place – *George, Nizhny Novgorod*, etc., – it is a **proper name**.

Words which refer to nouns without naming the phenomenon – *it, they, who, everything, someone*, etc., – are PRONOUNS.

Words which describe actions – *to hope*, he *is eating*, we *found* the dog, they *will be arrested*, etc., – are VERBS.

The **noun** or **pronoun** defining who or what is performing the action is called the SUBJECT of the **verb** – *he* is eating, *the student* was hoping, *cars* will be designed, etc.

The **noun** or **pronoun** defining whom or what the action is performed on is called the OBJECT of the **verb** – we found *the dog*, I'm reading *the paper*, airlines lose *money*.

Verbs which cannot take an **object** – *to fall, to appear, to sleep*, etc., – are called INTRANSITIVE VERBS. **Verbs** which describe an action affecting a phenomenon directly take a **direct object** and are called TRANSITIVE VERBS – *to find, to design, to break*, etc. Some may take a secondary or **indirect object** – to send *her* a letter (i.e. to her), I consider him *a genius* (i.e. as a genius). **Transitive verbs** may be used **intransitively**, without an **object**

– we were *painting*, the children *are eating*. The **verb** 'to be' takes not an object but a COMPLEMENT – her father is *a vet*.

Subject, verb and **object** comprise the main elements of a SENTENCE; a complete **sentence** must contain a **subject** and a **verb**. Everything in a **sentence** other than the **subject** is known collectively as the PREDICATE – I *like plums*; *after the concert* most of the players *stayed in the theatre to talk to the composer*.

Words giving the position, direction, or purpose of a **noun** or **pronoun** in space or time – *in, towards, for, until* – are called PREPOSITIONS.

Some languages, including Russian, alter the form – particularly the endings – of their words depending on which element of the **sentence** they represent; for this reason Russian is called an **inflected** language. The way in which individual words change according to their grammatical role is called MORPHOLOGY; **nouns** and **pronouns** DECLINE, **verbs** CONJUGATE.

The structure of a **sentence**, the grammatical relationship of its elements to one another is called its SYNTAX.

The **declension** of **nouns** in Russian depends on their GENDER, which is sometimes dependent on the sex of the person or animal referred to, but which often seems arbitrary – *дом* 'house' is MASCULINE, *кóмната* 'room' is FEMININE, *окнó* 'window' is NEUTER; *волк* 'wolf' (***masc.***), *лисá* 'fox' (***fem.***). The **declension** system comprises six CASES corresponding to the **syntactic** role of the word in the **sentence**, in both SINGULAR and PLURAL NUMBERS.

The six **cases** are:

NOMINATIVE, used for the **subject** of the verb – *рекá* течёт '*the river* flows', *дéти* играли '*the children* were playing.'
ACCUSATIVE, used for the **direct object** of the verb - он любит *мýзыку* 'he loves *music*', она учила *детéй* 'she was teaching *the children*' - and after certain **prepositions** – он éдет в *гóрод* на *недéлю* 'he's going to *town* for a *week*.'
GENITIVE, used to express possession – машина *отцá* '*father's* car', конéц *книги* 'the end *of the book*' – and after certain **prepositions** – из *гостиницы* 'out of *the hotel*.' It is also used in certain negative constructions – нет *мáсла* 'there's no *butter*', я не люблю *сыра* 'I don't like *cheese*' and after certain verbs (see pp. 185–6).
DATIVE, used to express the **indirect object** to or for whom something is done – мы послáли *емý* книгу 'we sent *him* the book', он готовит *женé* сюрприз 'he's preparing a surprise *for his wife*' – and after certain **prepositions** – идите к *окнý*! 'walk towards *the window*' – and after certain **verbs** (see pp. 188–91).

INSTRUMENTAL, used to express by whom or with what an action is performed – книга, напи́санная *жено́й* 'the book written *by his wife*', он уда́рил де́рево *топоро́м* 'he struck the tree *with an axe*' – and after certain **prepositions** – я е́ду с *бра́том* 'I'm going with *my brother*', они лежа́ли под *столо́м* 'they were lying under *the table*' – and after certain **verbs** (see pp. 193–6).

PREPOSITIONAL, used only after certain **prepositions** – она́ сиди́т в *библиоте́ке* 'she's sitting in the *library*', я ду́маю о *нём* 'I'm thinking about *him*.'

Cases other than the **nominative** are called OBLIQUE **cases**.

A word describing a **noun** – *fast* car, *interesting* story – is an ADJECTIVE. **Adjectives** in Russian **decline**, agreeing with the **noun** they describe in **case, number** and, in the singular, **gender** – *но́вые* студе́нты сидя́т в *ста́рой* библиоте́ке 'the *new* students are sitting in the *old* library'; the **plural declension** is common to all three **genders**.

A word describing the action of a **verb** – они *ско́ро* забы́ли 'they *soon* forgot', иди́ *осторо́жно* 'walk *carefully*' – is an ADVERB. **Adverbs** are usually formed from **adjectives**, but do not themselves decline. (Both **adjectives** and **adverbs** are sometimes known as 'qualifiers' or 'epithets'.)

The INFINITIVE of a **verb** is the basic form under which it is listed in dictionaries; this form does not **conjugate** or **decline** though it can be used like a **noun** as the **subject** or **object** of a **verb** – я люблю́ *слу́шать* его́ 'I love *to listen* to him', *поня́ть* зна́чит *проща́ть* '*to understand* means *to forgive*.'

The **conjugation** of a **verb** means the sytem of endings relating it to the **subject** by **number** (**singular** or **plural**) and by PERSON (FIRST, SECOND or THIRD): so that there are distinct endings for the **first person** I, **second person** you (informal or affectionate) and **third person singular** he, she, it or any **singular noun** or **pronoun** except I or you; there are also distinct endings for the **first person** we, **second person** you (formal or plural) and **third person plural** they or any **plural noun** or **pronoun** except we or you.

first person singular	я *ду́маю* 'I think, am thinking'
second person singular	ты *ду́маешь* 'you think, are thinking'
third person singular	он *ду́мает* 'he thinks, is thinking'
or, with a **noun** as subject,	врач *ду́мает* 'the doctor thinks, is thinking'
first person plural	мы *ду́маем* 'we think, are thinking'
second person plural	вы *ду́маете* 'you think, are thinking'
third person plural	они *ду́мают* 'they think, are thinking'
or, with a **noun** as subject	врачи́ *ду́мают* 'the doctors think . . .'

There are some differences between **first** and **second conjugations**.

The **conjugation** system also distinguishes actions by TENSE, i.e. by the time when an action takes place: PRESENT I *think*, I *am thinking*, PAST I *thought*, *was thinking*, etc. and FUTURE I *shall think*, I *shall be thinking*.

Only in the **present** and **future** are there endings for the **first**, **second** and **third persons**. In the **past tense** the ending corresponds to the **gender** of the subject in the **singular** with a **plural** ending for all three **genders**; from стоя́ть 'to stand' the **past tense** is:

masc.	я, ты, он, врач *стоя́л*	'I, you, he, the doctor stood'
fem.	я, ты, она́, жена́ *стоя́ла*	'I, you, she, the wife stood'
neut.	оно́, зда́ние *стоя́ло*	'it, the building stood'
plur.(all **genders**)	мы, вы, они́, де́ти *стоя́ли*	'we, you, they, the children stood.'

As well as **tenses** nearly all Russian **verbs** have two ASPECTS, distinguishing actions which are IMPERFECTIVE, i.e. thought of as general, continuous or regularly repeated, from those which are PERFECTIVE, i.e. thought of as completed.   An **imperfective verb** may form a **present, past** and **future tense**; a **perfective verb** may form a **past** and a **future tense**. The **aspects** cannot be equated with the **tenses** of English.

Verbs which express an action which the **subject** performs – она́ *поёт* 'she *sings*', они́ *надéялись* 'they *were hoping*', э́то *бýдет рабóтать* 'this *will work*' – are called ACTIVE **verbs**. Those which express an action which is performed on the **subject** – мы *поражены́* 'we *are amazed*', э́то *бы́ло разрабóтано* 'it *was developed*', собáка *бýдет нáйдена* 'the dog *will be found*' – are called PASSIVE **verbs**.

The **passive** voice may only be formed from **transitive verbs**. Russian and English do not always express the **passive** in the same way: for **sentences** like 'the book *is being read*' Russian is able to use the REFLEXIVE form – кни́га *читáется* – or the **third person plural** of the **active verb** without a subject – кни́гу *читáют* '(they) are reading the book.'

Reflexive verbs are not necessarily **passive** in meaning; often they represent **intransitive** forms of **transitive verbs** – мы начинáем игрý 'we are starting the game'; игрá *начинáется* 'the game *is starting.*'

Verbs have three MOODS which convey attitude. The INDICATIVE **mood** expresses a straightforward statement or question about an action as a fact that has happened, is happening or will happen – мы *откры́ли* письмó 'we *opened* the letter'; онá *лю́бит* егó? '*does* she *love* him?' This is the normal, everyday **mood** of the **verb**, and you may assume that unless otherwise stated the **verb** is **indicative**. The IMPERATIVE **mood** expresses the speakers' order or instruction – *откройте* дверь! '*open* the door'. The SUBJUNCTIVE **mood** expresses an action as something desired, advised, proposed or hypothesized – я хочу, чтобы он *решил* 'I wish he *would decide*'; он предложил, чтобы они *читали* газету 'he suggested that they *should read* the paper.' The **subjunctive** which is formed by the **past tense** + the particle бы also conveys the CONDITIONAL – она *сделала бы* это 'she *would have done* this'.

Other parts of speech may be formed from **verbs**; these are covered in other chapters: PARTICIPLES which define **nouns** in terms of an action performed by them, in which case the **participle** is **active** – человек, *читающий* газету 'the man *reading* the paper', поезд, *опоздавший* на час 'the train *which was* an hour *late*' – or in terms of an action performed on them, in which case the **participle** is **passive** – здание, *охраняемое* государством 'a building (*being*) *preserved* by the state', картина, *выставленная* в Петербурге 'a picture *exhibited* in Petersburg'. Like **adjectives**, **participles** decline, agreeing with the **noun** they refer to in **gender**, **number** and **case**; and GERUNDS which in Russian describe the action of the **verb** in terms of another action – он говорит, не *переставая* 'he talks without *stopping*', *открыв* окно, она заметила Бориса '*having opened* the window she noticed Boris'. Like **adverbs**, **gerunds** do not **decline**.

A word joining two **sentences** – *and, but, if, until, etc.,* – is a CONJUNCTION; the two or more parts containing a **verb** are called CLAUSES. If there are two or more **clauses** in a **sentence** it becomes a COMPOUND **sentence**. The MAIN CLAUSE of a **compound sentence** is the **clause** which contains the basic, essential fact to be communicated – *I'll come* if you ask me, *I don't know* whose dog it is, *that's the man* with whom she used to work. The **verb** in the **main clause** is called the MAIN **verb**.

When one **clause** merely qualifies the other – I'll come *if you ask me*, I don't know *whose dog it is*, that's the man *with whom she used to work* – it is called a SUBORDINATE **clause**.

INTERROGATIVE **sentences** are questions which may be introduced by an **interrogative pronoun** – *who, what, which* – or by an **interrogative adverb** – *how, when, where*. These **interrogative pronouns** and **adverbs** may introduce **subordinate clauses** known as INDIRECT QUESTIONS – I asked *who she was*, the pilot didn't know *where we were*, they tried to discover *whether it was time to go*. 'If' meaning 'whether' also introduces **indirect questions**.

CONDITIONAL **clauses** are **subordinate clauses** introduced by *if* specifying the conditions under which the action of the **main verb** takes place – *I'll come if you ask me.*

The **pronouns** *who* and *which* are also used to introduce RELATIVE **clauses** – *the tree which used to stand there*, I don't know *the man to whom she is talking.*

ABBREVIATIONS

masc.	masculine
fem.	feminine
neut.	neuter
sing.	singular
plur.	plural
nom.	nominative
acc.	accusative
gen.	genitive
dat.	dative
inst.	instrumental
pr.	prepositional
impf.	imperfective
pf.	perfective

RULES OF SPELLING

For historical reasons which may contradict modern pronunciation certain combinations of consonant + vowel are not possible in Russian spelling. These may be summarized thus:

1 after the chuintantes or 'hush'-type consonants ж, ч, ш and щ and the velar consonants г, к, and х the vowels а, и and у are written, (never я, ы or ю); after ц – а and у, (never я or ю);
2 after the chuintantes ж, ч, ш, and щ and the consonant ц, о is possible only if stressed; unstressed it is replaced by е.

Exceptions occasionally occur in words of foreign origin, e.g. парашю́т 'parachute'.

'HARD' AND 'SOFT'

Most consonants in Russian may be either 'hard' or 'soft'. By 'soft' we mean palatalized, articulated with a trace of the sound of 'y' in 'yes' by pressing the tongue against the roof of the mouth – the palate. Which vowel follows depends on the 'hardness' or 'softness' of the consonant, but since the letters for the hard and soft consonants are the same only the vowels show which is which. However, the distinction is crucial in Russian.

As well as words being distinguished from one another only by the hardness or softness of a single consonant, there is a hard and a soft version of virtually all the declension systems of nouns and adjectives in Russian.

In declensions 'hard' endings are based on vowels produced at the back or in the centre of the mouth – а, о, у, ы; 'soft' endings are based on the corresponding vowels beginning with the 'y' sound – я, е, ё, ю or the front vowel и; е occurs in endings of both 'hard' and 'soft' declensions.

Nouns ending in the soft sign ь and those ending in -я, -й or -е have 'soft' declensions, with the front vowels е and и corresponding to о and ы in the hard declension, and я and ю to а and у.

A neat division of all declensions into hard and soft is frustrated by the rules of spelling which result in several apparently 'mixed' declensions. So the nominative plural of оте́ц is отцы́, but of това́рищ is това́рищи – see, for example, the declension tables on p. 12.

In fact the phonetics are rather more consistent than the spelling because и is pronounced ы after the invariably hard ж, ц and ш, while а and у are pronounced я and ю after the invariably soft ч and щ.

1 DECLENSION OF THE NOUN

GENDER

Noun declensions vary in the first instance by gender; the gender of a noun and hence what endings it takes in the course of its declension are determined by the ending of its nominative case. Generally speaking nouns ending in a consonant or -й are masculine, those ending in -a or -я are feminine, and those ending in -o or -e are neuter. Some nouns ending in a soft sign ь are masculine and some feminine.

Declensions also vary, as indicated above, according to the 'hardness' or 'softness' of their endings, with 'mixed' declensions resulting from the rules of spelling.

A third criterion for choosing the model declensions tabulated below is their stress patterns; some declensions have stable stress throughout, but a significant number have stress which is mobile from singular to plural and even within each. There are no simple rules to help with these, so they are best learnt by ear.

MASCULINE NOUNS

1.1 Regular masculine hard declension

1.1.1	animate*		inanimate	
sing.	'engineer'	'ambassador'	'bus'	'wind'
nom.	инженéр	посóл	автóбус	вéтер
acc.	инженéра	послá	автóбус	вéтер
gen.	инженéра	послá	автóбуса	вéтра
dat.	инженéру	послý	автóбусу	вéтру
inst.	инженéром	послóм	автóбусом	вéтром
pr.	об инженéре	о послé	об автóбусе	о вéтре
plur.				
nom.	инженéры	послы́	автóбусы	вéтры
acc.	инженéров	послóв	автóбусы	вéтры
gen.	инженéров	послóв	автóбусов	вéтров
dat.	инженéрам	послáм	автóбусам	вéтрам
inst.	инженéрами	послáми	автóбусами	вéтрами
pr.	об инженéрах	о послáх	об автóбусах	о вéтрах

*Note: The accusative case of masculine animate nouns is the same as the genitive in both singular and plural.

1.1.2 Many masculine nouns have *nom. plur.* and, if inanimate, *acc. plur.* in
-á, including: áдрес 'address' – адресá; бéрег 'shore' – берегá; век
'century' – векá; вéчер 'evening' – вечерá; глаз 'eye' – глазá; гóлос 'voice;
vote' – голосá; гóрод 'town' – городá; дирéктор 'director' – директорá;
дóктор 'doctor' – докторá; дом 'house' – домá; кóлокол 'bell' –
колоколá; лес 'forest' – лесá; мáстер 'craftsman' – мастерá; нóмер
'(hotel) room' – номерá; óстров 'island' – островá; пáспорт 'passport' –
паспортá; пóезд 'train' – поездá; профéссор 'professor' – профессорá;
рукáв 'sleeve' – рукавá; том 'volume' – томá; цвет 'colour' – цветá.

1.2 Irregular masculine hard declensions

1.2.1

sing.	animate 'gosling'	'Englishman'	'citizen'	inanimate 'flower'
nom.	гусёнок	англичáнин	граждани́н	цветóк
acc.	гусёнка	англичáнина	граждани́на	цветóк
gen.	гусёнка	англичáнина	граждани́на	цветкá
dat.	гусёнку	англичáнину	граждани́ну	цветкý
inst.	гусёнком	англичáнином	граждани́ном	цветкóм
pr.	о гусёнке	об англичáнине	о граждани́не	о цветкé
plur.				
nom.	гусáта	англичáне	грáждане	цветы́
acc.	гусáт	англичáн	грáждан	цветы́
gen.	гусáт	англичáн	грáждан	цветóв
dat.	гусáтам	англичáнам	грáжданам	цветáм
inst.	гусáтами	англичáнами	грáжданами	цветáми
pr.	о гусáтах	об англичáнах	о грáжданах	о цветáх

Жемчýжины нарóдной мýдрости

рыбáк рыбакá ви́дит издалекá	a fisherman sees a fisherman from afar

1.2.2 Like **гусёнок**: the names of many small animals ending in -ёнок,
including: котёнок 'kitten'; поросёнок 'piglet'; слонёнок 'elephant calf';
телёнок 'calf'; утёнок 'duckling'; цыплёнок 'chick'; ягнёнок 'lamb', etc.
Note: ребёнок 'child' has *plur.*: дéти, детéй, детéй, дéтям, детьми́, о
дéтях. The *plur.* form ребя́та 'kids' is colloquial for 'young people'.

Note: щенóк 'puppy' is straightforward masculine mixed declension (see below): *gen.
sing.* щенкá; *plur.*: щенки́, щенкóв, etc. (also: щеня́та, etc.)

Жемчýжины нарóдной мýдрости

цыпля́т по óсени счита́ют	one counts one's chicks after autumn

1.2.3 Like **англича́нин**: the names of several nationalities, inhabitants of towns or areas and adherents of religious faiths ending in -анин or -янин including: **датча́нин** 'Dane'; **египтя́нин** 'Egyptian'; **израильтя́нин** 'Israeli'; **инопланетя́нин** 'extraterrestrial'; **киевля́нин** 'inhabitant of Kiev'; **крестья́нин** 'peasant'; **парижа́нин** 'Parisian'; **марсиа́нин** 'Martian'; **мусульма́нин** 'Moslem'.

1.2.4 Like **граждани́н**: several similar nouns denoting categories of people are end-stressed in the singular : **армяни́н** 'Armenian' *plur.*: **армя́не**; **дворяни́н** 'nobleman' *plur.*: **дворя́не**; **мещани́н** 'member of the petty bourgeoisie' *plur.*: **меща́не**; **славяни́н** 'Slav' *plur.*: **славя́не**; **христиани́н** 'Christian' *plur.*: **христиа́не**.

1.2.5 animate

sing.	'gypsy'	'Georgian'	'Bulgarian'	'master'	'gentleman'
nom.	цыга́н	грузи́н	болга́рин	хозя́ин	господи́н
acc.	цыга́на	грузи́на	болга́рина	хозя́ина	господи́на
gen.	цыга́на	грузи́на	болга́рина	хозя́ина	господи́на
dat.	цыга́ну	грузи́ну	болга́рину	хозя́ину	господи́ну
inst.	цыга́ном	грузи́ном	болга́рином	хозя́ином	господи́ном
pr.	о цыга́не	о грузи́не	о болга́рине	о хозя́ине	о господи́не

plur.					
nom.	цыга́не	грузи́ны	болга́ры	хозя́ева	господа́
acc.	цыга́н	грузи́н	болга́р	хозя́ев	госпо́д
gen.	цыга́н	грузи́н	болга́р	хозя́ев	госпо́д
dat.	цыга́нам	грузи́нам	болга́рам	хозя́евам	господа́м
inst.	цыга́нами	грузи́нами	болга́рами	хозя́евами	господа́ми
pr.	о цыга́нах	о грузи́нах	о болга́рах	о хозя́евах	о господа́х

1.3 Masculine mixed hard-soft declension

1.3.1 – и for ы after г, к, х

	animate		inanimate	
sing.	'boy'	'cockerel'	'tongue'	'circle'
nom.	ма́льчик	пету́х	язы́к	круг
acc.	ма́льчика	петуха́	язы́к	круг
gen.	ма́льчика	петуха́	языка́	кру́га
dat.	ма́льчику	петуху́	языку́	кру́гу
inst.	ма́льчиком	петухо́м	языко́м	кру́гом
pr.	о ма́льчике	о петухе́	о языке́	о кру́ге

plur.

nom.	ма́льчики	петухи́	языки́	круги́
acc.	ма́льчиков	петухо́в	языки́	круги́
gen.	ма́льчиков	петухо́в	языко́в	круго́в
dat.	ма́льчикам	петуха́м	языка́м	круга́м
inst.	ма́льчиками	петуха́ми	языка́ми	круга́ми
pr.	о ма́льчиках	о петуха́х	о языка́х	о круга́х

1.3.2 – о after ц only if stressed

	animate			inanimate	
sing.	'father'	'German'	'Chinaman'	'palace'	'month'
nom.	оте́ц	не́мец	кита́ец	дворе́ц	ме́сяц
acc.	отца́	не́мца	кита́йца	дворе́ц	ме́сяц
gen.	отца́	не́мца	кита́йца	дворца́	ме́сяца
dat.	отцу́	не́мцу	кита́йцу	дворцу́	ме́сяцу
inst.	отцо́м	не́мцем	кита́йцем	дворцо́м	ме́сяцем
pr.	об отце́	о не́мце	о кита́йце	о дворце́	о ме́сяце

plur.

nom.	отцы́	не́мцы	кита́йцы	дворцы́	ме́сяцы
acc.	отцо́в	не́мцев	кита́йцев	дворцы́	ме́сяцы
gen.	отцо́в	не́мцев	кита́йцев	дворцо́в	ме́сяцев
dat.	отца́м	не́мцам	кита́йцам	дворца́м	ме́сяцам
inst.	отца́ми	не́мцами	кита́йцами	дворца́ми	ме́сяцами
pr.	об отца́х	о не́мцах	о кита́йцах	о дворца́х	о ме́сяцах

1.3.3 – и for ы, о only if stressed after ж, ч, ш, щ

	animate		inanimate		
sing.	'hedgehog'	'comrade'	'storey'	'key'	'shower'
nom.	ёж	това́рищ	эта́ж	ключ	душ
acc.	ежа́	това́рища	эта́ж	ключ	душ
gen.	ежа́	това́рища	этажа́	ключа́	ду́ша
dat.	ежу́	това́рищу	этажу́	ключу́	ду́шу
inst.	ежо́м	това́рищем	этажо́м	ключо́м	ду́шем
pr.	о еже́	о това́рище	об этаже́	о ключе́	о ду́ше

plur.

nom.	ежи́	това́рищи	этажи́	ключи́	ду́ши
acc.	еже́й	това́рищей	этажи́	ключи́	ду́ши
gen.	еже́й	това́рищей	этаже́й	ключе́й	ду́шей
dat.	ежа́м	това́рищам	этажа́м	ключа́м	ду́шам
inst.	ежа́ми	това́рищами	этажа́ми	ключа́ми	ду́шами
pr.	о ежа́х	о това́рищах	об этажа́х	о ключа́х	о ду́шах

Note: The gen. plur. of all masculine nouns ending in ж, ч, ш, щ ends in -ей; also in this category are **врач** 'doctor'; **мяч** 'ball'; **нож** 'knife'; **рубе́ж** 'boundary' – all with end-stress.

Note: **сто́рож** 'watchman' has *plur.* **сторожа́, сторожей, сторожа́м,** etc. **муж** 'husband' has *plur.* **мужья́, муже́й, муже́й, мужья́м, мужья́ми, о мужья́х.**

1.4 Regular masculine soft declension

1.4.1 Nouns ending in -ь

	animate	inanimate	
sing.	'spectator'	'dictionary'	'coal'
nom.	зри́тель	слова́рь	у́голь
acc.	зри́теля	слова́рь	у́голь
gen.	зри́теля	словаря́	у́гля *or* угля́
dat.	зри́телю	словарю́	у́глю
inst.	зри́телем	словарём	у́глем
pr.	о зри́теле	о словаре́	об у́гле

plur.			
nom.	зри́тели	словари́	у́гли
acc.	зри́телей	словари́	у́гли
gen.	зри́телей	словаре́й	у́глей *or* угле́й
dat.	зри́телям	словаря́м	у́глям
inst.	зри́телями	словаря́ми	у́глями
pr.	о зри́телях	о словаря́х	об у́глях

1.4.2 Like **зри́тель**: over 400 masculine nouns ending in -атель or -итель, many denoting people or devices performing an action, *eg:* **жи́тель** 'inhabitant'; **дви́гатель** 'engine'; **писа́тель** 'writer'; **путеводи́тель** 'guidebook', etc. Also: **автомоби́ль** 'car'

Note: **учи́тель** 'schoolteacher' – *nom. plur.*: **учителя́**

1.4.3 Like **слова́рь**: **дождь** 'rain', etc.

1.4.4 Like **у́голь**: **день** 'day' (*gen.* дня; *inst.* днём); **ка́мень** 'stone' (*gen.* ка́мня; *inst.* ка́мнем); **ого́нь** 'fire', (*gen.* огня́; *inst.* огнём), etc.
Note: the *gen. plur.* of all nouns ending in -ь is in -ей.

1.4.5 Nouns ending in -й

	animate			inanimate	
sing.	'genius'	'hero'	'bourgeois'	'tram'	'museum'
nom.	ге́ний	геро́й	буржу́й	трамва́й	музе́й
acc.	ге́ния	геро́я	буржу́я	трамва́й	музе́й
gen.	ге́ния	геро́я	буржу́я	трамва́я	музе́я
dat.	ге́нию	геро́ю	буржу́ю	трамва́ю	музе́ю
inst.	ге́нием	геро́ем	буржу́ем	трамва́ем	музе́ем
pr.	о ге́нии	о геро́е	о буржу́е	о трамва́е	о музе́е

plur.

nom.	ге́нии	геро́и	буржу́и	трамва́и	музе́и
acc.	ге́ниев	геро́ев	буржу́ев	трамва́и	музе́и
gen.	ге́ниев	геро́ев	буржу́ев	трамва́ев	музе́ев
dat.	ге́ниям	геро́ям	буржу́ям	трамва́ям	музе́ям
inst.	ге́ниями	геро́ями	буржу́ями	трамва́ями	музе́ями
pr.	о ге́ниях	о геро́ях	о буржу́ях	о трамва́ях	о музе́ях

1.4.6 Like трамва́й: лентя́й 'lazybones'; поцелу́й 'kiss'; слу́чай 'case'; урожа́й 'harvest'.

Note: бой 'battle' (*gen. sing.* бо́я) *plur.*: бои́, бои́, боёв, боя́м, боя́ми, о боя́х; слой 'layer' (*gen. sing.* сло́я) *plur.*: слои́, слои́, слоёв, слоя́м, слоя́ми, о слоя́х; чай 'tea' (*gen. sing.* ча́я) *plur.*: чаи́, чаи́, чаёв, чая́м, чая́ми, о чая́х;   край 'edge; region' (*gen. sing.* кра́я) *plur.*: края́, края́, краёв, края́м, края́ми, о края́х.

1.5 Irregular masculine soft declensions

1.5.1   animate   inanimate

sing.	'devil'	'sparrow'	'way'
nom.	чёрт	воробе́й	путь
acc.	чёрта	воробья́	путь
gen.	чёрта	воробья́	пути́
dat.	чёрту	воробью́	пути́
inst.	чёртом	воробьём	путём
pr.	о чёрте	о воробье́	о пути́

plur.			
nom.	че́рти	воробьи́	пути́
acc.	черте́й	воробьёв	пути́
gen.	черте́й	воробьёв	путе́й
dat.	чертя́м	воробья́м	путя́м
inst.	чертя́ми	воробья́ми	путя́ми
pr.	о чертя́х	о воробья́х	о путя́х

1.5.2 Like чёрт: сосе́д 'neighbour *plur.*: сосе́ди, сосе́дей, etc.

Жемчу́жины наро́дной му́дрости

медве́ди – плохи́е сосе́ди	bears are not good neighbours

1.5.3 Like воробе́й: солове́й 'nightingale' *plur.*: соловьи́, соловьёв, etc. мураве́й 'ant' *plur.*: муравьи́, муравьёв, etc.

1.6   Irregular masculine plural declensions

1.6.1	animate			inanimate	
sing.	'brother'	'friend'	'son'	'leaf'	'chair'
nom.	брат	друг	сын	лист	стул
acc.	брáта	дрýга	сы́на	лист	стул
gen.	брáта	дрýга	сы́на	листá	стýла
dat.	брáту	дрýгу	сы́ну	листý	стýлу
inst.	брáтом	дрýгом	сы́ном	листóм	стýлом
pr.	о брáте	о дрýге	о сы́не	о листé	о стýле
plur.					
nom.	брáтья	друзья́	сыновья́	ли́стья	стýлья
acc.	брáтьев	друзéй	сыновéй	ли́стья	стýлья
gen.	брáтьев	друзéй	сыновéй	ли́стьев	стýльев
dat.	брáтьям	друзья́м	сыновья́м	ли́стьям	стýльям
inst.	брáтьями	друзья́ми	сыновья́ми	ли́стьями	стýльями
pr.	о брáтьях	о друзья́х	о сыновья́х	о ли́стьях	о стýльях

Note: человéк 'person' has the *plur.*: лю́ди, людéй, людéй, лю́дям, людьми́, о лю́дях.

Note: лист meaning 'sheet (of paper)' has the regular plural: листы́, листóв, листáм, etc.

Жемчýжины нарóдной мýдрости

друзья́ познаю́тся в бедé	friends are recognized in misfortune

1.7   Variations in case endings

1.7.1   Some masculine nouns can form a 'partitive' *gen. sing.* in -у or -ю, which generally has a colloquial flavour: мнóго нарóду (*or* нарóда) 'a lot of people'; килогрáмм сáхару (*or* сáхара) 'a kilo of sugar'; стакáн чáю (*or* чáя) 'a glass of tea'.

Note: the phrases: упусти́ть и́з виду 'to lose sight of'; и́з дому 'from home'; двáдцать лет óт роду 'twenty years from the day (he) was born'; ни рáзу 'not once'.

Жемчýжины нарóдной мýдрости

мнóго кри́ку, мáло тóлку	a lot of shouting, (but) little sense

1.7.2   Some masculine nouns, mainly monosyllables, form a locative case in -ý, used in place of the prepositional after the prepositions в or на: в лесý 'in the forest'; в садý 'in the garden'; в шкафý 'in the cupboard'; на летý 'in flight'.

Note: **на берегу́** 'on the bank'; **в, на углу́** 'in, on the corner'. This form may have a colloquial flavour: **в отпуску́** 'on holiday'.

Жемчу́жины наро́дной му́дрости

роди́лся в лесу́, моли́лся пню	(he) was born in the forest and prayed to a tree stump (he's rather thick)

1.7.3 Some masculine nouns have alternative *gen. plur.* forms:
сто грамм/сто гра́ммов '100 grammes'; **не́сколько помидо́р/помидо́ров** 'several tomatoes'.

1.8 Masculine animate nouns in - a and - я decline like feminines:

1.8.1

sing.	'man'	'young man'	'grandfather'	'uncle'
nom.	мужчи́на	ю́ноша	де́душка	дя́дя
acc.	мужчи́ну	ю́ношу	де́душку	дя́дю
gen.	мужчи́ны	ю́ноши	де́душки	дя́ди
dat.	мужчи́не	ю́ноше	де́душке	дя́де
inst.	мужчи́ной	ю́ношей	де́душкой	дя́дей
pr.	о мужчи́не	о ю́ноше	о де́душке	о дя́де

plur.				
nom.	мужчи́ны	ю́ноши	де́душки	дя́ди
acc.	мужчи́н	ю́ношей	де́душек	дя́дей
gen.	мужчи́н	ю́ношей	де́душек	дя́дей
dat.	мужчи́нам	ю́ношам	де́душкам	дя́дям
inst.	мужчи́нами	ю́ношами	де́душками	дя́дями
pr.	о мужчи́нах	о ю́ношах	о де́душках	о дя́дях

1.8.2 Many masculine 'diminutive' first names in -a or -я decline, normally only in the singular, like **ю́ноша** or **дя́дя**, including: **Воло́дя** (Влади́мир); **Же́ня** (Евге́ний); **Ми́ша** (Михаи́л); **Пе́тя** (Пётр); **Са́ша** (Алекса́ндр); **Серёжа** (Серге́й), etc.

Note: Adjectives qualifying such nouns are in the masculine, e.g. **мой дя́дя** 'my uncle'.

1.8.3 A few masculine nouns decline like neuters: **подмасте́рье** 'apprentice'; and those masculine nouns with suffices -ище or -ишко: **доми́ще** 'huge house'; **городи́шко** 'wretched little town', etc.

Note: **подмасте́рье** has an animate-accusative form only in the plural: **подмасте́рьев**.

FEMININE NOUNS

1.9 Regular feminine hard declension

Note: The *acc. plur.* of feminine animate nouns is the same as the *gen. plur.*

1.9.1

	animate		inanimate		
sing.	'fish'	'wife'	'car'	'side'	'price'
nom.	ры́ба	жена́	маши́на	сторона́	цена́
acc.	ры́бу	жену́	маши́ну	сто́рону	це́ну
gen.	ры́бы	жены́	маши́ны	стороны́	цены́
dat.	ры́бе	жене́	маши́не	стороне́	цене́
inst.	ры́бой	жено́й	маши́ной	стороно́й	цено́й
pr.	о ры́бе	о жене́	о маши́не	о стороне́	о цене́

plur.					
nom.	ры́бы	жёны	маши́ны	сто́роны	це́ны
acc.	рыб	жён	маши́ны	сто́роны	це́ны
gen.	рыб	жён	маши́н	сторо́н	цен
dat.	ры́бам	жёнам	маши́нам	сторона́м	це́нам
inst.	ры́бами	жёнами	маши́нами	сторона́ми	це́нами
pr.	о ры́бах	о жёнах	о маши́нах	о сторона́х	о це́нах

Note: сестра́ 'sister' *plur.*: сёстры, сестёр, сестёр, сёстрам, сёстрами, о сёстрах; and сосна́ 'pine' *plur.*: со́сны, со́сен, со́снам, со́снами, о со́снах.

1.10 Feminine mixed hard-soft declension

1.10.1 – и for ы after г, к, ж, х, ч, ш, щ; о after ж, ц, ч, ш, щ only if stressed.

	animate		inanimate		
sing.	'friend'	'sheep'	'difference'	'hand, arm'	'soul'
nom.	подру́га	овца́	ра́зница	рука́	душа́
acc.	подру́гу	овцу́	ра́зницу	ру́ку	ду́шу
gen.	подру́ги	овцы́	ра́зницы	руки́	души́
dat.	подру́ге	овце́	ра́знице	руке́	душе́
inst.	подру́гой	овцо́й	ра́зницей	руко́й	душо́й
pr.	о подру́ге	об овце́	о ра́знице	о руке́	о душе́

plur.					
nom.	подру́ги	о́вцы	ра́зницы	ру́ки	ду́ши
acc.	подру́г	ове́ц	ра́зницы	ру́ки	ду́ши
gen.	подру́г	ове́ц	ра́зниц	рук	душ
dat.	подру́гам	о́вцам	ра́зницам	рука́м	ду́шам
inst.	подру́гами	о́вцами	ра́зницами	рука́ми	ду́шами
pr.	о подру́гах	об о́вцах	о ра́зницах	о рука́х	о ду́шах

1.10.2 Before the suffix -ка, when the stem ends in ж, ч or ш insert -е- in

gen. plur. and animate *acc. plur.*:　**бóчка** 'barrel' – **бóчек**;　**дéвушка** 'girl' – **дéвушек**;　**кóшка** 'cat' – **кóшек**;　**лóжка** 'spoon' – **лóжек**;　**рýчка** 'handle' – **рýчек**, etc.

1.10.3　Before the suffix **-ка**, when the stem ends in *t* + ка (where *t* = any consonant except **ж, ч** or **ш**) insert **-о-** in *gen. plur.* and animate *acc. plur.*: **бáнка** 'jar, can' – **бáнок**;　**бутýлка** 'bottle' – **бутýлок**;　**группирóвка** 'gang' – **группирóвок**;　**ёлка** 'Christmas tree' – **ёлок**;　**загáдка** 'riddle' – **загáдок**;　**лóдка** 'boat' – **лóдок**;　**мáрка** 'stamp; (Deutsch)mark' – **мáрок**; **ошúбка** 'mistake' – **ошúбок**;　**скáзка** 'folk tale' – **скáзок**;　**скрúпка** 'violin' – **скрúпок**;　**сýмка** 'bag' – **сýмок**;　**улы́бка** 'smile' – **улы́бок**;　**ýтка** 'duck' – **ýток**, *etc.*

1.10.4　Before the suffix **-ка**, replace **-й-** by **-е-** in *gen. plur.* and animate *acc. plur.*:　**австралúйка** 'Australian (woman)' – **австралúек**;　**балалáйка** 'balalaika' – **балалáек**;　**двóйка** 'a mark of two' – **двóек**;　**индéйка** 'turkey' – **индéек**;　**хозя́йка** 'landlady' – **хозя́ек**;　**чáйка** 'seagull' – **чáек**, etc.

Before the suffix **-ка**, replace **-ь-** by **-е-** in *gen. plur.* and animate *acc. plur.*:　**кáпелька** 'droplet' – **кáпелек**;　**ступéнька** 'step' – **ступéнек**, etc.

Note: **кýкла** 'doll' – *gen. plur.*: **кýкол**;　**прóсьба** 'request' – *gen. plur.*: **прóсьб**; **свечá** 'candle' – *gen. plur.*: **свечéй** [but note the saying: **игрá** не стóит **свеч** 'the game isn't worth the candle(s)']; **дéньги** 'money' *(plur.)* – *gen.*: **дéнег**; **сéрьги** *(plur.)* 'earrings' – *gen.*: **серёг**; **судьбá** 'fate' – *gen. plur.*: **сýдеб**; **тюрьмá** 'prison' – *gen. plur.*: **тюрем**; **усáдьба** 'estate' – *gen. plur.*: **усáдеб**.

For the *gen. plur.* of **мечтá** 'dream' – use **мечтáний**.

1.11　Regular feminine soft declension

1.11.1

	animate			inanimate		
sing.	'nanny'	'storm'	'tower'	'series'	'idea'	'family'
nom.	ня́ня	бýря	бáшня	сéрия	идéя	семья́
acc.	ня́ню	бýрю	бáшню	сéрию	идéю	семью́
gen.	ня́ни	бýри	бáшни	сéрии	идéи	семьи́
dat.	ня́не	бýре	бáшне	сéрии	идéе	семьé
inst.	ня́ней	бýрей	бáшней	сéрией	идéей	семьёй
pr.	о ня́не	о бýре	о бáшне	о сéрии	об идéе	о семьé

plur.

nom.	ня́ни	бу́ри	ба́шни	се́рии	иде́и	се́мьи
acc.	нянь	бу́ри	ба́шни	се́рии	иде́и	се́мьи
gen.	нянь	бурь	ба́шен	се́рий	иде́й	семе́й
dat.	ня́ням	бу́рям	ба́шням	се́риям	иде́ям	се́мьям
inst.	ня́нями	бу́рями	ба́шнями	се́риями	иде́ями	се́мьями
pr.	о ня́нях	о бу́рях	о ба́шнях	о се́риях	об идеях	о се́мьях

1.11.2 Like бу́ря: **ба́ня** 'bath-house'; **ды́ня** 'melon'; **кастрю́ля** 'saucepan'; **неде́ля** 'week'; **поте́ря** 'loss'; **пу́ля** 'bullet'; **пусты́ня** 'desert'.

Note: **простыня́** 'sheet' – *inst. sing.*: **простынёй**, *plur.*: **про́стыни, про́стыни, просты́нь, простыня́м, простыня́ми, о простыня́х.**

Note: **тётя** 'aunt' – *gen. plur.*: **тётей.**

Note: **заря́** 'dawn' *sing.*: **заря́, зарю́, зари́, заре́, зарёй, о заре́;** *plur.*: **зо́ри, зо́ри, зорь, заря́м, заря́ми, о заря́х.**

1.11.3 Like ба́шня: **ви́шня** 'cherry'; **пе́сня** 'song'; **со́тня** 'a hundred'; **спа́льня** 'bedroom'; **сплётня** 'gossip'.

Note: **дере́вня** 'village' – *gen. plur.*: **дереве́нь;** **ку́хня** 'kichen' – *gen. plur.*: **ку́хонь;** **ка́пля** 'drop' – *gen. plur.*: **ка́пель;** **ту́фля** 'shoe' – *gen. plur.*: **ту́фель.**

Note: **земля́** 'earth; land' – *inst. sing.*: **землёй,** *plur.*: **зе́мли, зе́мли, земе́ль, зе́млям, зе́млями, о зе́млях.**

1.11.4 Like се́рия: about 1,400 nouns in -ия, many, like **психоло́гия** 'psychology', with no *plur.*

1.11.5 Like иде́я: **батаре́я** 'radiator'; **галере́я** 'gallery'; **ста́туя** 'statue'; **ста́я** 'flock; pack; shoal'; **фе́я** 'fairy'; **ше́я** 'neck'.

1.11.6 Like семья́: **свинья́** 'swine' (animate); **статья́** 'article' (end-stressed throughout); **судья́** 'judge, referee' (may be masculine or feminine).

1.12 Feminine declension in -ь: soft and mixed

1.12.1

sing.	animate 'mouse'	'horse'	inanimate 'part'	'stupidity'	'night'
nom.	мышь	ло́шадь	часть	глу́пость	ночь
acc.	мышь	ло́шадь	часть	глу́пость	ночь
gen.	мы́ши	ло́шади	ча́сти	глу́пости	но́чи
dat.	мы́ши	ло́шади	ча́сти	глу́пости	но́чи
inst.	мы́шью	ло́шадью	ча́стью	глу́постью	но́чью
pr.	о мы́ши	о ло́шади	о ча́сти	о глу́пости	о но́чи

plur.					
nom.	мы́ши	ло́шади	ча́сти	глу́пости	но́чи
acc.	мыше́й	лошаде́й	ча́сти	глу́пости	но́чи
gen.	мыше́й	лошаде́й	часте́й	глу́постей	ноче́й
dat.	мыша́м	лошадя́м	частя́м	глу́постям	ноча́м
inst.	мыша́ми	лошадьми́ *or* лошадя́ми	частя́ми	глу́постями	ноча́ми
pr.	о мыша́х	о лошадя́х	о частя́х	о глу́постях	о ноча́х

1.12.2 Like часть: ось 'axle'; о́чередь 'queue'; пло́щадь '(town) square'; сте́пень 'degree'; тень 'shadow'; пять 'five' (no *plur.*) (and many other numerals). Also дверь 'door', but note stress в двери́ 'in the doorway'.

1.12.3 Like глу́пость: крова́ть 'bed'; мысль 'thought'; связь 'connection'; and about 2,600 feminine abstract nouns in -ость, many, like гра́мотность 'literacy', having no *plur.*

1.12.4 Like ночь: вещь 'thing'; печь 'stove'.

Note: ложь 'lie': *sing.*: ложь, ложь, лжи, лжи, ло́жью, о лжи (no *plur.*); and любо́вь 'love': *sing.*: любо́вь, любо́вь, любви́, любви́, любо́вью, о любви́ (no *plur.*)

1.13 Irregular feminine soft declension

1.13.1 animate

sing.	'mother'	'daughter'	*plur.*	
nom.	мать	дочь	ма́тери	до́чери
acc.	мать	дочь	матере́й	дочере́й
gen.	ма́тери	до́чери	матере́й	дочере́й
dat.	ма́тери	до́чери	матеря́м	дочеря́м
inst.	ма́терью	до́черью	матеря́ми	дочерьми́/дочеря́ми
pr.	о ма́тери	о до́чери	о матеря́х	о дочеря́х

Жемчу́жины наро́дной му́дрости

му́дрость в голове́, а не в бороде́	wisdom is in the head, not in the beard

NOUNS OF COMMON GENDER

1.14 Professions, categories applicable to either sex

1.14.1 A few Russian nouns ending in -a or -я denote members of professions or categories of people of either sex, declining as feminine nouns but treated as masculine unless obviously referring to a female:

судья́ оказа́лся хоро́шим   the judge turned out to be a good one
but: она́ хоро́шая судья́   she is a good judge

1.14.2 Like **судья́**: **бродя́га** 'tramp'; **глава́** 'head (of an organization)'; **колле́га** 'colleague'; **кале́ка** 'cripple'; **левша́** 'left-hander'; **неве́жда** 'ignoramus'; **пья́ница** 'drunkard'; **сирота́** 'orphan'; **уби́йца** 'murderer'.

Note: **соба́ка** 'dog' and **же́ртва** 'victim' remain feminine, even when obviously referring to males (and же́ртва is considered inanimate).

1.14.3 Unlike судья́, etc., masculine-type nouns denoting members of professions or categories of people of either sex cannot change gender even when obviously referring to females:

мы нашли́ э́того врача́ случа́йно; она́ о́чень хоро́ший врач
we found this doctor by chance; she's a very good doctor

But if it is clear from the context that the person is female a feminine verb is used:

Како́й вы стра́нный челове́к, – улыбну́лась гла́вный врач
'What an odd person you are,' the senior doctor smiled

1.14.4 Like **врач**: **адвока́т** 'barrister'; **кандида́т нау́к** 'PhD'; **ма́стер спо́рта** 'master of sport'; **те́хник** 'technician', etc.

1.14.5 Some words denoting professions have masculine and feminine forms which are neutral in style and equally acceptable in literary or spoken Russian:
арти́ст, арти́стка 'actor, performer'; **писа́тель, писа́тельница** 'writer'; **портно́й, портни́ха** 'tailor'; **продаве́ц, продавщи́ца** 'shop assistant'; **спортсме́н, спортсме́нка** 'sportsman, sportswoman'; **студе́нт, студе́нтка** 'student'; **тракторист, трактори́стка** 'tractor driver'; **учени́к, учени́ца** 'pupil', etc.

Note: feminine forms in -ша are, however, not used in literary Russian: **библиоте́карша** 'librarian'; **касси́рша** 'cashier'; **конду́кторша** 'conductress'; **секрета́рша** 'secretary'; instead, use the masculine equivalents, qualifying them, if necessary, with masculine adjectives:

она́ отли́чный **библиоте́карь, касси́р, конду́ктор, секрета́рь**

1.14.6 In old Russian the accusative plural of animate nouns was the same as the nominative plural, and this form is preserved in some modern constructions referring to occupations:

его при́няли в бухга́лтеры
he was accepted into the accounts section

она́ отпра́вилась в медсёстры
she went off to become a nurse

кандида́т в президе́нты
presidential candidate

Жемчу́жины наро́дной му́дрости

из гря́зи не попадёшь в кня́зи	out of the mud you can't become a prince
куда́ сова́ться в во́лки, ко́ли хвост соба́чий	why join the wolves if your tail is a dog's

NAMES

1.15 Surnames

1.15.1 Russian surnames in -ов (-ова), -ев (-ева), -ёв (-ёва), -ин (-ина) and -ын (-ына) have masculine, feminine and plural forms and decline in a way showing some adjectival influence:

sing.	(masc.)	(fem.)	(masc.)	(fem.)
nom.	Петро́в	Петро́ва	Зо́рин	Зо́рина
acc.	Петро́ва	Петро́ву	Зо́рина	Зо́рину
gen.	Петро́ва	Петро́вой	Зо́рина	Зо́риной
dat.	Петро́ву	Петро́вой	Зо́рину	Зо́риной
inst.	Петро́вым	Петро́вой	Зо́риным	Зо́риной
pr.	о Петро́ве	о Петро́вой	о Зо́рине	о Зо́риной

plur.	(both genders)		(both genders)	
nom.	Петро́вы		Зо́рины	
acc.	Петро́вых		Зо́риных	
gen.	Петро́вых		Зо́риных	
dat.	Петро́вым		Зо́риным	
inst.	Петро́выми		Зо́риными	
pr.	о Петро́вых		о Зо́риных	

1.15.2 Russian and foreign surnames ending in a consonant and those ending in -ь decline like masculine nouns for males and in the plural: Пастерна́к, о Пастерна́ке, etc.; Шекспи́р, о Шекспи́ре; Да́рвин, с Да́рвином ; Даль, с Да́лем, etc. Referring to females they do not decline: о рома́нах Джейн О́стин 'about Jane Austen's novels'. However, names in -ых do not decline: мы встре́тили Ива́на Черны́х 'we met Ivan Chernykh'.

1.15.3 Russian surnames with adjectival endings -ый (-ая), -ий (-ая), -ой (-ая), e.g: Неизвéстный (Неизвéстная), Мúрский (Мúрская), Толстóй (Толстáя) decline like adjectives.

1.15.4 Russian surnames ending in -a decline like feminine nouns, regardless of ~~sex, in the singular only: Глúшка, Глúнку, Глúнки, *etc* Foreign surnames in~~ stressed -a do not normally decline: у Андрé Морyá 'in André Maurois' work'.

1.15.5 Surnames ending in letters not associated with masculine or feminine declensions do not decline in literary Russian: surnames in -енко, common in Ukrainian, may decline in colloquial Russian (with *acc. sing.* in -енку, *gen. sing.* in -енки).

1.16 First names

1.16.1 Masculine and feminine first names decline like masculine and feminine nouns if their endings are appropriate, i.e. ending in a consonant or -й or -ь for masculines, e.g. Борис, Сергéй, Úгорь; and in -a or -я for feminines, e.g. Нúна, Мáрья. Some masculine first names ending in -a and -я decline like feminine nouns, e.g. Никúта, Ильá.

Note: Любóвь as a feminine first name declines without losing the -o-: Любóвь, Любóвь, Любóви, Любóви, Любóвью, о Любóви.

1.16.2 If non-Russian first names have inappropriate endings they do not decline, e.g. Стéнли (Stanley); Мáргарет (Margaret); роднóй гóрод Мáргарет Тéтчер 'Margaret Thatcher's home town'.

1.17 Patronymics

1.17.1 Masculine patronymics ('son of . . .') end in -**ич**: Михáйлович, Николáевич, Ильúч; they decline like товарищ or, if end-stressed, with an *inst.* like ёж (see p. 12):
с Николáем Михáйловичем 'with Nikolai Mikhailovich'; у Борúса Николáевича 'at Boris Nikolaevich's'; с Владúмиром Ильичóм 'with Vladimir Ilyich'.

1.17.2 Feminine patronymics ('daughter of . . . .') end in -**на**: Михáйловна, Николáевна, Ильúнична; they decline like regular feminine nouns (see p. 17):
с Людмúлой Михáйловной 'with Lyudmila Mikhailovna'; у Вéры Николáевны 'at Vera Nikolaevna's'; с Любóвью Ильúничной 'with Lyubov Ilyinichna'.

NEUTER NOUNS

1.18 Regular neuter hard declension

1.18.1

sing.	'business'	'village'	'window'	'number'	'feeling'
nom.	де́ло	село́	окно́	число́	чу́вство
acc.	де́ло	село́	окно́	число́	чу́вство
gen.	де́ла	села́	окна́	числа́	чу́вства
dat.	де́лу	селу́	окну́	числу́	чу́вству
inst.	де́лом	село́м	окно́м	число́м	чу́вством
pr.	о де́ле	о селе́	об окне́	о числе́	о чу́встве

plur.					
nom.	дела́	сёла	о́кна	чи́сла	чу́вства
acc.	дела́	сёла	о́кна	чи́сла	чу́вства
gen.	дел	сёл	о́кон	чи́сел	чувств
dat.	дела́м	сёлам	о́кнам	чи́слам	чу́вствам
inst.	дела́ми	сёлами	о́кнами	чи́слами	чу́вствами
pr.	о дела́х	о сёлах	об о́кнах	о чи́слах	о чу́вствах

Note: the common stress shifts between *sing.* and *plur.*

1.18.2 Like де́ло: **зе́ркало** 'mirror' – *nom. plur.*: **зеркала́**, *gen. plur.*: **зерка́л**; **ме́сто** 'place' – *nom. plur.*: **места́**, *gen. plur.*: **мест**; **сло́во** 'word' – *nom. plur.*: **слова́**, *gen. plur.*: **слов**; **ста́до** 'herd' – *nom. plur.*: **стада́**, *gen. plur.*: **стад**.

Note: **о́зеро** 'lake' – *nom. plur.*: **озёра**, *gen. plur.*: **озёр**.

Note: **о́блако** 'cloud' – *nom. plur.*: **облака́**, *gen. plur.*: **облако́в**.

1.18.3 Like село́: **бедро́** 'hip' – *gen. plur.*: **бёдер**; **ведро́** 'bucket' – *gen. plur.*: **вёдер**; **гнездо́** 'nest' – *gen. plur.*: **гнёзд**; **зерно́** 'grain' – *gen. plur.*: **зёрен**; **лицо́** 'face; person' – *gen. plur.*: **лиц**; **ребро́** 'rib' – *gen. plur.*: **рёбер**; **яйцо́** 'egg' – *gen. plur.*: **яи́ц**.

Note: **воро́та** 'gate', **дрова́** 'firewood' have no *sing.*

1.18.4 Like число́: **письмо́** 'letter' – *gen. plur.*: **пи́сем**; **полотно́** 'canvas' – *nom. plur.*: **поло́тна**, *gen. plur.*: **поло́тен**; **пятно́** 'spot' – *gen. plur.*: **пя́тен**; **ядро́** 'nucleus; cannon-ball' – *gen. plur.*: **я́дер**; *Note:* **стекло́** 'glass' – *gen. plur.*: **стёкол**.

1.18.5 Like чу́вство (no stress shift): **блю́до** 'dish'; **боло́то** 'marsh'; **нача́ло** 'beginning'; **одея́ло** 'blanket' and about 900 nouns ending in -ство, most of which, like **любопы́тство** 'curiosity', have no *plur.*

Жемчу́жины наро́дной му́дрости

слов мно́го, а де́ла ма́ло	a lot of words, but little action

1.19 Regular neuter soft and mixed declension

1.19.1

sing.	'field'	'heart'	'saucer'	'building'	'ravine'
nom.	по́ле	се́рдце	блю́дце	зда́ние	ущéлье
acc.	по́ле	се́рдце	блю́дце	зда́ние	ущéлье
gen.	по́ля	се́рдца	блю́дца	зда́ния	ущéлья
dat.	по́лю	се́рдцу	блю́дцу	зда́нию	ущéлью
inst.	по́лем	се́рдцем	блю́дцем	зда́нием	ущéльем
pr.	о по́ле	о се́рдце	о блю́дце	о зда́нии	об ущéлье

plur.					
nom.	поля́	сердца́	блю́дца	зда́ния	ущéлья
acc.	поля́	сердца́	блю́дца	зда́ния	ущéлья
gen.	поле́й	серде́ц	блю́дец	зда́ний	ущéлий
dat.	поля́м	сердца́м	блю́дцам	зда́ниям	ущéльям
inst.	поля́ми	сердца́ми	блю́дцами	зда́ниями	ущéльями
pr.	о поля́х	о сердца́х	о блю́дцах	о зда́ниях	об ущéльях

1.19.2 Like по́ле: **мо́ре** 'sea'.

1.19.3 Like блю́дце: **чудо́вище** 'monster'.

1.19.4 Like зда́ние (no stress shift): over 3,000 neuter nouns in -ие; many are abstract and, like **сочу́вствие** 'sympathy', have no plural. Archaically some may be spelt ending in -ье and decline like ущéлье: **сча́стье** 'happiness'.

Жемчу́жины наро́дной му́дрости

молча́ние – знак согла́сия	silence is a sign of agreement
повторе́нье – мать уче́нья	repetition is the mother of learning

1.20 Uncommon or irregular neuter declensions

1.20.1

sing.	'gun'	'name'	'banner'	'feather'	'dress'
nom.	ружьё	и́мя	зна́мя	перо́	пла́тье
acc.	ружьё	и́мя	зна́мя	перо́	пла́тье
gen.	ружья́	и́мени	зна́мени	пера́	пла́тья
dat.	ружью́	и́мени	зна́мени	перу́	пла́тью
inst.	ружьём	и́менем	зна́менем	перо́м	пла́тьем
pr.	о ружье́	об и́мени	о зна́мени	о пере́	о пла́тье

plur.					
nom.	ру́жья	имена́	знамёна	пе́рья	пла́тья
acc.	ру́жья	имена́	знамёна	пе́рья	пла́тья
gen.	ру́жей	имён	знамён	пе́рьев	пла́тьев
dat.	ру́жьям	имена́м	знамёнам	пе́рьям	пла́тьям
inst.	ру́жьями	имена́ми	знамёнами	пе́рьями	пла́тьями
pr.	о ру́жьях	об имена́х	о знамёнах	о пе́рьях	о пла́тьях

1.20.2 Like и́мя: вре́мя 'time'; пле́мя 'tribe'; се́мя 'seed' – *gen. plur.*: семя́н.

Жемчу́жины наро́дной му́дрости

де́лу вре́мя, а поте́хе час	(all the) time (in the world) for work, but (only) an hour for fun

1.20.3 Like перо́: де́рево 'tree' – *plur.*: дере́вья, дере́вья, дере́вьев, дере́вьям, дере́вьями, о дере́вьях; звено́ 'link (in chain)' – *plur.*: зве́нья, зве́ньев, etc.; крыло́ 'wing' – *plur.*: кры́лья, кры́льев, etc.

1.20.4 Like пла́тье: верхо́вье 'upper reaches (of river)'; у́стье 'mouth (of river)'.

Note: не́бо 'sky; heaven' – *plur.*: небеса́, небеса́, небе́с, небеса́м, небеса́ми, о небеса́х; чу́до 'miracle' – *plur.* чудеса́, etc.

Note: су́дно 'vessel, ship' – *plur.*: суда́, суда́, судо́в, суда́м, суда́ми, о суда́х.

Note: коле́но 'knee' – *plur.*: коле́ни, коле́ни, коле́ней (*or*, if used with a Preposition, коле́н), коле́ням, коле́нями, о коле́нях;
плечо́ 'shoulder' – *plur.*: пле́чи, пле́чи, плеч, плеча́м, плеча́ми, о плеча́х;
о́ко 'eye' [obsolete] – *plur.*: о́чи, о́чи, оче́й, оча́м, оча́ми, об оча́х;
у́хо 'ear' – *plur.*: у́ши, у́ши, уше́й, уша́м, уша́ми, об уша́х;
я́блоко 'apple' – *plur.*: я́блоки, я́блоки, я́блок, я́блокам, я́блоками, о я́блоках.

Жемчу́жины наро́дной му́дрости

и со́лнце не без пя́тен	even the sun is not without spots
от плохо́го се́мени не жди хоро́шего пле́мени	from poor seed don't expect a good breed

1.21 Indeclinable nouns

A number of nouns of foreign origin, some with inappropriate endings for their gender, do not decline (they stay the same in all cases, singular and plural); they do, however, have a definite gender and adjectives agreeing with them must be in the appropriate case.

1.21.1 Masculine: **атташе́** 'attaché' – e.g. с вое́нным атташе́ 'with the military attaché'; likewise: **ко́фе** 'coffee' (colloquially neuter); **по́ни** 'pony'; **шимпанзе́** 'chimpanzee'.

Towns tend to be masculine (like го́род): се́верный То́кио 'northern Tokio' в совреме́нном Тбили́си 'in modern Tbilisi'.

1.21.2 Feminine: **ле́ди** 'lady' – e.g. ста́рая ле́ди 'an elderly lady'; **мада́м** 'madame; lady'.

Rivers tend to be feminine (like река́): широ́кая Миссиси́ппи 'the broad Mississippi'.

1.21.3 Neuter: **бюро́** 'bureau'; **кафе́** 'café'; **кино́** 'cinema'; **пальто́** 'coat'; **ра́дио** 'radio'; **такси́** 'taxi'; **шоссе́** 'highway'.

EXERCISES

(i)   *Decline in the singular and plural, indicating stressed vowels; check with a dictionary if unsure about animate or inanimate meaning:*

стари́к; медве́дь; ребёнок; ка́мень; мяч; по́езд; кенгурёнок; ирла́ндец; урожа́й; солове́й;

му́ха; ли́ния; ра́дость; продавщи́ца; кни́жка; неде́ля; пое́здка; сте́пень; скамья́; свеча́;

ме́сто; мо́ре; кре́сло; после́дствие; одея́ло; зре́лище; кольцо́; сре́дство; полоте́нце; зна́ние.

(ii)   *Give the nom. and gen. plur. of:*

дом; райо́н; газе́та; пе́сня; па́ртия; и́мя; ночь; уро́к; сло́во; мысль; гость; слу́чай; врач; де́рево; мать; оте́ц; сын; дочь; брат; сестра́; муж; друг; ме́сто; судья́; письмо́; де́вушка; окно́; кружо́к; плечо́; атташе́.

(iii)   *Translate into Russian using the prepositions and cases provided, e.g.*

In (в + *pr.*) the town centre: в це́нтре го́рода

1   By (у + *gen.*) the factory wall.
2   On (на + *pr.* [*locative*, see p. 15]) the river bank.

3   During (на + *pr.*) the maths lesson.
4   Without (без + *gen.*) the ambassador's name and patronymic.
5   Thanks to (благодаря + *dat.*) the price of apples.
6   In (*inst.*) the eyes of the citizens.
7   Among (среди + *gen.*) the peasants' children.
8   Into (в + *acc.*) the Englishman's car.
9   In (на + *pr.*) Revolution Square.
10   Under (под + *inst.*) the writer's table.
11   In (в + *pr.* [*locative*, see p. 15]) the Zhukovs' garden.
12   Between (между + *inst.*) the teacher's windows.
13   Above (над + *inst.*) the palace door.
14   From (от + *gen.*) the Chinaman's friends.
15   Onto (на + *acc.*) the side of the Americans.
16   Through (через + *acc.*) the region's forests.
17   Into (в + *acc.*) Lyubov Andreyevna's hands.
18   In (на + *pr.*) the language of love.
19   According to (по + *dat.*) the engineer's opinion.
20   About (о + *pr.*) their attitude to (к + *dat.*) world peace.

2 DECLENSION OF THE ADJECTIVE

Adjectives have masculine, feminine and neuter singular declensions and a plural declension common to all three genders. There are 'hard' and 'soft' declensions, 'mixed' declensions affected by the rules of spelling and declensions with unstressed and stressed endings.

2.1 Adjectives with unstressed endings

2.1.1 Hard declension: most adjectives, including about 8,000 ending in -ный, such as типи́чный 'typical', decline like но́вый 'new' and are said to have hard endings – i.e. with a stem ending in a hard consonant as indicated by the vowels ы, а, о, у in the endings:

sing.	masc.	fem.	neut.	plur.
nom.	но́вый	но́вая	но́вое	но́вые
acc.	но́вый / но́вого	но́вую	но́вое	но́вые / но́вых
gen.	но́вого	но́вой	но́вого	но́вых
dat.	но́вому	но́вой	но́вому	но́вым
inst.	но́вым	но́вой	но́вым	но́выми
pr.	о но́вом	но́вой	но́вом	о но́вых

2.1.2 All passive participles, present and past: чита́емый '(which is being) read'; прочи́танный '(which has been) read' (see pp. 120–1, 123–6).

2.1.3 Soft declension: a much smaller number of adjectives have soft endings, that is, the stem ends in a soft consonant as indicated by the vowels и, я, е, ю in the endings, e.g. ли́шний 'extra, superfluous'

sing.	masc.	fem.	neut.	plur.
nom.	ли́шний	ли́шняя	ли́шнее	ли́шние
acc.	ли́шний / ли́шнего	ли́шнюю	ли́шнее	ли́шние / ли́шних
gen.	ли́шнего	ли́шней	ли́шнего	ли́шних
dat.	ли́шнему	ли́шней	ли́шнему	ли́шним
inst.	ли́шним	ли́шней	ли́шним	ли́шними
pr.	о ли́шнем	ли́шней	ли́шнем	о ли́шних

2.1.4 Like ли́шний: бли́жний 'near'; ве́рхний 'upper'; весе́нний 'spring'; вече́рний 'evening'; вне́шний 'external'; вну́тренний 'internal'; вчера́шний 'yesterday's'; да́льний 'far, distant'; дома́шний 'domestic';

за́втрашний 'tomorrow's'; зде́шний 'local'; зи́мний 'winter'; ле́тний 'summer'; ни́жний 'lower'; ны́нешний 'present day'; осе́нний 'autumn'; после́дний 'last, latest'; сего́дняшний 'today's, modern'; си́ний 'bright blue'; тепе́решний 'present day'; тогда́шний 'of that time'; у́тренний 'morning', etc.

Жемчу́жины наро́дной му́дрости

ли́шние де́ньги – ли́шняя забо́та	extra money is extra worry
за́дним умо́м де́ла не попра́вишь	you can't put the matter right with hindsight

2.1.5   A distinct group of soft adjectives is formed mainly from nouns denoting animals or categories of people, e.g. **ли́сий** 'fox's'

sing.	masc.	fem.	neut.	plur.
nom.	ли́сий	ли́сья	ли́сье	ли́сьи
acc.	ли́сий / ли́сьего	ли́сью	ли́сье	ли́сьи / ли́сьих
gen.	ли́сьего	ли́сьей	ли́сьего	ли́сьих
dat.	ли́сьему	ли́сьей	ли́сьему	ли́сьим
inst.	ли́сьим	ли́сьей	ли́сьим	ли́сьими
pr.	о ли́сьем	ли́сьей	ли́сьем	ли́сьих

Like ли́сий: **бо́жий** 'God's'; **вдо́вий** 'widow's'; **во́лчий** 'wolf'; **ко́шачий** 'cat'; **медве́жий** 'bear'; **о́тчий** 'father's'; **охо́тничий** 'hunter's'; **пти́чий** 'bird'; **ры́бий** 'fish'; **соба́чий** 'dog'; **тре́тий** 'third', etc.

Жемчу́жины наро́дной му́дрости

у хи́трости тарака́ньи но́жки	cunning has cockroach legs

2.1.6   Mixed declension: due to the rules of spelling, adjectives with a stem ending in г, ж, к, х, ч, ш, щ and ц have a 'mixed' declension, eg: (-кий, -гий, -хий) **ти́хий** 'quiet'

sing.	masc.	fem.	neut.	plur.
nom.	ти́хий	ти́хая	ти́хое	ти́хие
acc.	ти́хий / ти́хого	ти́хую	ти́хое	ти́хие / ти́хих
gen.	ти́хого	ти́хой	ти́хого	ти́хих
dat.	ти́хому	ти́хой	ти́хому	ти́хим
inst.	ти́хим	ти́хой	ти́хим	ти́хими
pr.	о ти́хом	ти́хой	ти́хом	ти́хих

2.1.7   Like ти́хий: **вели́кий** 'great'; **высо́кий** 'high'; **глубо́кий** 'deep'; **гро́мкий** 'loud'; **далёкий** 'far'; **ди́кий** 'wild'; **жа́лкий** 'pathetic';

жа́ркий 'hot'; жесто́кий 'cruel'; кре́пкий 'firm'; лёгкий 'light, easy'; ло́вкий 'dexterous'; ме́лкий 'small, fine'; мя́гкий 'soft'; ни́зкий 'low'; ре́дкий 'rare'; сла́дкий 'sweet'; стро́гий 'strict'; то́нкий 'subtle'; у́зкий 'narrow'; широ́кий 'wide'; я́ркий 'bright', etc., and several hundred adjectives ending in -ский.

2.1.8 Mixed-declension adjectives in -жий, -чий, -ший, -щий, *eg*: о́бщий - 'general, common':

sing.	masc.	fem.	neut.	plur.
nom.	о́бщий	о́бщая	о́бщее	о́бщие
acc.	о́бщий / о́бщего	о́бщую	о́бщее	о́бщие / о́бщих
gen.	о́бщего	о́бщей	о́бщего	о́бщих
dat.	о́бщему	о́бщей	о́бщему	о́бщим
inst.	о́бщим	о́бщей	о́бщим	о́бщими
pr.	об о́бщем	о́бщей	о́бщем	об о́бщих

2.1.9 Like о́бщий: бы́вший 'former'; горя́чий 'hot'; могу́чий 'mighty'; ры́жий 'ginger (coloured)'; све́жий 'fresh'; хоро́ший 'good';
and the superlatives: вы́сший 'highest'; лу́чший 'best'; ху́дший 'worst'; and all those in -ейший or -айший: нове́йший 'newest'; тонча́йший 'subtlest', etc. (see p. 51–2);
all present active participles: чита́ющий '(who is) reading'; стро́ящий '(who is) building'; несу́щий '(who is) carrying'; интересу́ющийся '(who is) interested', etc. (see pp. 114–15); and all past active participles: чита́вший '(who was) reading'; постро́ивший 'who has built'; принёсший 'who had brought'; заинтересова́вшийся 'who has got interested in', etc. (see pp. 116–17).

Жемчу́жины наро́дной му́дрости

пе́ший ко́нному не това́рищ	pedestrian is no partner for equestrian

2.1.10 Adjectives in -цый are very rare; e.g: ку́цый 'short, tailless'

sing.	masc.	fem.	neut.	plur.
nom.	ку́цый	ку́цая	ку́цее	ку́цые
acc.	ку́цый / ку́цего	ку́цую	ку́цее	ку́цые / ку́цых
gen.	ку́цего	ку́цей	ку́цего	ку́цых
dat.	ку́цему	ку́цей	ку́цему	ку́цым
inst.	ку́цым	ку́цей	ку́цым	ку́цыми
pr.	о ку́цем	ку́цей	ку́цем	о ку́цых

Like ку́цый: бледноли́цый 'pale-faced'; круглоли́цый 'round-faced', etc.

2.2 Adjectives with stressed endings

2.2.1   Adjectives with stress on the ending may have hard or 'mixed' declensions. Most are hard, i.e. with a stem ending in a hard consonant as indicated by the vowels ы, а, о, у in the endings e.g. немо́й 'dumb':

sing.	masc.	fem.	neut.	plur.
nom.	немо́й	нема́я	немо́е	немы́е
acc.	немо́й / немо́го	нему́ю	немо́е	немы́е / немы́х
gen.	немо́го	немо́й	немо́го	немы́х
dat.	немо́му	немо́й	немо́му	немы́м
inst.	немы́м	немо́й	немы́м	немы́ми
pr.	о немо́м	немо́й	немо́м	о немы́х

2.2.2   Like немо́й: больно́й 'ill'; восьмо́й 'eighth'; второ́й 'second'; голубо́й 'pale blue, gay (of men)'; живо́й 'alive'; земно́й 'terrestrial'; злой 'angry'; лесно́й 'forest'; ночно́й 'nocturnal'; основно́й 'fundamental'; пусто́й 'empty'; речно́й 'river'; ручно́й 'tame'; седьмо́й 'seventh'; слепо́й 'blind'; смешно́й 'funny'; тупо́й ' blunt, dull'; шесто́й 'sixth', etc.

Жемчу́жины наро́дной му́дрости

перелива́ть из пусто́го в поро́жнее	to pour from one empty (vessel) into another (to say the same old things, state the obvious)

2.2.3   Due to the rules of spelling, adjectives with end stress and a stem ending in г, к, х, ж, ш have a 'mixed' declension e.g. сухо́й 'dry'

sing.	masc.	fem.	neut.	plur.
nom.	сухо́й	суха́я	сухо́е	сухи́е
acc.	сухо́й / сухо́го	суху́ю	сухо́е	сухи́е / сухи́х
gen.	сухо́го	сухо́й	сухо́го	сухи́х
dat.	сухо́му	сухо́й	сухо́му	сухи́м
inst.	сухи́м	сухо́й	сухи́м	сухи́ми
pr.	о сухо́м	сухо́й	сухо́м	о сухи́х

2.2.4   Like сухо́й: большо́й 'big'; дорого́й 'dear'; друго́й 'other'; како́й 'what (sort of)'; морско́й 'marine'; плохо́й 'bad'; чужо́й 'someone else's', etc.

Жемчу́жины наро́дной му́дрости

на чужо́м коне́ далеко́ не уе́дешь	you won't get far on another's horse

2.3 Adjectives used as nouns:

Adjectives used as nouns decline like adjectives, e.g.:
  столо́вая 'dining room; canteen'
  пере́дняя entrance hall'
  живо́тное 'animal'

EXERCISES

(i) *Translate into Russian:*

1   In a new winter coat
2   The Ministry of Internal Affairs
3   In the fresh air
4   On the open sea
5   In the seventh heaven
6   There are no serious problems
7   How many superfluous men are there?
8   Thanks to the former director
9   Beyond the distant mountains
10 Under the third tall tree
11 In second place
12 Away from the pale blue flowers

(ii) *Decline in sing. and plur.:*

  ти́хий ве́тер; большо́й сканда́л; пуста́я буты́лка; молодо́е поколе́ние; чужа́я ша́пка; осе́нний день; бледноли́цый челове́к; ближа́йшая остано́вка; медве́жье у́хо; злой медве́дь.

---

3   SHORT ADJECTIVES

DIFFERENCES BETWEEN LONG AND SHORT FORMS

3.1 Most Russian adjectives have a long (or attributive) form and a short (or predicative) form, e.g.

> краси́вый, краси́вая, краси́вое; краси́вые   – *long form* 'beautiful'
> **краси́в, краси́ва, краси́во; краси́вы**   – *short form*

3.1.1 The short form has masculine, feminine, neuter and plural forms but does not decline (except in a few archaic set phrases) and can only be used as a complement or predicate, i.e. after the verb 'to be':

> **она́ умна́**   she is intelligent

while only the long form can be used as an attribute, 'qualifying' a noun:

> она́ у́мная де́вушка   she is an intelligent girl

Like the short form, it may be used on its own after the verb 'to be' :

> она́ у́мная *or* она́ умна́   she is intelligent

3.1.2 In impersonal constructions of the type 'it's cold', 'it was easy', 'it'll be interesting' the neuter short form is used without any equivalent to the English 'it':

> **хо́лодно**   it's cold
> **ей бы́ло легко́**   it was easy for her
> **интере́сно бу́дет** уви́деть его́   it'll be interesting to see him

Жемчу́жины наро́дной му́дрости

парши́вому поросёнку и в Петро́в день холодно́	a mangy piglet feels cold even on St Peter's day [12 July] (some people are never satisfied)

3.1.3 The meaning of the adjective may be intensified by 'so' or 'such': for short forms the indeclinable так is used, and for long forms the long form adjective такой:

бы́ло так хо́лодно, что река́ замёрзла
it was so cold (that) the river froze

соба́ка так умна́, что она́ сама́ зна́ет, когда́ у нас бу́дут го́сти
or: соба́ка **така́я у́мная**, что она́ сама́ зна́ет, когда́ у нас бу́дут го́сти
the dog is so intelligent (that) it knows itself when we are going to have visitors

он прие́хал **в тако́м шика́рном костю́ме**, что мы не узна́ли его́
he arrived in such a smart suit (that) we didn't recognize him

Жемчу́жины наро́дной му́дрости

не так стра́шен чёрт, как его́ малю́ют	the devil is not as terrible as he is painted

3.2 Formation of the short form

3.2.1 Masculine short forms are based on the root of the adjective, inserting a fleeting vowel, usually -e-, if an awkward combination of consonants results. For the feminine, neuter and plural forms add only -a, -o and -ы , respectively to the root:

ми́лый 'beloved'	*short form:* мил, мила́, ми́ло; ми́лы
глубо́кий 'deep'	*short form:* глубо́к, глубока́, глубо́ко *or* глубоко́; глубо́ки *or* глубоки́
акти́вный 'active'	*short form:* акти́вен, акти́вна, акти́вно; акти́вны
дли́нный 'long'	*short form:* дли́нен, длинна́, дли́нно; дли́нны *or* длинны́
све́тлый 'light'	*short form:* све́тел, светла́, све́тло *or* светло́; све́тлы
типи́чный 'typical'	*short form:* типи́чен, типи́чна, типи́чно; типи́чны
дово́льный 'contented, happy'	*short form:* дово́лен, дово́льна, дово́льно; дово́льны

3.2.2 Before -к the fleeting vowel is -o- :

кре́пкий 'strong'	*short form:* кре́пок, крепка́, кре́пко; кре́пки
лёгкий 'light, easy'	*short form:* лёгок, легка́, легко́; легки́
у́зкий 'narrow'	*short form:* у́зок, узка́, у́зко; у́зки

except when the preceding consonant is ж, ч, ш, or is soft:

тя́жкий 'hard, heavy'	*short form:* тя́жек, тяжка́, тя́жко; тя́жки
го́рький 'bitter'	*short form:* го́рек, горька́, го́рько; го́рьки

3.2.3 The letter -й- becomes -e- in the masculine short form:

споко́йный 'calm'	*short form:* споко́ен, споко́йна, споко́йно; споко́йны

Note that рад, ра́да; ра́ды 'glad' has no long form.

Note the following oddities:

злой 'angry, malicious'	*short form:* зол, зла, зло; злы
досто́йный 'worthy'	*short form:* досто́ин, досто́йна, досто́йно; досто́йны
о́стрый 'sharp'	*short form:* остр, остра́, о́стро; о́стры
о́стрый 'witty'	*short form:* остёр, остра́, остро́; остры́
по́лный 'full'	*short form:* по́лон, полна́, по́лно; по́лны
си́льный 'strong'	*short form:* силён, сильна́, си́льно; си́льны
смешно́й 'funny'	*short form:* смешо́н, смешна́, смешно́; смешны́
у́мный 'intelligent'	*short form:* умён, умна́, у́мно *or* умно́; у́мны *or* умны́
хи́трый 'cunning'	*short form:* хитёр, хитра́, хи́тро; хи́тры

3.2.4 Some adjectives which might be expected to acquire a fleeting vowel do not in fact do so:

бо́дрый 'cheerful'	*short form:* бодр, бодра́, бо́дро; бо́дры
го́рдый 'proud'	*short form:* горд, горда́, го́рдо; го́рды
до́брый 'good, kind'	*short form:* добр, добра́, до́бро; до́бры *or* добры́
мёртвый 'dead'	*short form:* мёртв, мертва́, мёртво; мёртвы
ту́склый 'dim'	*short form:* тускл, тускла́, ту́скло; ту́склы

3.2.5 Some adjectives formed with the suffix -енный have only one -н- on the end of the masculine short form:

му́жественный 'brave'	*short form:* му́жествен, му́жественна, – енно; -енны

But a growing number have an alternative masculine or standard masculine form in -енен:

есте́ственный 'natural'	*short form:* есте́ствен *or* есте́ственен, есте́ственна. . .
ме́дленный 'slow'	*short form:* ме́дленен, ме́дленна. . .
обыкнове́нный 'ordinary'	*short form:* обыкнове́нен, обыкнове́нна. . .
отве́тственный 'responsible'	*short form:* отве́тственен, отве́тственна. . .

3.2.6 Like му́жественный, adjectives formed from past passive participles have only one -н in the masculine short form, but two in the other genders and plural:

образо́ванный (*adj.*) 'educated'	*short form:* образо́ван, образо́ванна. . .
она́ умна́ и образо́ванна	she is clever and educated

Note: the short form of the past passive participle has only one -н throughout:
образо́ванный   *short form:* образо́ван, образо́вана (see pp. 127, 131)

коми́ссия была́ образо́вана в декабре́   the commission was formed in
December

3.2.7 'Soft' adjectives in -ний do not have short forms, except:
си́ний 'blue'   *short form:* **синь**, (синя́, си́не); **си́ни** (rare)
и́скренний 'sincere'   *short form:* **и́скренен, и́скренна, и́скренне** *or*
                        и́скренно; и́скренни *or* **и́скренны**

3.2.8 Short forms of the following categories of adjective do not exist or are
very rarely used:
*   Adjectives ending in -ский:
        ру́сский, демократи́ческий 'democratic', типи́ческий 'typical'

(alternative forms in -ный, e.g. демократи́чный, типи́чный have short
forms: демократи́чен, демократи́чна . . . ; типи́чен, типи́чна . . .)

*   Adjectives formed with the suffix -овый, -ово́й, -ево́й:
        ро́зовый 'pink, gay (of women)'
        делово́й 'business'
        боево́й 'fighting, combat'

Note: но́вый, суро́вый 'grim', здоро́вый 'healthy' are *not* in the category formed with
a suffix.They are formed by adding the adjectival endings to a stem in -ов or -ев and
they do have short forms: нов, нова́, etc.

*   Adjectives formed from verbs and archaic participles and ending in -лый:
        отста́лый 'backward'
        про́шлый 'past'

*   The adjectives большо́й and ма́ленький (for short form of большо́й use:
    вели́к, велика́, велико́; велики́ or вели́ки, and for ма́ленький use: мал,
    мала́, мало́; малы́)

*   Adjectives which identify
    a substance, e.g. кирпи́чный 'brick';
    or a time, e.g. дневно́й 'daytime';
    or a particular object, e.g. автомоби́льный 'automobile';
    or a place or geographical feature, e.g. степно́й 'steppe', лесно́й 'forest';
    or a person or animal, e.g. соба́чий 'dog's'.
It may be useful to remember that there cannot normally be a comparative
formed from these adjectives.

*   In this connection colours derived from substances or objects, e.g.:

голубо́й 'pale blue, gay (of men)'; шокола́дный 'chocolate'; кори́чневый 'brown' (from кори́ца 'cinnamon') have no short form, while 'ordinary' colours do:

кра́сный 'red'   *short form:* кра́сен, красна́ . . .

Note: some adjectives have more than one meaning and may have a short form in one meaning, but not in another. For example: серде́чный; with the medical meaning 'heart, cardiac' as in серде́чный при́ступ 'heart attack' referring to the heart literally has no short form, but in its second meaning of 'cordial, heartfelt' it has: серде́чен, серде́чна . . .

Жемчу́жины наро́дной му́дрости

куй желе́зо, пока́ горячо́	forge the iron while it's hot

EXERCISES

(i) *Give the English for the following adjectives and say whether they could have a short form:*

англи́йский; бе́лый; бли́зкий; больно́й; большо́й; бы́стрый; весёлый; вре́дный; высо́кий; гла́вный; головно́й; гото́вый; гру́стный; далёкий; де́тский; дли́нный; до́брый; дома́шний; живопи́сный; зелёный; знамени́тый; иностра́нный; кру́пный; ли́шний; любопы́тный; ма́ленький; мясно́й; наро́дный; нового́дний; ночно́й; обы́чный; опа́сный; поле́зный; по́лный; постоя́нный; про́шлый; прямо́й; ра́вный; ра́нний; рожде́ственский; ску́чный; сосе́дний; тру́дный; трудово́й; тяжёлый; удо́бный; ую́тный; фина́нсовый; чуде́сный; шокола́дный.

(ii) *Where possible, form short forms, masculine and feminine, from the adjectives in* (i) *above.*

3.3 Use of the short form

3.3.1 With the past and future tenses of the verb 'to be' and the infinitive and imperative, the long form may be used in the nominative or instrumental case, so that 'she was very intelligent' could be translated into Russian as:

either   она́ была́ о́чень умна́
or   она́ была́ о́чень у́мная
or   она́ была́ о́чень у́мной

(the *inst.* is more *literary*, though with future, conditional, infinitive and imperative the *inst* is preferred – see pp. 175–9).

3.3.2 Short-form adjectives should be used only as predicates (complements), but even so there is a choice here between long and short forms:

лékция была́ **интере́сна** *or* интере́сная   the lecture was interesting

- The difference seems to be that the long form implies the presence or repetition of the noun it qualifies, so that ле́кция была́ интере́сная suggests 'the lecture was an interesting lecture' *or* 'the lecture was an interesting one'. If the subject is a person, the long adjective implies that he or she is that type of person:

  Ива́н Бори́сович умён Ivan Borisovich is intelligent
  Ива́н Бори́сович у́мный Ivan Borisovich is an intelligent person

There is little practical difference in the above example, but with some adjectives there is need for care, for example, гото́вый 'ready':

  пора́ е́хать. **Ты гото́в?** it's time to go. Are you ready?

(It would be distinctly odd to ask: 'are you a ready type of person?')

3.3.3 It follows from the above that if the context indicates that the characteristic is only *temporary*, the short form may be preferred. This is particularly clear with some adjectives, e.g. больно́й:

  он больно́й he is a sick person, *ie.* an invalid
  он бо́лен сего́дня he is unwell today

This cannot, however, be given as a firm rule; it is quite correct to say:

  она́ весёлая she is a cheerful person
and **она́ сего́дня весела́** she is cheerful today,

but *Note:* 'Ты сего́дня не весёлая, Ма́ша.' (Chekhov) You seem sad today, Masha

3.3.4 The short form is used where the scope of the characteristic is *delimited* by words or phrases which the adjective governs:

  их дочь о́чень спосо́бная their daughter is very talented
            (generally)
but: их дочь **спосо́бна к му́зыке** their daughter has a talent for music

3.3.5 Some other adjectival predicate constructions of this type are:

бога́т (бога́та, бога́то; бога́ты) + *inst.* 'rich in'
  на́ша страна́ бога́та не́фтью our country is rich in oil

дово́лен (дово́льна; дово́льны) + *inst.* 'pleased with, content'
    он дово́лен ва́ми   he's pleased with you

по́лон (полна́, по́лно *or* **полно́; по́лны** *or* **полны́)** + *gen.* 'full of'
    зал по́лон наро́ду   the hall is full of people

Similarly: **благода́рен** + *dat.* 'grateful to'; **гото́в на** + *acc.* 'ready for'; **гото́в к** + *dat.* 'ready for'; **добр к** + *dat.* 'kind towards'; **знако́м с** + *inst.* 'acquainted, familiar with'; **похо́ж на** + *acc.* 'similar to'; **равноду́шен к** + *dat.* 'indifferent to'; **спосо́бен на** + *acc.* or: **к** + *dat.* 'competent in' ; **спосо́бен** + *infin.* 'capable of'.

With these adjectives the same general principle applies. It is perfectly natural to say, using the short form:

    я благода́рен вам   I'm grateful to you
    or **я благода́рна вам**

On the other hand 'I'm a grateful type of person to you' is hardly possible.

3.3.6   The short form sometimes indicates that the characteristic is relative and excessive for the circumstances:

    э́та ку́ртка больша́я   this jacket is a large one
    э́та ку́ртка велика́   this jacket is too large

The scope of the short-form adjective in such sentences is delimited, even if the precise limitation is not expressed. The jacket is too large *for somebody*, e.g. for me, for him. Similarly:

потоло́к ни́зкий	the ceiling is a low one
потоло́к ни́зок	the ceiling is too low (e.g. for this furniture)
чемода́н тяжёлый	the case is heavy
чемода́н тяжёл для ребёнка	the case is too heavy for the child
боти́нки ма́ленькие	the boots are small
боти́нки малы́ ему́	the boots are too small for him

3.3.7 The neuter short form has to be used in impersonal constructions:
    бы́ло хо́лодно   it was cold *or* it was too cold
    мне всё равно́   it's all the same to me, I couldn't care less

or where the subject is э́то:

    э́то бы́ло о́чень интере́сно   that was very interesting or where the subject is an infinitive:

рабóтать там бы́ло невозмóжно it was impossible to work there

Note: in such instances there is no noun, either present or 'understood', which an adjective could qualify, and *э́то* is only used if 'it' refers to something specific.

3.3.8 Much is written about the criteria used to determine whether the long or short form should be used, the short form being described as more literary, more categorical and sometimes more blunt, whilst the long form is neutral and denotes inherent characteristics. These criteria, however, sometimes contradict each other and are not then of great practical help.

Remember: only the *long* form can be used attributively, while the *short* form can be used only predicatively: both the *long* and the *short* form can be used as a predicate to the verb 'to be':

он был óчень дóбрый
он был óчень добр he was very kind

3.3.9 It is therefore safer to use the long form if you are in doubt, but, if you know the short form exists, use it after the verb 'to be' in the present ('understood'), past and future tenses (bearing in mind the points above.)

Note: that after other parts of the verb 'to be', i.e. the infinitive быть, the gerund бу́дучи, and the imperative будь! бу́дьте! , the long form of the adjective in the instrumental can be used, even in the circumstances outlined above (see also p.175):

'Пра́вда, он в тече́ние всего́ э́того вре́мени постоя́нно чу́вствовал, как бу́дто ему́ сле́довало быть ей благода́рным.' (Turgenev)
Admittedly, all this time he had felt constantly as if he ought to have been grateful to her.

'Я доста́точно образóван, чтóбы не быть суеве́рным, но я суеве́рен.' (Dostoevsky)
I am sufficiently educated not to be superstitious, but I am.

Note: The short form of хорóший: **хорóш, хороша́; хороши́** often means 'beautiful, pretty, handsome'.
The short form of живóй 'lively': **жив, жива́; жи́вы** means 'alive'.

Жемчу́жины нарóдной му́дрости

тяжела́ ты ша́пка Мономáха	you are heavy, crown of Monomakh

3.3.10 Occasionally the short form (instead of the Instrumental, see p. 175) is met after verbs other than 'to be' but in the same general category of 'being', 'seeming', 'becoming', 'turning out to be', *etc.*:

'Отчего́ мы ... стано́вимся ску́чны, се́ры, неинтере́сны, лени́вы, равноду́шны, беспол́езны, несча́стны ...' (Chekhov)
'Why are we becoming dull, colourless, uninteresting, lazy, indifferent, useless and unhappy ...'

EXERCISES

(i) *Translate into English and comment on the use of the adjectives in italics:*
1 'Он был сли́шком для неё *мо́лод*' (Turgenev).
2 'Ру́ки твои́ *хороши́* ... то́лько *велики́*' (Turgenev).
3 'Челове́ческая ли́чность должна́ быть *крепка́*, как скала́, и́бо на ней всё стро́ится' (Turgenev).
4 'Ли́бо я глуп, ли́бо э́то всё вздор. Должно́ быть, я *глуп*' (Turgenev).
5 'Па́вел Петро́вич сошёл в гости́ную у́же *гото́вый* к бо́ю' (Turgenev).
6 'Па́вел Петро́вич сошёл в гости́ную. Он уже́ был *гото́в* к бо́ю. Он скоре́е сожале́ния *досто́ин*, чем насме́шки' (Turgenev).
7 'О́стров Капри́ был *сыр* и *тёмен* в э́тот ве́чер' (Bunin).
8 'Бенга́льский стоя́л *кра́сный*, а Ри́мский был *бле́ден*' (Bulgakov).
9 'День был *тёплый*. Ле́то в 1995 году́ бы́ло необы́чно *жа́рким*' (Press).
10 'Он гляде́л так, как бу́дто бы для него́ бы́ло реши́тельно всё равно́, гори́т ли пе́ред ним ого́нь, и́ли нет, вку́сно ли вино́, и́ли *проти́вно*, *ве́рны* ли счёты, кото́рые он проверя́л, и́ли нет ...' (Chekhov).
11 'Он ре́дко быва́л *резв*, да́же ре́дко *ве́сел*, но все, взгляну́в на него́, то́тчас ви́дели, что э́то во́все не от како́й-нибудь в нём угрю́мости, что, напро́тив, он *ро́вен* и *ве́сел*' (Dostoevsky).
12 'Се́рый пиджа́к, застёгнутый све́рху до́низу, на широ́кой, кре́пкой спине́ был си́льно натя́нут, – ви́дно, хозя́ину он был *те́сен*' (N. Ostrovsky).
13 '*Краси́в*, как Диони́с, *му́жественен*, как Аполло́н, Алекса́ндр в шестна́дцать лет на́чал кома́ндовать войска́ми' (Tendryakov).
14 'Во́здух был *тёпел* и *чист*; си́льно мерца́ли звёзды' (Kazakov).
15 'Во́здух в избе́ *густо́й* и *вя́зкий*. Я *мо́крый* от по́та' (Gladkov).
16 'Язы́к реалисти́ческих, модерни́стских и постмодерни́стских произведе́ний по́сле 60-х гг. нере́дко про́сто *гря́зен*. Вы́бор слов *ужа́сен*, а́вторские сенте́нции *далеки́* от изя́щества' (Yu. Rozhdestvensky).
17 'Совреме́нное состоя́ние ру́сского языка́ *плохо́е*' (ibid.)
18 'Мы, опьянённые во́здухом свобо́ды, стано́вимся *гру́бы*, *однолине́йны*, *криклвы*' (V. Lakshin).

(ii) *Translate into Russian, explaining your choice of short or long form adjective:*
1 He was ill yesterday, but he is well today.
2 My grandmother was an invalid.

3 It's very cold today.
4 Jeans are expensive because they are fashionable.
5 The skirt was too short for her.
6 At the beginning of term the lecture rooms were full of students.
7 He will not be satisfied with your work.
8 That is just like him!
9 She's terribly pale – don't you think she's hungry?
10 Russia is rich in natural resources.
11 Russia is a country rich in natural resources.
12 They were very cheerful today.

4 COMPARATIVE OF THE ADJECTIVE

There are two ways of forming the comparative degree of the adjective in Russian:

4.1 The comparative with бо́лее

бо́лее 'more' precedes the basic positive adjective, *either* in its long form:

бо́лее у́мный, бо́лее у́мная, etc.   more intelligent, cleverer
(бо́лее does not change, but the adjective declines in the normal way;)

or in its short impersonal form:

бо́лее интере́сно   it's more interesting

4.1.1 Like the long form of the positive adjective, the comparative with бо́лее can be used attributively, in the oblique cases, if required:
он рабо́тает то́лько с бо́лее у́мными ученика́ми
he works only with the more intelligent pupils

мы тепе́рь живём в бо́лее краси́вой кварти́ре
we now live in a more beautiful apartment

4.1.2 The comparative with бо́лее can also be used predicatively, with both long and short-form adjectives, as complement to the verb 'to be':
на́ша кварти́ра бо́лее шика́рная   our apartment is more chic
у нас бо́лее интере́сно   it's more interesting at our place

4.1.3 'Than' is expressed by **чем**:
э́то бо́лее но́вая маши́на, чем ва́ша
this is a newer car than yours

они́ живу́т в бо́лее удо́бных усло́виях, чем мы
they live in more comfortable conditions than us

в их кварти́ре бо́лее удо́бно, чем у нас
it's more comfortable in their apartment than in our place

4.2 Adjectives with declinable comparative

There are eight adjectives with a declinable comparative form used without бóлее:

4.2.1 большóй 'big' has the comparative   **бóльший** 'bigger'
мáленький 'small' has the comparative   **мéньший** 'smaller'

они живýт в бóльшей квартúре, чем мы
they live in a bigger apartment than us

Note: бóлее is never used with большóй oг мáленький.

4.2.2 With the other six a normal comparative of **бóлее** + positive adjective may be used; but with:
хорóший 'good' the comparative   **лýчший** 'better'
and   плохóй 'bad' the comparative   **хýдший** 'worse'

are preferred to бóлее хорóший, бóлее плохóй.

With the other four a difference in meaning is apparent; the single-word declinable comparative has an expressive edge:

молодóй 'young' has the comparative   **млáдший** 'younger, junior'
стáрый 'old' has the comparative   **стáрший** 'elder, senior'

(compare: млáдший брат 'younger brother', стáршая сестрá 'elder sister', млáдшая сотрýдница 'junior colleague', стáрший преподавáтель 'senior lecturer' with он предпочитáет рабóтать с бóлее молоды́м музыкáнтом 'he prefers to work with a younger musician' [merely younger literally, with no hint of inferiority].)

нúзкий 'low' has a comparative   **нúзший** 'lower, inferior'
which is rare.
высóкий 'high' has the comparative   **вы́сший** 'higher, superior'

(compare: вы́сшее образовáние 'higher education' with бóлее высóкое здáние 'higher building', бóлее нúзкий ýровень 'lower level', бóлее нúзкий мост 'the lower bridge'.)

With these four adjectives бóлее gives a truer, more literal comparative than the single-word declinable form, whose meaning shades off towards the superlative: is стáршее поколéние 'the elder generation' or 'the eldest'?

4.3   The short-form comparative

4.3.1 After the verb 'to be' and such verbs as станови́ться 'to become' and
каза́ться 'to seem' an indeclinable short form of the comparative is normally
used:

он **умне́е**	he is more intelligent
пье́са **интере́снее**, чем фильм	the play is more interesting than the film

It is possible to use бо́лее with the short form of the adjective in these
situations (он бо́лее умён; э́та пье́са бо́лее интере́сна), but the short-form
comparative is preferred: он умне́е, э́та пье́са интере́снее.

4.3.2 This comparative is normally formed with the suffix -ee replacing the
endings of the positive adjective; if, in the feminine short form, the ending -a
is stressed, the suffix -е́е will also be stressed; this means that for most
adjectives consisting of a single syllable root + endings the stress on the
comparative will fall on -е́е:

но́вый	нова́	**нове́е** 'newer'
сло́жный	сложна́	**сложне́е** 'more complex'

Otherwise the stress falls on the same syllable as in the positive adjective:

интере́сный	интере́сна	**интере́снее** 'more interesting'

Note: these polysyllabic adjectives:

весёлый	весела́	**веселе́е** 'more cheerful'
тяжёлый	тяжела́	**тяжеле́е** 'heavier'
холо́дный	холодна́	**холодне́е** 'colder'

(There is an alternative form of the ending -ee, sometimes met in literature, in
-ей: **нове́й, тяжеле́й**, etc.)

4.3.3 There are also a number of irregular short-form comparatives,
including:

бли́же 'nearer' (from бли́зкий)   **бога́че** 'richer' (from бога́тый)
бо́льше 'bigger' (from большо́й)   **вы́ше** 'higher' (from высо́кий)
глу́бже 'deeper' (from глубо́кий)   **гро́мче** 'louder' (from гро́мкий)
гу́ще 'denser' (from густо́й)   **да́льше** 'farther' (from далёкий)
деше́вле 'cheaper' (from дешёвый)   **доро́же** 'dearer' (from дорого́й)
жа́рче 'hotter' (from жа́ркий)   **коро́че** 'shorter' (from коро́ткий)

кре́пче 'stronger' (from кре́пкий)
лу́чше 'better' (from хоро́ший)
моло́же *or:* мла́дше 'younger'
  (from молодо́й)
мя́гче 'softer' (from мя́гкий)
по́зже *or:* поздне́е 'later'
  (from по́здний)
ра́ньше 'earlier' (from ра́нний)
ста́рше 'older' [of people] *or:* старе́е
  'older' [of things] (from ста́рый)
стро́же 'stricter' (from стро́гий)
ти́ше 'quieter' (from ти́хий)
ху́же 'worse' (from плохо́й)
ши́ре 'wider' (from широ́кий).

ле́гче 'lighter, easier' (from лёгкий)
ме́ньше 'smaller' (from ма́ленький)

ни́же 'lower' (from ни́зкий)

про́ще 'simpler' (from просто́й)
сла́ще 'sweeter' (from сла́дкий)

твёрже 'harder' (from твёрдый)
то́ньше 'finer' (from то́нкий)
ча́ще 'more frequent' (from ча́стый)

4.3.4 Positive adjectives which have no short form have no short predicative comparative; in general they are not required as comparatives because they refer to objects or substances (e.g. кирпи́чный 'brick').

4.3.5 Adjectives in -ский, even those denoting qualities, have no short-form comparative, e.g. реалисти́ческий 'realistic', which may be used with бо́лее:

бо́лее реалисти́ческий подхо́д a more realistic approach

In some cases an adjective with the suffix -ный on the same root can be substituted, *eg:* реалисти́чный:

его́ подхо́д **реалисти́чнее** his approach is more realistic

4.4 Constructions with the comparative

4.4.1 'Than' with the short-form comparison may be expressed *either* by **чем** (as with the comparative with бо́лее) *or* by putting the object to which comparison is being made in the **genitive**:

either: она́ умне́е, чем брат she's cleverer than her brother
or: она́ умне́е бра́та she's cleverer than her brother

either: река́ Во́лга длинне́е, чем Нева́ the river Volga is longer
or: река́ Во́лга длинне́е Невы́ than the Neva

Note: the genitive of comparison may *not* be used with бо́лее; with the longer comparative with бо́лее, чем must be used :

Во́лга бо́лее дли́нная река́, чем Нева́
the Volga is a longer river than the Neva

Note: to translate 'than his', 'than hers' or 'than theirs' чем must be used:

> на́ша маши́на старе́е, чем их
> our car is older than theirs
> (на́ша маши́на старе́е их would mean 'our car is older than they are'.)

Жемчу́жины наро́дной му́дрости

ла́сковое сло́во сла́ще мёда	a kind word is sweeter than honey
у́тро ве́чера мудрене́е	morning is wiser than evening (better sleep on it)
для свиньи́ нет ху́же, чем двор без лу́жи	for a pig there's nothing worse than a (farm)yard without a puddle

4.4.2 Чем . . ., тем . . . are used with short-form comparatives in balanced sentences of the kind:

> чем ра́ньше, тем лу́чше   the earlier, the better
> чем сильне́е идёт дождь, тем печа́льнее вы́глядит тре́нер
> the harder it rains, the sadder coach looks

4.4.3 Как мо́жно . . . is used with the short-form comparative after the infinitive to express 'as . . . as possible':

> уро́ки всегда́ должны́ быть как мо́жно содержа́тельнее
> lessons must always be as informative as possible

4.4.4 'Less' is expressed by **ме́нее** with the positive adjective; as with бо́лее, comparison is made only with чем, and not the genitive:

> он ме́нее спосо́бный, чем его́ брат   he's less able than his brother

> они́ живу́т в ме́нее удо́бных усло́виях, чем мы
> they live in less comfortable conditions than we do

4.4.5 'Much more', 'much less' is expressed by **гора́здо** *or* **намно́го** and either comparative:

> она́ гора́здо умне́е меня́   she's much cleverer than me
> *or:* она́ намно́го умне́е меня́

> в гора́здо бо́лее удо́бных усло́виях   in much more comfortable conditions
> *or* в намно́го бо́лее удо́бных усло́виях

> с гора́здо ме́нее интере́сным спу́тником
> with a much less interesting travelling companion

4.4.6 'By how much' with the comparative can be expressed by на+*acc.* or the straight *inst.*:

either: он на два го́да ста́рше сестры́ he's two years older than his sister
or: он двумя́ года́ми ста́рше сестры́ he's two years older than his sister

4.4.7 'More of...', or **'less of...'** something in the nominative or accusative is translated by бо́льше or ме́ньше plus the genitive:

ну́жно бо́льше молока́ more milk is needed

сего́дня бы́ло ме́ньше францу́зов, чем не́мцев
there were fewer Frenchmen than Germans today

дай мне бо́льше де́нег give me some more money

Жемчу́жины наро́дной му́дрости

в гостя́х хорошо́, а до́ма лу́чше	it's nice visiting, but home is better

---

EXERCISES

(i) *Give the short-form comparative of:*
бога́тый; бы́стрый; высо́кий; глубо́кий; жа́ркий; коро́ткий; лёгкий; просто́й; стро́гий; твёрдый; широ́кий

(ii) *Translate into English:*
Здоро́вье лу́чше бога́тства.
Большинство́ из нас бо́лее счастли́вые, чем несча́стные геро́и Достое́вского.
Э́то вы́ше моего́ понима́ния.
'Он находи́л либера́льное направле́ние бо́лее разу́мным, потому́ что оно́ подходи́ло бли́же к его́ о́бразу жи́зни' (Turgenev).
Никола́й, ста́рший брат Константи́на, проигра́л бо́льшую до́лю своего́ состоя́ния.
Весь у́жас мете́ли показа́лся ей ещё бо́лее прекра́сен тепе́рь.
'База́ров владе́л осо́бенным уме́ньем возбужда́ть к себе́ дове́рие в лю́дях ни́зших' (Turgenev).
'Поря́дочный хи́мик в два́дцать раз поле́знее вся́кого поэ́та, – сказа́л он' (Turgenev).
'Э́то вре́мя бы́ло трудне́е для Па́вла Петро́вича, чем для вся́кого друго́го' (Turgenev).
'Она́ каза́лась ещё моло́же при све́те весе́ннего со́лнца' (Turgenev).
'Фрукто́за в два ра́за сла́ще са́хара. На консерви́рование я́год, фру́ктов и

овощей фруктозы тратится в 4 раза меньше, чем сахара' (press).
'Будет выгоднее производить мясо, колбасу, молоко и другие продукты в стране, потому что привозить их из-за рубежа окажется гораздо дороже' (press).

(iii) *Translate into Russian, using short-form comparatives where possible:*
1   This lecture is more interesting than I expected.
2   She's much younger than he is.
3   The more he works, the less he learns.
4   They'll come as quickly as possible.
5   I think it's colder here in the spring than in the winter.
6   She was wearing a longer skirt yesterday.
7   They make better furniture than in all the other factories.
8   The older generation doesn't understand that for students conditions are more difficult than they were earlier.
9   Russian grammar is certainly more complicated than English grammar.
10 I consider Russian grammar more complicated than nuclear physics.

5 SUPERLATIVE OF THE ADJECTIVE

5.1 Ways of forming the superlative

The superlative degree of the adjective can be formed in more than one way: if you want to define something as literally 'the most (interesting, tall, green' or whatever) use the compound superlative with **са́мый, са́мая, са́мое; са́мые**, etc:

са́мый интере́сный рома́н   the most interesting novel
са́мая ра́нняя пье́са   the earliest play

5.1.1 Са́мый agrees with the noun, as does the positive adjective itself, in gender, number and case:

в са́мом коро́тком стихотворе́нии   in the shortest poem

Compare: бы́страя маши́на   a fast car   [positive]
           бо́лее бы́страя маши́на   a faster car   [comparative]
           са́мая бы́страя маши́на   the fastest car   [superlative]

Note: 'best' is **лу́чший** *or* **са́мый лу́чший**,
        'worst' **ху́дший** *or* **са́мый ху́дший**

'Лу́чшим, са́мым люби́мым о́тдыхом на Капри́ ста́ла для Го́рького ры́бная ло́вля' (L. Bykovtseva)
Fishing became Gorky's best, most favourite relaxation on Capri

Note: In literary style са́мый may be replaced by the indeclinable **наибо́лее**:
        в наибо́лее ра́звитых стра́нах in the most developed countries

5.2 -ейший and айший

5.2.1 If you want to express your feeling about something as being 'most extraordinarily (interesting, tall, green' or whatever) you can sometimes use the suffix -**ейший** added to the stem of the adjective:

интере́снейший рома́н   a *most* interesting novel
быстре́йшая маши́на   a really fast car
без мале́йшего сомне́ния   without the slightest doubt

5.2.2 When the stem of the positive adjective ends in -к, -г or -х, these velar consonants are palatalized to -ч, -ж and -ш respectively and the suffix -**айший** is used:

высоча́йшее зда́ние	an amazingly high building
строжа́йший режи́м	an extremely strict regime

Note, also: ближа́йший from бли́зкий, and нижа́йший from ни́зкий; дража́йший from дорого́й, and кратча́йший from коро́ткий; велича́йший from вели́кий is used for 'biggest', 'greatest'.

5.3 всё and все

Yet another form of the superlative can be formed with the short-form comparative and the genitive of всё or its plural все; this construction, like the short-form adjective, may only be used as complement to the verb 'to be' (i.e. as predicate):

> она́ быстре́е всех (*literally*) she is faster than all, i.e. the fastest
> его́ пе́рвый рома́н интере́снее всего́
> his first novel is the most interesting, i.e. more interesting than anything (he wrote)
> его́ пе́рвый рома́н интере́снее всех
> his first novel is the most interesting i.e. more interesting than all (the novels he wrote)

It is also correct to use the 'compound' form as complement:

> э́та маши́на са́мая бы́страя, его́ пе́рвый рома́н са́мый интере́сный,

and this form may be qualified by из and the genitive of всё or its plural все:

> э́та маши́на са́мая бы́страя из всех   this car is the fastest of all
> его́ пе́рвый рома́н са́мое интере́сное изо всего́, что он написа́л
> his first novel is the most interesting (thing) of everything he wrote

Жемчу́жины наро́дной му́дрости

о́пыт – лу́чший учи́тель	experience is the best teacher

EXERCISES

(i) *Put the following phrases into the superlative, using both the 'compound' and the expressive forms in nominative singular and genitive plural forms:*
добрый челове́к; ста́рый го́род; ску́чная газе́та; чи́стое о́зеро; сла́бое чу́вство; просто́й вопро́с; сканда́льная исто́рия; о́пытный врач; широ́кая река́; высо́кое зда́ние; жесто́кие слова́; бли́зкий телефо́н; кру́пный заво́д.

(ii) *Translate into English:*

1 Они́ е́хали в грома́днейшем авто́бусе.
2 Э́то был челове́к велича́йшего ума́.
3 Студе́нты сиде́ли в глубоча́йшем молча́нии без мале́йшего движе́ния.
4 Бори́с нашёл вы́ход оригина́льнейшим спо́собом.
5 Ничего́ не́ было ви́дно да́же при ярча́йшем све́те.
6 Он до сих пор пи́шет э́ти ужа́снейшие расска́зы?
7 Мы ча́сто вспомина́ли на́ших ближа́йших друзе́й.
8 Э́то интере́снейшая же́нщина!
9 У нас была́ ую́тнейшая кварти́ра в са́мой ую́тной ча́сти го́рода.
10 У бедне́йших крестья́н ча́сто сильне́йшая ве́ра.
11 Он оказа́лся богате́йшим бизнесме́ном.
12 Они́ не уме́ли перевести́ просте́йшие ве́щи, не пропуска́я грубе́йших оши́бок.
13 'Когда́ спроси́ли у Бро́дского о состоя́нии совреме́нной ру́сской поэ́зии, он отве́тил, что она́ нахо́дится на высоча́йшем у́ровне' (press).
14 'Совреме́нный Ло́ндон – крупне́йший центр развлече́ний, тури́зма и о́чень весёлый го́род, мо́жет быть, са́мый весёлый го́род ми́ра' (press).

(iii) *Translate into Russian:*

1 This is the most famous shop in Moscow.
2 His films were the most interesting of all.
3 He had the brightest talent of all the writers of that time.
4 To listen to this programme is the most boring thing of all.
5 In the coldest places there aren't even any wolves.
6 She used to work with the most inexperienced of all the doctors.
7 There is a university in all the largest towns.
8 My mother once gave me the most useful advice.
9 They worked in the most difficult conditions.
10 Who is your closest friend?

6   ADVERBS

6.1 Adverbs are used to qualify verbs, adjectives and other adverbs

он идёт **ме́дленно**	he is walking *slowly*
он **удиви́тельно** спосо́бный	he is *amazingly* capable
он идёт **удиви́тельно** ти́хо	he is walking *amazingly* quietly

Adverbs come in many shapes and sizes.

6.1.1 A large number of adverbs are formed from adjectives adopting a form identical to the neuter short form:

бы́стрый –	**бы́стро**	fast, quickly
обыкнове́нный –	**обыкнове́нно**	usually, ordinarily
раска́тистый –	**раска́тисто**	staccato
серьёзный –	**серьёзно**	seriously
высо́кий –	**высоко́**	highly
ди́кий –	**ди́ко**	wildly
ни́зкий–	**ни́зко**	low

Similarly: гро́мкий 'loud' – **гро́мко**; жа́ркий 'hot' – **жа́рко**; коро́ткий 'short' – **ко́ротко**; кре́пкий 'strong' – **кре́пко**; ре́дкий 'rare' – **ре́дко**; стро́гий 'strict' – **стро́го**; ти́хий 'quiet' – **ти́хо**; я́ркий 'bright' – **я́рко**.

6.1.2 Adverbs formed from adjectives ending in -ий are not all regular. Most of the common ones form adverbs in -o:

по́здний –	**по́здно**	late
ра́нний –	**ра́но**	early

A few, including those with stem in -ш-, -щ- and -ж- whose adverb is not end-stressed, form adverbs in -e:

вне́шний –	**вне́шне**	externally, outwardly
кра́йний –	**кра́йне**	extremely
неуклю́жий –	**неуклю́же**	clumsily

but: хоро́ший – **хорошо́** well

And и́скренний allows *either* **и́скренно** *or* **и́скренне** 'sincerely'.

6.1.3 Adjectives ending in -ский form adverbs in -и:

категори́ческий –	**категори́чески** categorically	
фантасти́ческий –	**фантасти́чески** fantastically	

' Adjectives in -ский are sometimes prefixed by по- to form adverbs:

англи́йский –	**по англи́йски**	in English, in the English way
ки́евский –	**по-ки́евски**	à la Kiev

Жемчу́жины наро́дной му́дрости

с волка́ми жить – по-во́лчьи выть live with wolves, (and you must) howl like a wolf

6.2 Adverbs may also be formed from participles (see pp. 131–2)

досяга́емый –	**досяга́емо**	attainably
неисправи́мый –	**неисправи́мо**	incorrigibly
неузнава́емый –	**неузнава́емо**	unrecognizably
припо́днятый –	**припо́днято**	exaltedly
сде́ржанный –	**сде́ржанно**	restrainedly
отдалённый –	**отдалённо**	distantly, remotely

Note: the adverb from the past passive participle in -нный preserves the double -нн-, while the short form of these participles retains only one (see pp. 131–2):
отдалённый – отдалённо, *but:* отдалён, отдалена́, отдалено́; отдалены́ – removed

• Adverbs may also be formed from some present active participles; the ending -щий gives an adverbial ending in -ще (see pp. 114–15, 131):

угрожа́ющий –	**угрожа́юще**	threateningly
соблазня́ющий –	**соблазня́юще**	seductively
блестя́щий –	**блестя́ще**	brilliantly

6.3 There are both comparative and superlative forms of the adverb

6.3.1 The comparative adverb is formed in the same way as the comparative adjective, with бо́лее or with the suffix -ее:

	она́ хо́дит бо́лее бы́стро, чем я	she walks faster than me
or:	она́ хо́дит быстре́е меня́	she walks faster than me

Жемчу́жины наро́дной му́дрости

ти́ше е́дешь – да́льше бу́дешь	slow and steady wins the race
осе́нняя му́ха больне́е куса́ет	the autumn fly bites more painfully

6.3.2 Like comparative adjectives, short-form comparative adverbs are liable to be qualified:

онá хóдит **горáздо** быстрéе меня́   she walks much faster than me

Жемчýжины нарóдной мýдрости

чем дáльше в лес, тем бóльше дров	the further into the forest, the more the firewood

6.3.3 A superlative adverb is only formed from those adjectives which have a 'short' comparative, using the genitive of comparison from всё *or* все (*plur.*):

он кýпит мáсло **бы́стрее всегó** на ры́нке
he'll buy butter quickest at the market, i.e. it's quicker *than anywhere else*

он кýпит мáсло **бы́стрее всех** на ры́нке
he'll buy butter quickest at the market, i.e. he'll be quicker *than anyone else*

Жемчýжины нарóдной мýдрости

кто бóльше всех спит, тот мéньше всех живёт	who sleeps most, lives least

- An adverb may also be formed from the 'expressive' superlative adjective:

стрóгий – строжáйший – **строжáйше**   most severely
покóрнейше прошý   I most humbly beg; be my guest

6.4 Like adjectives, adverbs may be intensified or qualified by other adverbs

óчень мéдленно	very slowly
весьмá стрóго	extremely severely
необы́чно деликáтно	unusually politely
я́вно нейскренно	blatantly insincerely

6.5 Like adverbs, nouns in the instrumental case qualify the actions of verbs

онá удáрила егó ключóм   she hit him with a spanner

6.5.1 Several are used frequently enough to be considered adverbs:

ýтром; днём; вéчером; нóчью
in the morning; in the afternoon; in the evening; at night

весно́й; ле́том; о́сенью; зимо́й
in the spring; in summer; in the autumn; in winter
круго́м; ря́дом; верхо́м around; beside; on horseback
ле́сом; чи́стым по́лем through the wood; across the open fields
времена́ми, поро́й at times
да́ром free, for nothing
не да́ром not for nothing, not in vain

Жемчу́жины наро́дной му́дрости

ле́сом шёл, а дере́вьев не ви́дел	(he) didn't see the wood for the trees
Москва́ века́ми стро́илась	Moscow wasn't built in a day

6.5.2 Many adverbs can be seen to derive from other cases of the noun or from preposition + noun combinations:

вверх; вниз upwards, upstairs; downwards, downstairs
во́время; вокру́г in time; around
вслух aloud
вдали́; и́здали in the distance; from a long way off
вме́сте together
вперёд; наза́д forwards;backwards
впереди́; позади́ in front; behind
кста́ти by the way, incidentally, opportunely
наверху́; внизу́ above, upstairs; below, downstairs
назло́; наоборо́т for spite; on the contrary
све́рху; сни́зу; сза́ди from above; from below; from behind
снача́ла; наконе́ц initially, to start with; finally
сра́зу at once, immediately

6.6 Adverbs can also be formed from combinations of preposition + adjective

за́ново; сно́ва anew; again
и́зредка; издалека́ now and again; from far away
напра́во; нале́во to the *or* on the right; . . . left
по-друго́му; по-но́вому in another way; in a new way
по-мо́ему in my opinion
смо́лоду; вручну́ю since childhood; by hand

6.7 The gerund of the verb is adverbial in the sense that it qualifies the action of another verb (see pp. 134–6)

он упа́л, поднима́ясь по ле́стнице   he fell down climbing the stairs

(the gerund поднима́ясь answers the question: 'how or when did he fall?')

Some gerunds are common enough to be considered as adverbs, divorced from their verbal connotation:

мо́лча	silently, without a word
неме́для	without delay

6.8 Some common adverbs

о́чень; ещё; уже́	very (much); still, yet, again; already
ещё не; уже́ не	not yet; no longer
вдруг; одна́жды; два́жды	suddenly; once; twice
чуть; едва́; то́лько	just a bit; only just, very nearly; only
вчера́; сего́дня; за́втра	yesterday; today; tomorrow
как? где? куда́? когда́?	how? where? where (to)? when?
тепе́рь; тогда́; иногда́; всегда́	now; then; sometimes; always
здесь; там; туда́	here; there; there (thither)
так; почти́; совсе́м	so, like that; almost; completely
сли́шком; весьма́; во́все не	too (much); extremely; not at all
опя́ть; то́же; та́кже	again; also, too; also, besides
почему́?	why?

EXERCISES

(i)　a.　*Form adverbs from these adjectives:*
си́льный; интере́сный; тяжёлый; бли́зкий; лёгкий; да́вний; тя́жкий; вну́тренний; физи́ческий; фантасти́ческий;

　　b.　*Now form comparative adverbs from them;*

　　c.　*Now form superlative adverbs from the first five.*

(ii)　*Translate into Russian:*

1　She looked at him cheerfully.
2　She looked at him unwillingly.
3　She looked at him sceptically.
4　She looked at him greedily.
5　She looked at him frankly.

7 PRONOUNS

7.1 Personal pronouns

7.1.1

	1st person	2nd person	3rd person			Reflexive
sing.	'I'	'you'	'he/it'	'she/it'	'it'	'-self'
nom.	я	ты	он	она́	оно́	–
acc.	меня́	тебя́	его́	её	его́	себя́
gen.	меня́	тебя́	его́	её	его́	себя́
dat.	мне	тебе́	ему́	ей	ему́	себе́
inst.	мной	тобо́й	им	ей	им	собо́й
pr.	обо мне	о тебе́	о нём	о ней	о нём	о себе́

	'we'	'you'	'they'	'-selves'
plur.				
nom.	мы	вы	они́	–
acc.	нас	вас	их	себя́
gen.	нас	вас	их	себя́
dat.	нам	вам	им	себе́
inst.	на́ми	ва́ми	и́ми	собо́й
pr.	о нас	о вас	о них	о себе́

Note: его́, её and их, the *acc.* of он, она́, оно́ and они́, are used for both animate and inanimate *masc., fem., neut.* and *plur.* objects respectively.

Note: When a preposition governs any of the 3rd person pronouns, all of which start with a vowel, the letter н- is prefixed to the pronoun:

	у неё краси́вый го́лос	she has a beautiful voice
(*cf:*	её го́лос о́чень краси́вый	her voice is very beautiful)

	она́ зашла́ к ним	she called in on them
(*cf:*	она́ дала́ им нож	she gave them the knife)

	мы пошли́ без него́	we went without him
(*cf:*	мы пошли́ без его́ соба́ки	we went without his dog

here без is governing соба́ка, 'dog': его́ 'his' is genitive of possession)

7.1.2 Себя the reflexive pronoun has no nominative case; this is because it always refers back to the subject of the verb – it cannot be the subject:

ты ду́маешь то́лько **о себе́**	you're thinking only of yourself
я найду́ **себе́** но́вую кварти́ру	I'll find myself a new apartment
они́ спра́шивали **себя́**, где он	they were asking themselves where he was

Note: себя́ is close in meaning, but not identical, to the reflexive particle -ся:

он счита́ет себя́ отли́чным шахмати́стом
he considers himself an excellent chess player
он счита́ется отли́чным шахмати́стом
he is considered an excellent chess player
я чу́вствую себя́ си́льным   I feel strong
э́то чу́вствуется си́льно   this is felt strongly

EXERCISES

(i)   a.   *Complete the following sentences by inserting the correct form of the pronoun* я:
они́ лю́бят . . .
они́ живу́т недалеко́ от . . .
. . . всё равно́
за́втра она́ пое́дет со . . . в Минск
что он говори́л обо . . .

      b.   *Now insert the appropriate form of* мы:

(ii) a.   *Complete the following sentences by inserting the correct form of the pronoun* ты:
они́ не зна́ют . . .
она́ зави́сит от . . .
Бори́с и А́нна посла́ли . . . пода́рок
что с . . . ?
о . . . пи́шут в газе́те

      b.   *Now insert the appropriate form of* вы.

(iii) a.   *Complete the following sentences by inserting the correct form of the pronoun* он:
я понима́ю . . .
она́ получи́ла письмо́ от . . .
она посла́ла . . . откры́тку
мы о́чень дово́льны . . .
мать беспоко́ится о . . .

b. *Now insert the appropriate form of* онá.

c. *Now insert the appropriate form of* они́.

(iv) *Translate into Russian:*
1 I respect him, but I worry about his son.
2 Where is her dictionary? I can't see it.
3 Where are his cassettes? I can't see them.
4 We'll do it for him and for his family.
5 He can't live without her; he can't live without her money.
6 When they got used to him they allowed him to sit with them.
7 We know nothing about them or their plans.
8 Yesterday evening I had a talk with her and her husband and their children.

(v) a. *Insert the correct form of the pronoun* себя *in the gaps in the following sentence:*

Он ужáсный эгои́ст: он óчень лю́бит . . . , покупáет . . . дороги́е подáрки, интересу́ется тóлько . . . , беспокóится тóлько о . . . .

b. *Now put the sentence above into the plural.*

(vi) *Translate into Russian:*
1 She considers herself a good pianist
2 He bought a new motorcycle for himself
3 Did you take your camera with you?
4 How do you feel?

7.2 Demonstrative pronouns

7.2.1

sing.	'this'			'that'		
	masc.	*fem.*	*neut.*	*masc.*	*fem.*	*neut.*
nom.	э́тот	э́та	э́то	тот	та	то
acc.	э́тот/э́того	э́ту	э́то	тот/тогó	ту	то
gen.	э́того	э́той	э́того	тогó	той	тогó
dat.	э́тому	э́той	э́тому	томý	той	томý
inst.	э́тим	э́той	э́тим	тем	той	тем
pr.	об э́том	об э́той	об э́том	о том	о той	о том

plur.	'these'	'those'
nom.	э́ти	те
acc.	э́ти/э́тих	те/тех
gen.	э́тих	тех
dat.	э́тим	тем
inst.	э́тими	тéми
pr.	об э́тих	о тех

7.3   Interrogative pronouns

7.3.1   'who?'   'what?'   'whose?'

sing.			*masc.*	*fem.*	*neut.*	*plur.*
nom.	кто	что	чей	чья	чьё	чьи
acc.	кого	что	чей/чьего	чью	чьё	чьи/чьих
gen.	кого	чего	чьего	чьей	чьего	чьих
dat.	кому	чему	чьему	чьей	чьему	чьим
inst.	кем	чем	чьим	чьей	чьим	чьими
pr.	о ком	о чём	о чьём	о чьей	о чьём	о чьих

Note: the negative pronouns никто, ничто and ничей (see pp. 204–5) decline like кто, что, чей.

Note: the gender of **кто** is *masc.* even when it is clear that the speaker is referring to a woman: кто пришёл? 'who's that?' even if you can hear a woman's voice and even when it could only be referring to a woman:

кто вышел замуж в этом году?   who got married this year?

But if **кто** is qualified by a feminine noun or pronoun it may take on feminine gender:

кто из девушек нашла мои очки?   which of the girls found my glasses?
кто она такая?   who is she?

* **что** is always neuter
  что случилось?   what's happened?

* the interrogative Adjective **чей** agrees with the noun which it qualifies, *not* the person; in simple questions of the sort 'whose house is this?' the accompanying demonstrative это remains neuter singular, 'this thing':

чей это дом?   whose house is this?
чья это была квартира?   whose apartment was this?
чьи это носки?   whose socks are these?
о чьём портрете ты говорила?   whose portrait were you talking about?

Жемчужины народной мудрости

чует кошка, чьё мясо съела	the cat senses whose meat it has eaten

---

EXERCISES

(i) a. *Insert the correct form of* **этот** *in the following phrases:*
       для ... студента

с ... студе́нткой
в ... сло́ве
на ... берегу́
в ... ко́мнату
по ... у́лицам
над ... го́родом
с ... сто́роны
по ... направле́нию

b. *Insert the correct form of* **тот** *in the same phrases.*

(ii) *Translate into Russian:*

a. Who do you know? What are you writing? Who are you writing to? Who are you going to Scotland with? What are you interested in? Who are they talking about? What are they talking about?

b. Whose is this umbrella? Whose room is this? Whose book did she take? Whose name had he forgotten? In whose house did they find her? Whose parents did he write to?

7.4 Indefinite pronoun

Russian distinguishes two levels of the indefinite pronouns 'someone' and 'something':

- **кто-то** and **что-то** are used if an actual person or thing is being referred to but not named for some reason – you've forgotten, you don't want to say, or you're not sure who or what it actually was:

  кто-то звони́л   someone rang
  что-то случи́лось   something's happened

  она́ всегда́ хо́дит в теа́тр с кем-то из свое́й шко́лы
  she always goes to the theatre with someone from her school

- **кто́-нибудь** and **что́-нибудь** are used if the person or thing cannot be specified – it could be anyone or anything, someone or something or other:

  я наде́юсь, что кто́-нибудь придёт   I hope someone comes

  что́-нибудь невероя́тное обяза́тельно случи́тся
  something incredible is bound to happen

  чего́-нибудь хо́чешь?   do you want anything?

- **че́й-то** or **че́й-нибудь** are used for 'someone's', depending on whether reference is to an actual, theoretically definable 'someone' or to a vague, unidentifiable or hypothetical 'anyone':

мы услы́шали че́й-то знако́мый го́лос
we heard someone's familiar voice

возьми́ че́й-нибудь зо́нтик – всё равно́, ско́ро придёшь
take anyone's umbrella – you'll be back soon, anyway

Note: the pronouns decline normally, but none of the suffixes change:
он разгова́ривал с кем-то о чём-то соверше́нно неинтере́сном
he was talking to someone about something totally boring

расскажи́ мне о чём-нибудь интере́сном! – tell me about something interesting

Note: the suffixes -то and -нибудь are also used with the interrogative adjective како́й 'which? what sort of?' (како́й-то, како́й-нибудь 'some, some kind of') and the interrogative adverbs как 'how?' (ка́к-то, ка́к-нибудь 'somehow'), где 'where?' (где́-то, где́-нибудь 'somewhere'), куда́ 'where (to)?' (куда́-то, куда́-нибудь 'somewhere' [implying movement]), отку́да 'where from?' (отку́да-то, отку́да-нибудь 'from somewhere'), когда́ 'when?' (когда́-то, когда́-нибудь 'sometime; ever'); почему́ 'why?' (почему́-то 'for some reason' [no equivalent with -нибудь])

Note: an alternative to -нибудь is -либо: кто́-либо, где́-либо, etc.

EXERCISES

(i) *Translate into English and explain the difference between these pairs of sentences:*

она́ должна́ люби́ть кого́-то
она́ должна́ люби́ть кого́-нибудь

ты что́-то слы́шал о нём?
ты что́-нибудь слы́шал о нём?

он всё вре́мя разгова́ривает с ке́м-то
он хо́чет поговори́ть с ке́м-нибудь

она́ дала́ мне чью́-то кни́гу
дай мне чью́-нибудь кни́гу!

(ii) *Translate into Russian:*

1 If you want to see anything ask the guide.
2 I think I saw something in the water.
3 She found someone's glasses in the bus.
4 It's raining – we'll have to go in someone's car.
5 He always says something nice to me.
6 He found out about this from one of his acquaintances.
7 Did you notice anyone in the corridor?
8 We noticed someone in the corridor.

7.5   Possessive pronoun

1st person singular 'my'

sing.	*masc.*	*fem.*	*neut.*	*plur.*
nom.	мой	моя́	моё	мои́
acc.	мой/моего́	мою́	моё	мои́/мои́х
gen.	моего́	мое́й	моего́	мои́х
dat.	моему́	мое́й	моему́	мои́м
inst.	мои́м	мое́й	мои́м	мои́ми
pr.	о моём	о мое́й	о моём	о мои́х

* 2nd person singular 'your' (informal) **твой, твоя́, твоё** declines in the same way: **твою́, твоего́, твои́ми**, etc.

1st person plural 'our'

sing.	*masc.*	*fem.*	*neut.*	*Plur.*
nom.	наш	на́ша	на́ше	на́ши
acc.	наш/на́шего	на́шу	на́ше	на́ши/на́ших
gen.	на́шего	на́шей	на́шего	на́ших
dat.	на́шему	на́шей	на́шему	на́шим
inst.	на́шим	на́шей	на́шим	на́шими
pr.	о на́шем	о на́шей	о на́шем	о на́ших

* 2nd person plural 'your' (and formal singular) **ваш, ва́ша, ва́ше; ва́ши** declines in the same way: **ва́шу, ва́шего, ва́ших**, etc.

7.6 The reflexive pronoun

The reflexive pronoun **свой** '(one's) own' declines like мой. It can refer to any person of the verb, singular or plural, – 'my (own)', 'your (own)', 'their (own)', etc. It refers back to the subject of the verb in the same clause, but cannot normally qualify, or itself be, the subject, so:

| я принесу́ свою́ скри́пку | I'll bring my violin |
| ты забы́ла о своём дне рожде́ния | you forgot about your birthday |

мы пи́шем свои́м друзья́м   we're writing to our friends

Note: in these examples свой can be replaced by the appropriate personal pronoun : я принесу́ *мою́* скри́пку, ты забы́ла о *твоём* дне рожде́ния, мы пи́шем *на́шим* друзья́м; there is no change in meaning. This goes for the 1st and 2nd persons, singular and plural. But in the 3rd person singular 'his', 'her', 'its' and 3rd person plural 'their' care must be taken:
if 'his', 'her', 'its' or 'their' refers back to the subject *only* свой may be used:

он встреча́ет свою́ сестру́   he's meeting his (own) sister
они́ спо́рят о свои́х пла́нах   they're arguing about their (own) plans

Жемчу́жины наро́дной му́дрости

со свои́м самова́ром в Ту́лу не е́здят	you don't go to Tula with your own samovar (coals to Newcastle)
ка́ждый кули́к в своём боло́те вели́к	every sandpiper is a giant in its own marsh

- Otherwise, when 'his', 'her', 'its' or 'their' does not refer back to the subject, the genitive case of the personal pronoun is used:
  его́ 'his', 'its'; **её** 'her', 'its'; **их** 'their'

These stay in the genitive, whatever the case of the noun they qualify:

она́ идёт к **его́** до́му   she's walking towards his house
(*lit:* 'towards the house of him')
cf. к моему́ до́му   towards my house (here мой agrees with дом)

Similarly: с **её** друзья́ми   with her friends (её remains in the *gen.*)
cf. с твои́ми друзья́ми   with your friends (твой has to agree with друзья́)

and   на **их** маши́не   in their car
по **его́** мне́нию   in his opinion
об **их** пробле́мах   about their problems

Note: when following a 3rd-person subject these forms of possessive pronoun do not refer back to it, so:

он встреча́ет его́ сестру́   he's meeting his (someone else's) sister
они́ спо́рят об их пла́нах   they're arguing about their (others') plans

Compare:

они́ про́дали свой ста́рый дом   they've sold their old house

они́ не зна́ют, кому́ тепе́рь принадлежи́т их ста́рый дом
they don't know whom their old house belongs to now

они́ не зна́ют, кто купи́л их ста́рый дом
they don't know who's bought their old house

Only in the first of these does 'their' refer back to the *subject* of the verb in the same clause, so only there can свой be used.

• свой normally refers back to the subject of the verb, but does not normally agree with the subject, i.e. it does not normally occur in the nominative case. But it is used in the nominative in some idiomatic or proverbial sayings:

он свой челове́к	he's one of us
здесь то́лько свои́ лю́ди	we're all friends here

Жемчу́жины наро́дной му́дрости

своя́ руба́шка бли́же к те́лу	blood is thicker than water

Note: when его́, её *or* их are used as adjectives 'his', 'her(s)', 'its' *or* 'their' they do *not* take initial -н after prepositions:

у него́ 'he has', *but:* у его́ отца́ 'his father has', к их до́му 'towards their house'

EXERCISES

(i) a. *Insert the correct form of* мой *in the following phrases:*
для ... бра́та; у ... сестры́; по ... мне́нию; к ... ра́дости;
в ... ча́шку; на ... ме́сто; над ... голово́й; в ... положе́нии;
до ... экза́менов; в ... интере́сах.

b. *Insert the correct form of* твой *in the same phrases.*

c. *Insert the correct form of* ваш *in the same phrases.*

(ii) *Translate into Russian:*

1 She met his brother in the bookshop.
2 She met her brother in the bookshop.
3 Her brother met her in her bookshop.
4 Her brother met her in his bookshop.
5 Did you find your dog?
6 Did they find their dog?

7   She stayed at home to finish her homework.
8   She stayed at home to help her brother with his homework.
9   We asked him to mend our window.
10 We advised him to mend his window.

7.7 The pronoun весь 'all', 'the whole ...'

sing.	masc.	fem.	neut.	plur.
nom.	весь	вся	всё	все
acc.	весь/всего	всю	всё	все/всех
gen.	всего	всей	всего	всех
dat.	всему	всей	всему	всем
inst.	всем	всей	всем	всёми
pr.	обо всём	о всей	обо всём	обо всех

Note: the neuter form всё is used for 'everything':

всё хорошо   everything's fine
мы всё забыли   we've forgotten everything

The plural form все is used for 'everyone', 'everybody':

все пришли   everyone's arrived
у всех ручка?   has everybody got a pen?

Жемчужины народной мудрости

все за одного – один за всех	all for one and one for all

EXERCISE

Insert the correct form of весь *and give the English for:*

во ... голос; во... мочь; от ... сердца; ... хорошего;
он ... в отца; нам ... равно; спасибо за ...;
во ... времена; изо... сил; во ... отношениях

7.8 Relative pronouns

A relative pronoun is used to refer to a preceding noun or pronoun, e.g. 'the man *who* lives next door', 'in the club *from which* we got the invitation'.

7.8.1 With nouns, Russian uses the relative pronoun **который** 'who, which':

sing.	masc.	fem.	neut.	plur.
nom.	кото́рый	кото́рая	кото́рое	кото́рые
acc.	кото́рый/кото́рого	кото́рую	кото́рое	кото́рые/кото́рых
gen.	кото́рого	кото́рой	кото́рого	кото́рых
dat.	кото́рому	кото́рой	кото́рому	кото́рым
inst.	кото́рым	кото́рой	кото́рым	кото́рыми
pr.	о кото́ром	о кото́рой	о кото́ром	о кото́рых

- The noun to which кото́рый refers may be in any case; кото́рый agrees with this noun in gender and number (*sing.* or *plur.*) but its own case depends on its grammatical role in the relative clause.

Note: in colloquial English 'who' and 'which' are sometimes omitted:
где же́нщина, **кото́рая** стоя́ла здесь пять мину́т наза́д?
where is the woman who was standing here five minutes ago?

but: э́то челове́к, **у кото́рого** рабо́тает мой брат
this is the man my brother works for (. . . for whom my brother works)

вот врач, **к кото́рому** обрати́лся наш оте́ц
here's the doctor our father went to (. . . to whom our father turned)

где маши́на, **на кото́рой** пое́дем в го́род?
where's the car we're going to town in?

де́рево, **под кото́рым** он сиди́т, бы́ло поса́жено его́ де́душкой
the tree he's sitting under was planted by his grandfather

иду́т де́вушки, **с кото́рыми** у́чится моя́ сестра́
here come the girls my sister goes to school with

- The case of the noun to which кото́рый refers is irrelevant to it: the main clauses in the examples above can be changed without affecting кото́рый or the relative clause:

он и́щет же́нщину, **кото́рая** стоя́ла здесь пять мину́т наза́д
he's looking for the woman who was standing here five minutes ago

дава́й помо́жем челове́ку, **у кото́рого** рабо́тает мой брат
let's help the man my brother works for

она́ е́хала в трамва́е с врачо́м, **к кото́рому** обрати́лся наш оте́ц
she was riding in a tram with the doctor our father went to

он во́дит маши́ну, **на кото́рой** мы пое́дем в го́род
he's driving the car we're going to town in

мы то́лько что прошли́ ми́мо де́рева, **под кото́рым** он сиди́т
we've just walked past the tree he's sitting under

я хочу́ познако́миться с де́вушками, **с кото́рыми** сестра́ у́чится
I want to get to know the girls my sister goes to school with

Note: the relative pronoun кото́рый is used in some expressions of time as an interrogative: кото́рый час? – what's the time? в кото́ром часу́? – at what time?

EXERCISES

(i) *Translate into English:*

1 В магази́не, кото́рый принадлежи́т моему́ дя́де, продаётся фи́нская ме́бель.
2 Но нет той ме́бели, о кото́рой мечта́ет моя́ тётя.
3 На трамва́е, кото́рый идёт в университе́т, е́здят одни́ студе́нты.
4 Он потеря́л ми́шку, без кото́рого он спать не мо́жет.
5 Они́ терпе́ть не мо́гут преподава́телей, у кото́рых нет чу́вства ю́мора.
6 Дере́вья, вокру́г кото́рых стоя́ли лю́ди, бу́дут руби́ть.

(ii) *Translate into Russian:*

1   We saw the businessman who visited us last week.
2   We saw the businessman we visited last month.
3   We saw the businessman whose wife opened the exhibition.
4   We saw the businessman we wrote to last year.
5   We saw the businessman we went to Moscow with.
6   We saw the businessman we were talking about yesterday.
7   The car standing under that tree belongs to her father.
8   We went to London in the car her father bought her.
9   I don't like a car which doesn't have a radio.
10 The books my friend is interested in are too expensive.
11 There was a lot of philosophy in all the books we talked about.
12 Among the papers he hasn't read yet there are some very interesting articles.

7.8.2 **То, что . . .; тот, кто . . .** When the relative pronoun refers to a pronoun, not a noun in phrases like 'those who', 'everything which', etc. the pronouns что *or* кто replace кото́рый:

то, что мы ви́дели на вы́ставке, порази́ло нас
what we saw at the exhibition amazed us (i.e. that which we saw . . .)

он де́лает **то, чем** он интересу́ется
he does what he's interested in (. . . that in which he's interested)

он занима́ется **тем, что** интересу́ет его
he occupies himself with what interests him (. . . with that which . . .)

всё, что она говори́т о нём, отно́сится ко мне
everything that she says about him relates to me

мы не понима́ли **всего́, что** они́ говори́ли
we didn't understand everything they said

им показа́ли **всё, от чего́** зави́сит програ́мма
they were shown everything the programme depends on

тот, кто откры́л дверь, очеви́дно, взял су́мку
the one who opened the door obviously took the bag

те, кто ду́мает так, обы́чно схо́дят с ума́
those who think like that usually go mad

Note: even if the pronoun to which кто refers is plural, кто remains singular, taking the 3rd person singular of the verb and generally masculine in the past tense (see p. 79); so too:

мы согла́сны со **все́ми, кто** хо́чет постро́ить тунне́ль
we agree with all those who want to build a tunnel

Note: if the pronoun is attached to a noun кото́рый replaces the pronoun in the relative clause:

мы согла́сны **со все́ми инжене́рами, которые** хотя́т постро́ить тунне́ль
we agree with all the engineers who want to build a tunnel

Жемчу́жины наро́дной му́дрости

Не всё то зо́лото, что блести́т	not all is gold that glitters
Кто не рабо́тает, тот не ест	he who doesn't work, doesn't eat

EXERCISES

(i) *Translate into English:*

1   Тот, кто найдёт ключ, полу́чит награ́ду.
2   Мы получи́ли пи́сьма от всех тех, кто был в на́шей гру́ппе.
3   Она́ сра́зу узна́ла того́, с кем она́ говори́ла по телефо́ну.
4   Э́то был тот, о ком нас предупреди́ли.
5   То, что нам говори́ли, совсе́м не повлия́ло на нас.
6   То, о чём они́ говори́ли, о́чень заинтересова́ло нас.
7   Мы бы́ли поражены́ тем, что они́ сообщи́ли нам.
8   Они́ удивля́лись всему́, что происходи́ло.
9   'Хорошо́ смеётся тот, кто стреля́ет пе́рвым' (General Lebed').

(ii) *Translate into Russian:*

1   The one who opened the door obviously saw this man.
2   She's gone to Odessa with the one who lives on the third floor.
3   What she said was extraordinarily interesting.
4   We were thinking about what she said.
5   He hears everything they do.
6   I'm interested in everything she writes.
7   Everyone who hears this music falls asleep.
8   She wrote to everyone who had sent her a present.
9   These books belong to the ones we used to go to the theatre with.
10 I never pay attention to those who argue loudly.

7.8.3   **Чей**: relative clauses may also be formed with the interrogative adjective чей? 'whose?'; чей is normally used with the demonstrative э́то and a noun to form direct questions such as:

чей э́то слова́рь?   whose dictionary is this?
чья э́то соба́ка?   whose dog is this?

от чьих роди́телей она́ получи́ла приглаше́ние?
from whose parents did she get the invitation?

When used in relative clauses чей means 'whose' but does not imply a question; it has the sense of the genitive — 'of whom' — and is equivalent to the genitive of кото́рый. Again it agrees with the noun it qualifies:

наш сосе́д, **чей оте́ц** был изве́стным музыка́нтом, не лю́бит джа́за
our neighbour whose father was a famous musician doesn't like jazz

This could also be rendered by:

наш сосе́д, оте́ц кото́рого был изве́стным музыка́нтом, не лю́бит
джа́за

у же́нщины, **в чьей кварти́ре** вспы́хнул пожа́р, тепе́рь нет ме́бели
(*or:* у же́нщины, в кварти́ре кото́рой вспы́хнул пожа́р, . . .)
the woman in whose flat the fire burst out hasn't got any furniture now

тем друзья́м, **без чьей по́мощи** мы не постро́или бы гара́ж, мы
бесконе́чно благода́рны
to those friends without whose help we would not have built the garage
we are eternally grateful

EXERCISES

(i) *Translate into English:*

1 Чья э́то маши́на?
2 Чьи э́то де́ти?
3 Лю́ди, с чьи́ми детьми́ мы идём сего́дня в кино́, на́ши сосе́ди.
4 На чьей маши́не мы пое́дем сего́дня в шко́лу?
5 Челове́к, на чьей маши́не мы пое́дем сего́дня в шко́лу, знако́мый отца́.
6 На́шего дру́га, чья соба́ка укуси́ла почтальо́на, арестова́ли вчера́.

(ii) *Translate into Russian:*

1 Whose dog bit the postman?
2 I never met the person on whose help my fate depended.
3 Whose dictionary is this?
4 The woman whose dictionary you found likes reading.
5 The director without whose influence I would not have got the job turned out to
  be my wife's uncle.

8 CONJUGATION OF THE VERB

8.1 Aspect

You will already be familiar with the general principles of the formation and use of the imperfective and perfective aspects, but they are sufficiently complex for English speakers to warrant enumeration and repetition:

- the **perfective** aspect expresses or draws attention to the **completion** or **result** of an action performed on one occasion:
  сего́дня ве́чером я хочу́ **прочита́ть** э́ту главу́
  I want to read this chapter (and finish it, get it read) this evening

  она́ **написа́ла** сочине́ние вчера́
  she wrote the essay yesterday (has got it written, and as a result is now free).

- It follows that the perfective is used for a **series** of actions, each of which must be completed before the next can take place:
  он **закры́л** дверь, **откры́л** окно́ и **на́чал** писа́ть
  he closed the door, opened the window and began to write

  я **приду́** в во́семь, **уберу́** кварти́ру, **пригото́влю** у́жин и **ля́гу** спать
  I'll come at eight, tidy the apartment, make supper and go to bed.

The **imperfective** aspect is used for all other purposes, i.e. principally:

- to draw attention to the **process** or **duration** of the action itself:
  сего́дня ве́чером я хочу́ **чита́ть** э́тот но́вый рома́н;
  я **бу́ду чита́ть** его́ весь ве́чер
  this evening I want to read this new novel; I'll be reading it all evening

- to express **general** or **repeated** action:
  в тече́ние семе́стра мы **чита́ли** ру́сские рома́ны и **писа́ли** сочинения
  in the course of the semester we read Russian novels and wrote essays

Only the imperfective can form a present tense – describing actions that are continuing in the present or which are repeated, i.e. which are not thought of as completed. Past and future tenses may be imperfective or perfective.

The use of aspects is dealt with in more detail in chapter 10.

Note: from now on imperfective/perfective infinitive pairs may be shown separated by the oblique stroke 'slash' (/), e.g. де́лать/сде́лать, реша́ть/реши́ть.

8.2 Conjugation of regular verbs

There are two main conjugations in Russian, distinguished by what happens in the present tense or, if perfective, the perfective future :

8.2.1 Verbs in the 1st Conjugation have the 3rd person singular (ie. with он, она́ or оно́ as subject) in -ет or -ёт and the 3rd person plural in -ют or -ут:

Present tense

	чита́ть	писа́ть	идти́	пить	интересова́ться
	'to read'	'to write'	'to go'	'to drink'	'to be interested'
я	чита́ю	пишу́	иду́	пью	интересу́юсь
ты	чита́ешь	пи́шешь	идёшь	пьёшь	интересу́ешься
он, etc.	чита́ет	пи́шет	идёт	пьёт	интересу́ется
мы	чита́ем	пи́шем	идём	пьём	интересу́емся
вы	чита́ете	пи́шете	идёте	пьёте	интересу́етесь
они́	чита́ют	пи́шут	иду́т	пьют	интересу́ются

Perfective future tense

	прочита́ть	написа́ть	принести́	прожи́ть	заня́ться
	'to read'	'to write'	'to bring'	'to live'	'to engage in'
я	прочита́ю	напишу́	принесу́	проживу́	займу́сь
ты	прочита́ешь	напи́шешь	принесёшь	проживёшь	займёшься
он	прочита́ет	напи́шет	принесёт	проживёт	займётся
мы	прочита́ем	напи́шем	принесём	проживём	займёмся
вы	прочита́ете	напи́шете	принесёте	проживёте	займётесь
они́	прочита́ют	напи́шут	принесу́т	проживу́т	займу́тся

8.2.2 Verbs in the 2nd Conjugation have the 3rd person singular in -ит and the 3rd person plural in -ят or -ат:

Present tense

	вари́ть	учи́ться	стоя́ть	лежа́ть	ви́деть
	'to cook'	'to learn'	'to stand'	'to lie'	'to see'
я	варю́	учу́сь	стою́	лежу́	ви́жу
ты	ва́ришь	у́чишься	стои́шь	лежи́шь	ви́дишь
он	ва́рит	у́чится	стои́т	лежи́т	ви́дит
мы	ва́рим	у́чимся	стои́м	лежи́м	ви́дим
вы	ва́рите	у́читесь	стои́те	лежи́те	ви́дите
они́	ва́рят	у́чатся	стоя́т	лежа́т	ви́дят

Perfective future tense

	сварить	решить	улететь	превратиться
	'to cook'	'to decide'	'to fly away'	'to turn into'
я	сварю́	решу́	улечу́	превращу́сь
ты	сва́ришь	реши́шь	улети́шь	преврати́шься
он	сва́рит	реши́т	улети́т	преврати́тся
мы	сва́рим	реши́м	улети́м	преврати́мся
вы	сва́рите	реши́те	улети́те	преврати́тесь
они́	сва́рят	реша́т	улетя́т	превратя́тся

Жемчу́жины наро́дной му́дрости

на воре́ ша́пка гори́т	on a thief the cap burns (it's easy to see who did it)

Note: There are some consonant changes which regularly occur in the first person singular of the present or perfective future tense of 2nd Conjugation verbs:

- Epenthetic -л-: this appears in all 2nd Conjugation verbs whose stem ends in

-б, -в, -м, -п or **-ф:**

Infinitive	*Present tense*
гото́вить 'to prepare'	гото́влю, гото́вишь ... гото́вят
графи́ть 'to rule (paper)'	графлю́, графи́шь ... графя́т
люби́ть 'to love'	люблю́, лю́бишь ... лю́бят
спать 'to sleep'	сплю, спишь ... спят
станови́ться 'to become'	становлю́сь, стано́вишься ... стано́вятся

- Stems ending in -д, -т, -з, -с, -ст: these consonants are changed to chuintantes ('hush-type' consonants) in the 1st person singular of the present and perfective future tenses of 2nd Conjugation verbs:

	Infinitive	*Present tense*
д > ж	ви́деть 'to see'	ви́жу, ви́дишь ... ви́дят
	е́здить 'to travel'	е́зжу, е́здишь ... е́здят
т > ч	лете́ть 'to fly'	лечу́, лети́шь ... летя́т
	плати́ть 'to pay'	плачу́, пла́тишь ... пла́тят
з > ж	вози́ть 'to transport'	вожу́, во́зишь ... во́зят
с > ш	проси́ть 'to ask, request'	прошу́, про́сишь ... про́сят
ст > щ	чи́стить 'to clean'	чи́щу, чи́стишь ... чи́стят

	Perfective future	
д > ж	утверди́ть 'to assert'	утвержу́, утверди́шь ... утвердя́т
т > ч	встре́тить 'to meet'	встре́чу, встре́тишь ... встре́тят
з > ж	сни́зить 'to lower'	сни́жу, сни́зишь ... сни́зят
с > ш	согласи́ться 'to agree'	соглашу́сь, согласи́шься ... соглася́тся
ст > щ	пусти́ть 'to release, let go'	пущу́, пу́стишь ... пу́стят

Note: some -т stem verbs derived from the old literary language Church Slavonic show the change т > щ:

Infinitive	*Perfective future*
защити́ть 'to defend'	**защищу́, защити́шь ... защитя́т**
просвети́ть 'to enlighten'	**просвещу́, просвети́шь ... просветя́т**

Жемчу́жины наро́дной му́дрости

лес ру́бят – ще́пки летя́т	(if they) chop down the forest the chips fly

---

EXERCISES

(i) a.   *Give the present tense of:*
      гра́бить; гото́вить; знако́мить; спать; терпе́ть

   b.   *Give the perfective future tense of:*
      изуми́ть; купи́ть; осла́бить; поздра́вить; укрепи́ть

   c.   *Give their English meanings.*

(ii) a.   *Give the present tense of:*
      вреди́ть; грози́ть; плати́ть; проси́ть; суди́ть; чи́стить

   b.   *Give the perfective future tense of:*
      разбуди́ть; порази́ть; пригласи́ть; пусти́ть; заме́тить

   c.   *Give their English meanings.*

8.3 Verbs of 'mixed' conjugation

8.3.1 There are two verbs which have mixed (1st and 2nd) Conjugation:

Present tense

	хоте́ть	бежа́ть
	'to want'	'to run'
я	хочу́	бегу́
ты	хо́чешь	бежи́шь
он	хо́чет	бежи́т
мы	хоти́м	бежи́м
вы	хоти́те	бежи́те
они́	хотя́т	бегу́т

8.3.2 And there are two verbs which have traces of an old 'athematic' Conjugation (in which there was no 'stem' and endings were added to the root):

Present tense	Perfective future tense
есть	дать
'to eat'	'to give'
я ем	дам
ты ешь	дашь
он ест	даст
мы еди́м	дади́м
вы еди́те	дади́те
они́ едя́т	даду́т

8.3.3 Only the 3rd person singular of the present tense of быть 'to be' survives in modern Russian: **есть**. This is used for emphasis ('there *is* . . .') and it may be used for any person:

вы и есть мой лу́чший друг	you *are* my best friend

Есть is commonly used to express possession or location:

у нас есть соба́ка	we have a dog
в го́роде есть кино́	there is a cinema in the town

8.4 There is a complete future tense of быть, 'I shall be, you will be, etc.':

я	бу́ду	мы	бу́дем
ты	бу́дешь	вы	бу́дете
он	бу́дет	они́	бу́дут

мы бу́дем в Вашингто́не за́втра	we'll be in Washington tomorrow
она́ бу́дет отли́чным врачо́м	she'll be an excellent doctor

8.5 The ending of the infinitive is not a reliable indication of conjugation

There is, for instance, a group of 2nd Conjugation verbs whose infinitive ends in **-ать**, including:

Infinitive	*Present tense*
держа́ть 'to hold'	держу́, де́ржишь . . . де́ржат
(likewise **содержа́ть** 'to contain')	
дыша́ть 'to breathe'	дышу́, ды́шишь . . . ды́шат
крича́ть 'to shout'	кричу́, кричи́шь . . . крича́т
лежа́ть 'to lie (flat)'	лежу́, лежи́шь . . . лежа́т
(likewise **принадлежа́ть** 'to belong' принадлежу́, принадлежи́шь . . .	
принадлежа́т)	
молча́ть 'to be silent'	молчу́, молчи́шь . . . молча́т
слы́шать 'to hear'	слы́шу, слы́шишь . . . слы́шат

Note: The rules of spelling affect the 3rd person plural of 2nd Conjugation verbs with stem endings in -ж, -ч, -ш or -щ.

Note: Not all verbs with stem endings in -ж, -ч or -ш and infinitive ending in -ать are 2nd Conjugation; most are regular 1st Conjugation, e.g.

Infinitive	*Present tense*
выража́ть 'to express'	выража́ю, выража́ешь . . . выража́ют
отвеча́ть 'to answer'	отвеча́ю, отвеча́ешь . . . отвеча́ют
слу́шать 'to listen'	слу́шаю, слу́шаешь . . . слу́шают

8.6 Formation of the past tenses and the imperfective future tense

These are formed in the same way in both conjugations.

8.6.1 Formation of the imperfective past and perfective past is normally from the respective infinitive by removing -ть and adding an ending appropriate to the gender and number of the subject: -л, -ла, -ло and -ли for *masc.*, *fem.*, *neut.* and *plur.* (all genders), respectively:

impf.	де́лать 'to do, make'	>	де́лал, де́лала, де́лало; де́лали
pf.	сде́лать	>	сде́лал, сде́лала, сде́лало; сде́лали
impf.	вари́ть 'to boil'	>	вари́л, вари́ла, вари́ло; вари́ли
pf.	свари́ть	>	свари́л, свари́ла, свари́ло; свари́ли
Note:	быть	>	был, была́, бы́ло; бы́ли

Жемчу́жины наро́дной му́дрости

от во́лка бежа́л, да на медве́дя напа́л	he was running away from a wolf, and fell upon a bear

8.6.2 The **imperfective future** tense is formed with the future tense of быть (see p. 78) and the imperfective infinitive:

он бу́дет рабо́тать в Сиби́ри	he will work in Siberia *or* he will be working . . .
вы бу́дете чита́ть э́ту статью́?	are you going to read this article?
я бу́ду говори́ть о́коло ча́са	I shall talk for about an hour
мы бу́дем возвраща́ться ка́ждый год	we shall come back every year

8.7 Stress patterns in 2nd Conjugation verbs

8.7.1 2nd Conjugation verbs follow three main stress patterns in the present or perfective future tenses (these and the consonant changes outlined on pp. 76–7 are also invoked when forming the past passive participle of 2nd Conjugation verbs: see p. 126).

- stress on the stem in the infinitive and throughout the tense
e.g. **поста́вить** 'to put' (**поста́влю, поста́вишь . . . поста́вят**);

- stress on the ending of the infinitive and throughout the tense
e.g. **соедини́ть** 'to unite' (**соединю́, соедини́шь . . . соединя́т**);

- stress on the ending of the infinitive and the first person singular, but on the stem for the rest of the tense
e.g. **запусти́ть** 'to launch' (**запущу́, запу́стишь . . . запу́стят**).

There are no rules which could help in memorizing which pattern a verb belongs to, but some common verbs are shown grouped below according to stress pattern:

- stress on stem throughout as in **поста́вить**:

Imperfective – **беспоко́ить** 'to worry'; **ви́деть** 'to see'; **гла́дить** 'to stroke, iron'; **гото́вить** 'to prepare, cook'; **гра́бить** 'to rob'; **е́здить** 'to travel'; **жа́рить** 'to fry, roast'; **знако́мить** 'to acquaint'; **зна́чить** 'to mean'; **кле́ить** 'to glue'; **кра́сить** 'to paint'; **ла́дить** 'to be on good terms with'; **ме́рить** 'to measure'; **му́чить** 'to torment'; **мы́слить** 'to think'; **по́ртить** 'to spoil'; **пра́вить** 'to rule, correct'; **ра́нить** 'to wound'; **ста́вить** 'to put, stand'; **стро́ить** 'to build'; **трево́жить** 'to alarm'; **чи́стить** 'to clean'.

Perfective – **бро́сить** 'to throw'; **встре́тить** 'to meet'; **доба́вить** 'to add'; **заме́тить** 'to notice'; **ко́нчить** 'to finish'; **ограни́чить** 'to limit'; **одо́брить** 'to approve'; **осве́домить** 'to inform'; **осла́бить** 'to weaken'; **отве́тить** 'to answer'; **поздра́вить** 'to congratulate'; **разру́шить** 'to destroy'; **расши́рить** 'to widen'; **увели́чить** 'to increase'; **уда́рить** 'to hit'; **уме́ньшить** 'to decrease'; **уси́лить** 'to strengthen'; **уско́рить** 'to speed up'.

- stress on ending throughout as in **соедини́ть**:

Imperfective – **вреди́ть** 'to harm'; **годи́ться** 'to suit'; **грози́ть** 'to threaten'; **кипяти́ть** 'to boil'; **мири́ться** 'to be reconciled'; **роди́ть** 'to give birth to'; **сади́ться** 'to sit down'; **сиде́ть** 'to sit'; **спеши́ть** 'to hurry'; **стреми́ться** 'to rush; aspire'; **стыди́ться** 'to be ashamed'; **храни́ть** 'to keep'; **щади́ть** 'to spare'.

Perfective – **включи́ть** 'to include; switch on'; **вооружи́ть** 'to arm'; **заключи́ть** 'to conclude'; **запрети́ть** 'to forbid'; **изуми́ть** 'to amaze'; **награди́ть** 'to reward'; **обвини́ть** 'to accuse'; **обрати́ть** 'to turn'; **определи́ть** 'to define'; **освободи́ть** 'to free'; **осуществи́ть** 'to bring about'; **повтори́ть** 'to repeat'; **помести́ть** 'to accommodate'; **порази́ть** 'to strike, amaze'; **посети́ть** 'to visit'; **прекрати́ть** 'to cease'; **пригласи́ть** 'to invite'; **соедини́ть** 'to unite'; **убеди́ть** 'to convince'; **удиви́ть** 'to surprise'; **укрепи́ть** 'to strengthen'; **употреби́ть** 'to use'; **утверди́ть** 'to affirm'.

• end stress in infinitive and first person singular, then on stem as in **запусти́ть**:

Imperfective — **броди́ть** 'to roam'; **буди́ть** 'to awaken'; **вари́ть** 'to boil'; **води́ть** 'to lead; drive'; **вози́ть** 'to convey'; **гаси́ть** 'to extinguish'; **губи́ть** 'to ruin'; **дави́ть** 'to press'; **дари́ть** 'to give'; **дразни́ть** 'to tease'; **корми́ть** 'to feed'; **крести́ть** 'to baptise'; **крути́ть** 'to twist'; **кури́ть** 'to smoke'; **лечи́ть** 'to treat, cure'; **лови́ть** 'to catch'; **люби́ть** 'to love'; **моли́ться** 'to pray'; **носи́ть** 'to carry; wear'; **плати́ть** 'to pay'; **проси́ть** 'to request'; **руби́ть** 'to chop'; **служи́ть** 'to serve'; **смотре́ть** 'to look'; **станови́ться** 'to become'; **суди́ть** 'to judge'; **тащи́ть** 'to drag'; **терпе́ть** 'to endure'; **труди́ться** 'to labour'; **туши́ть** 'to extinguish'; **учи́ть** 'to teach; learn'; **хвали́ть** 'to praise'; **ходи́ть** 'to go, walk'; **цени́ть** 'to value'; **шути́ть** 'to joke'.

Perfective — **впусти́ть** 'to let in'; **застрели́ть** 'to shoot'; **наклони́ть** 'to incline, tilt'; **объяви́ть** 'to announce'; **останови́ть** 'to stop'; **перемени́ть** 'to change'; **положи́ть** 'to put, lay'; **получи́ть** 'to receive'; **посади́ть** 'to seat; plant'; **пусти́ть** 'to allow; release'; **раздели́ть** 'to divide'; **ступи́ть** 'to step'; **урони́ть** 'to drop'; **хвати́ть** 'to seize; suffice'.

Note: stress in сади́ться (сади́шься, etc.) and посади́ть (поса́дишь, etc.)

Жемчу́жины наро́дной му́дрости

за ле́сом ви́дит, а под но́сом нет	(he) sees beyond the forest, but not under his nose

EXERCISE

(i) *Give the present tense of the following verbs and indicate their stress patterns:*

беспоко́ить; буди́ть; вари́ть; годи́ться; кури́ть; по́ртить; служи́ть; спеши́ть; ста́вить; храни́ть.

(ii) *Give the perfective future tense of the following verbs and indicate their stress patterns:*

бро́сить; встре́тить; обвини́ть; объяви́ть; определи́ть; повтори́ть; положи́ть; разреши́ть; уда́рить; урони́ть.

9 IRREGULAR VERBS

Some irregular or at least unpredictable verbs fall into groups, making it a little easier to learn them. They nearly all belong to the 1st Conjugation.

9.1 Monosyllabic verbs in -ить:

Infinitive		*Present tense*
бить	'to hit, beat'	бью, бьёшь ... бьют
вить	'to wind, weave'	вью, вьёшь ... вьют
лить	'to pour'	лью, льёшь ... льют
пить	'to drink'	пью, пьёшь ... пьют
шить	'to sew'	шью, шьёшь ... шьют

9.1.1 With prefixes these verbs are perfective, so that their perfective future conjugates in the same way, e.g.

Infinitive	*Perfective future*
пробить 'to knock through'	пробью, пробьёшь ... пробьют
убить 'to kill'	убью, убьёшь ... убьют
вы́лить 'to pour out'	вы́лью, вы́льешь ... вы́льют

When the prefix ends in a consonant a fleeting 'o' appears, e.g.

вбить 'to knock, drive in'	вобью, вобьёшь ... вобьют
испить 'to drain'	изопью, изопьёшь ... изопьют
развить 'to develop'	разовью, разовьёшь ... разовьют

- As mentioned in chapter 17, where prefixes add new shades of meaning to perfective verbs new imperfectives with this new meaning have to be formed. These are known as secondary imperfectives and are straight-forward 1st Conjugation verbs, e.g. from the above, respectively: пробива́ть, убива́ть, вылива́ть, вбива́ть, испива́ть, развива́ть; *Present Tense:* пробива́ю, пробива́ешь ... etc. (see p. 75)

Note: жить 'to live' is not in this group (*present tense:* живу́, живёшь... живу́т); but from perfectives прожи́ть 'to live through, spend (time)', вы́жить 'to survive', зажи́ть 'to heal', пережи́ть 'to survive', etc., secondary imperfectives: прожива́ть, выжива́ть, зажива́ть, пережива́ть, etc. are regular.

EXERCISES

(i) a. *Give the infinitives of the following future perfective verbs:*
разовью́; привью́; волью́; пропью́; зашью́

b. *Give the corresponding imperfective infinitives and give their English meaning.*

(ii) *Give the perfective future of:*
отбива́ть/отби́ть; завива́ть/зави́ть; пролива́ть/проли́ть;
запива́ть/запи́ть; пришива́ть/приши́ть

9.2 Note these present tenses from imperfective 1st Conjugation verbs

	смея́ться 'to laugh'	наде́яться 'to hope'	жать 'to press'	жать 'to reap'	иска́ть 'to seek'	брать 'to take'
я	смею́сь	наде́юсь	жму	жну	ищу́	беру́
ты	смеёшься	наде́ешься	жмёшь	жнёшь	и́щешь	берёшь
он	смеётся	наде́ется	жмёт	жнёт	и́щет	берёт
мы	смеёмся	наде́емся	жмём	жнём	и́щем	берём
вы	смеётесь	наде́етесь	жмёте	жнёте	и́щете	берёте
они́	смею́тся	наде́ются	жмут	жнут	и́щут	беру́т

- Perfectives formed by adding prefixes to these verbs conjugate in the same way as the basic verb, e.g.

Infinitive
засмея́ться 'to burst out laughing'
пожа́ть 'to press'
вы́брать 'to choose'

Perfective future
засмею́сь, засмеёшься ... засмею́тся
пожму́, пожмёшь ... пожму́т
вы́беру, вы́берешь ... вы́берут

Жемчу́жины наро́дной му́дрости

как посе́ешь, так и пожнёшь	as you will sow, so will you also reap

9.3 Note also

	Present tense		Perfective future	
	каза́ться	мочь	нача́ть	стать
	'to seem'	'to be able'	'to begin'	'to become
	(see p. 269)	(see pp. 254–5)		
я	кажу́сь	могу́	начну́	ста́ну
ты	ка́жешься	мо́жешь	начнёшь	ста́нешь
он	ка́жется	мо́жет	начнёт	ста́нет
мы	ка́жемся	мо́жем	начнём	ста́нем
вы	ка́жетесь	мо́жете	начнёте	ста́нете
они	ка́жутся	мо́гут	начну́т	ста́нут

- Perfective verbs formed with prefixes from the same root conjugate like каза́ться:

Infinitive		Perfective future
доказа́ть	'to prove'	докажу́, дока́жешь . . . дока́жут
заказа́ть	'to place an order'	закажу́, зака́жешь . . . зака́жут
наказа́ть	'to punish'	накажу́, нака́жешь . . . нака́жут
показа́ть	'to show'	покажу́, пока́жешь . . . пока́жут
приказа́ть	'to command'	прикажу́, прика́жешь . . . прика́жут
сказа́ть	'to say, tell'	скажу́, ска́жешь . . . ска́жут
указа́ть	'to indicate'	укажу́, ука́жешь . . . ука́жут

Except **сказа́ть** these all form regular 1st Conjugation secondary imperfectives (see pp. 83, 95–7): **дока́зывать, зака́зывать, нака́зывать, пока́зывать, прика́зывать, ука́зывать; сказа́ть** has the imperfective **говори́ть** (regular 2nd Conjugation).

Жемчу́жины наро́дной му́дрости

я тебе́ покажу́, где ра́ки зиму́ют	I'll show you where the crayfish spend the winter (i.e. I have a bone to pick with you)

9.3.1 Compounds of -(н)ять such as взять, занять, понять, etc., all of which are perfective:

Imperfective/perfective infinitive		*Perfective future*
брать/взять	'to take'	возьму́, возьмёшь ... возьму́т
занима́ть/заня́ть	'to occupy'	займу́, займёшь ... займу́т
нанима́ть/наня́ть	'to hire, rent'	найму́, наймёшь ... найму́т
обнима́ть/обня́ть	'to embrace'	обниму́, обни́мешь ... обни́мут
отнима́ть/отня́ть	'to take away'	отниму́, отни́мешь ... отни́мут
поднима́ть/подня́ть	'to lift, raise'	подниму́, подни́мешь ... подни́мут
понима́ть/поня́ть	'to understand'	пойму́, поймёшь ... пойму́т
принима́ть/приня́ть	'to accept'	приму́, при́мешь ... при́мут
предпринима́ть/ предприня́ть	'to undertake'	предприму́, предпри́мешь ... предпри́мут
снима́ть/снять	'to take off; snap; rent'	сниму́, сни́мешь ... сни́мут
изыма́ть/изъя́ть	'to take out of service'	изыму́, изы́мешь ... изы́мут

EXERCISE

(i) *Give the 3rd person singular and 2nd person plural of the perfective future of:*
взять; поня́ть; подня́ть; отня́ть; заня́ть; приня́ть

(ii) *Give the corresponding imperfective infinitives and their English meanings.*

9.4 Verbs in -овать, -евать

Most of these replace -ов-, -ев- with -у-, -ю-, respectively, in conjugation like интересова́ться (see p. 75), e.g.

Infinitive		*Present tense*
сове́товать/по-	'to advise'	сове́тую, сове́туешь ... сове́туют
чу́вствовать/по-	'to feel'	чу́вствую, чу́вствуешь ... чу́вствуют
рисова́ть/на-	'to draw'	рису́ю, рису́ешь ... рису́ют
малева́ть/на-	'to paint'	малю́ю, малю́ешь ... малю́ют

• Many verbs of this type are based on word roots adopted from other languages and are the same in the imperfective and perfective:

| арестова́ть | 'to arrest' | аресту́ю, аресту́ешь ... аресту́ют |
| приватизи́ровать | 'to privatize' | приватизи́рую, приватизи́руешь ... приватизи́руют |

- A few are stressed on the ending:

жева́ть (*impf.* only)	'to chew'	жую́, жуёшь . . . жую́т
сова́ть/су́нуть	'to poke, stick'	сую́, суёшь . . . сую́т
плева́ть/наплева́ть *or* /плю́нуть	'to spit'	плюю́, плюёшь . . . плюю́т

- There are some exceptions to this pattern, i.e. verbs in -овать, -евать which conjugate normally:

здоро́ваться/по- 'to greet'	здоро́ваюсь, здоро́ваешься . . . здоро́ваются
зева́ть/про- 'to yawn' *or* /зевну́ть	зева́ю, зева́ешь . . . зева́ют
намерева́ться (*Impf.* only) 'to intend'	намерева́юсь, намерева́ешься . . . намерева́ются
подозрева́ть/заподо́зрить 'to suspect'	подозрева́ю, подозрева́ешь . . . подозрева́ют

- The verb дева́ть/деть 'to put' and the reflexive дева́ться/де́ться 'to hide, get to' are colloquial (куда́ он де́лся? – 'where did he get to?'; не́куда дева́ться – there's no way out). But compounds of these are normal for standard Russian; the imperfectives do not contract, but the perfectives are irregular:

Infinitive

Present tense	Perfective future
надева́ть/наде́ть 'to put on (clothing)'	
надева́ю, надева́ешь . . . надева́ют	наде́ну, наде́нешь . . . наде́нут
одева́ть/оде́ть 'to dress (someone)'	
одева́ю, одева́ешь . . . одева́ют	оде́ну, оде́нешь . . . оде́нут
одева́ться/оде́ться 'to dress (oneself)'	
одева́юсь, одева́ешься . . . одева́ются	оде́нусь, оде́нешься . . . оде́нутся
раздева́ть /разде́ть 'to undress (someone)'	
раздева́ю, раздева́ешь . . . раздева́ют	разде́ну, разде́нешь . . . разде́нут
раздева́ться /разде́ться 'to undress (oneself), take one's coat off'	
раздева́юсь, раздева́ешься . . . раздева́ются	разде́нусь, разде́нешься . . . разде́нутся
переодева́ться /переоде́ться 'to change (clothes)'	
переодева́юсь, переодева́ешься . . . переодева́ются	переоде́нусь, переоде́нешься . . . переоде́нутся

• Several in this 'regular' category of verbs in - евать are secondary imperfectives formed from perfectives:

успева́ть (успева́ю, успева́ешь … успева́ют)
  from perfective успе́ть 'to succeed, manage, have time to'
заболева́ть (заболева́ю …)   <   заболе́ть 'to fall ill'
застрева́ть (застрева́ю …)   <   застря́ть 'to get stuck'
нагрева́ть (нагрева́ю …)   <   нагре́ть 'to warm up'
обозрева́ть (обозрева́ю …)   <   обозре́ть 'to survey, review'
продлева́ть (продлева́ю …)   <   продли́ть 'to prolong', etc.

EXERCISES

(i) *Give the present tense of:*
   организова́ть; жева́ть; сова́ть; здоро́ваться; зева́ть; одева́ться; намерева́ться; ликвиди́ровать; ориенти́роваться

(ii) *Give their English meanings.*

9.5 Verbs in -авать, – not many in number, but commonly used

Infinitive
Present tense   *Perfective future*
дава́ть 'to give'
   даю́, даёшь … даю́т   (Perfective: дать – see p. 78)
and its compounds, such as: продава́ть/прода́ть 'to sell'
   продаю́, продаёшь … продаю́т   **прода́м, прода́шь … продаду́т**
выдава́ть/вы́дать 'to give out'
   выдаю́, выдаёшь … выдаю́т   **вы́дам, вы́дашь … вы́дадут**
издава́ть/изда́ть 'to publish
   издаю́, издаёшь … издаю́т   **изда́м, изда́шь … издаду́т**
передава́ть/переда́ть 'to hand over; transmit'
   передаю́, передаёшь … передаю́т   **переда́м, переда́шь … передаду́т**
создава́ть/созда́ть 'to create'
   создаю́, создаёшь … создаю́т   **созда́м, созда́шь … создаду́т**
встава́ть/встать 'to get up'
   встаю́, встаёшь … встаю́т   **вста́ну, вста́нешь … вста́нут**
and other compounds from the same root: достава́ть/доста́ть 'to get'
   достаю́, достаёшь … достаю́т   **доста́ну, доста́нешь … доста́нут**
остава́ться /оста́ться 'to stay, remain'
   остаю́сь, остаёшься … остаю́тся   **оста́нусь, оста́нешься … оста́нутся**

отставáть/отстáть 'to lag; desist'
    отстаю́, отстаёшь ... отстаю́т   **отстáну, отстáнешь ... отстáнут**
переставáть/перестáть 'to cease, stop'
    перестаю́, перестаёшь ... перестаю́т
                               перестáну, перестáнешь ...
                               перестáнут
приставáть/пристáть 'to stick to; pester'
    пристаю́, пристаёшь ... пристаю́т   **пристáну, пристáнешь ...**
                               пристáнут
расставáться/расстáться 'to part'
    расстаю́сь, расстаёшься ... расстаю́тся
                               расстáнусь, расстáнешься ...
                               расстáнутся
уставáть/устáть 'to tire, get tired'
    устаю́, устаёшь ... устаю́т   **устáну, устáнешь ... устáнут**
узнавáть/узнáть 'to find out, recognize'
    узнаю́, узнаёшь ... узнаю́т   **узнáю, узнáешь ... узнáют**
and other compounds: осознавáть/осознáть 'to realize'
    осознаю́, осознаёшь ... осознаю́т   **осознáю, осознáешь ... осознáют**
признавáть/признáть 'to recognize'
    признаю́, признаёшь ... признаю́т   **признáю, признáешь ... признáют**
признавáться/признáться 'to admit, confess'
    признаю́сь, признаёшься ...   **признáюсь, признáешься ...**
    признаю́тся   **признáются**
сознавáть/сознáть 'to acknowledge'
    сознаю́, сознаёшь ... сознаю́т   **сознáю, сознáешь ... сознáют**

Note: плáвать 'to swim, float' is regular: **плáваю, плáваешь ... плáвают.**

EXERCISES

(i) *Give the present tense of:*
    признавáть; узнавáть; отставáть; уставáть

(ii) *Give their English meanings.*

9.6 Epenthetic -л-

Some 1st Conjugation verbs with a stem ending in a bilabial consonant (б, п, or м) insert the letter -л- between the stem and the ending of the present or future perfective tense:

Infinitive	*Present tense*
дремáть 'to doze'	дремлю́, дрéмлешь ... дрéмлют
сы́пать 'to sprinkle, strew'	сы́плю, сы́плешь ... сы́плют
щипáть 'to pinch'	щиплю́, щи́плешь ... щи́плют
колебáться 'to hesitate'	колéблюсь, колéблешься ... колéблются

EXERCISE

(i) *Give the 3rd person singular and 2nd person plural of the present tense of:*
дремáть; колебáться; сы́пать; щипáть

(ii) *Give their English meanings.*

9.7 Other irregular 1st Conjugation verbs are not so readily categorized

Infinitive	*Present tense*
везти́ 'to transport, convey'	везу́, везёшь ... везу́т
вести́ 'to lead'	веду́, ведёшь ... веду́т
грести́ 'to row'	гребу́, гребёшь ... гребу́т
ждать 'to wait'	жду, ждёшь ... ждут
жечь 'to burn (something)'	жгу, жжёшь ... жгут
жить 'to live'	живу́, живёшь ... живу́т
звать 'to call'	зову́, зовёшь ... зову́т
класть 'to put, lay flat'	кладу́, кладёшь ... кладу́т (see p. 266)
кля́сться 'to take an oath'	кляну́сь, клянёшься ... кляну́тся
красть 'to steal'	краду́, крадёшь ... краду́т
лезть 'to climb'	лéзу, лéзешь ... лéзут
мыть 'to wash'	мóю, мóешь ... мóют
нести́ 'to carry (on foot)'	несу́, несёшь ... несу́т
пасти́ 'to graze (cattle)'	пасу́, пасёшь ... пасу́т
пасть 'to fall'	паду́, падёшь ... паду́т
петь 'to sing'	пою́, поёшь ... пою́т
печь 'to bake'	пеку́, печёшь ... пеку́т
писáть 'to write'	пишу́, пи́шешь ... пи́шут
плáкать 'to cry'	плáчу, плáчешь ... плáчут
пляса́ть 'to dance' (folk)	пляшу́, пля́шешь ... пля́шут
ползти́ 'to crawl'	ползу́, ползёшь ... ползу́т
расти́ 'to grow'	расту́, растёшь ... расту́т
рéзать 'to cut'	рéжу, рéжешь ... рéжут

	Future perfective
лечь 'to lie down'	ля́гу, ля́жешь . . . ля́гут
откры́ть 'to open'	откро́ю, откро́ешь . . . откро́ют
ошиби́ться 'to make a mistake'	ошибу́сь, ошибёшься . . . ошибу́тся
посла́ть 'to send'	пошлю́, пошлёшь . . . пошлю́т
предпоче́сть 'to prefer'	предпочту́, предпочтёшь . . . предпочту́т
сесть 'to sit down'	ся́ду, ся́дешь . . . ся́дут
умере́ть 'to die'	умру́, умрёшь . . . умру́т

Жемчу́жины наро́дной му́дрости

ба́ба пля́шет, а дед пла́чет	grandma's dancing while grandad's crying

9.8 A few irregular verbs are 2nd conjugation

Infinitive	*Present tense*
гнать 'to chase'	гоню́, го́нишь . . . го́нят
спать 'to sleep'	сплю, спишь . . . спят
терпе́ть 'to bear, tolerate'	терплю́, те́рпишь . . . те́рпят

9.9 The past tense

Problems may arise in forming the past tense when the infinitive does not end in -ть or ends in a consonant + ть; common examples are listed below:

Imperfective infinitive:	*Past tense*
бере́чь 'to save, keep'	берёг, берегла́, берегло́; берегли́
везти́ 'to transport'	вёз, везла́, везло́; везли́
вести́ 'to lead'	вёл, вела́, вело́; вели́
грести́ 'to row'	грёб, гребла́, гребло́; гребли́
грызть 'to gnaw'	грыз, гры́зла, гры́зло; гры́зли
есть 'to eat'	ел, е́ла, е́ло; е́ли
жечь 'to burn'	жёг, жгла, жгло; жгли
идти́ 'to go'	шёл, шла, шло; шли
класть 'to put, lay down'	клал, кла́ла, кла́ло; кла́ли
клясть 'to curse'	клял, кляла́, кля́ло; кля́ли
красть 'to steal'	крал, кра́ла, кра́ло; кра́ли
лезть 'to climb, crawl'	лез, ле́зла, ле́зло; ле́зли
мочь 'to be able'	мог, могла́, могло́; могли́
нести́ 'to carry'	нёс, несла́, несло́; несли́
пасти́ 'to tend (cattle)'	пас, пасла́, пасло́; пасли́
пасть 'to fall'	пал, па́ла, па́ло; па́ли
печь 'to bake'	пёк, пекла́, пекло́; пекли́
ползти́ 'to crawl'	полз, ползла́, ползло́; ползли́
расти́ 'to grow'	рос, росла́, росло́; росли́

течь 'to flow'	тёк, текла́, текло́; текли́
цвести́ 'to bloom'	цвёл, цвела́, цвело́; цвели́
влечь 'to draw, attract'	влёк, влекла́, влекло́; влекли́

Perfective infinitive:

лечь 'to lie down'	лёг, легло́, легло́; легли́
предпоче́сть 'to prefer'	предпочёл, предпочла́; предпочли́
сесть 'to sit down'	сел, се́ла, се́ло; се́ли
спасти́ 'to save'	спас, спасла́, спасло́; спасли́

Note: the past tense of prefixed compounds of the same roots are formed the same way e.g. сбере́чь (perfective of бере́чь): сберёг, сберегла́ . . . ; ввезти́ 'to import': ввёз, ввезла́ . . . ; найти́ 'to find': нашёл, нашла́ . . . , etc.

Note: irregular past tenses are formed from a few perfective verbs with the infinitive ending -нуть:

возни́кнуть 'to crop up'	возни́к, возни́кла, возни́кло; возни́кли
исче́знуть 'to disappear'	исче́з, исче́зла, исче́зло; исче́зли
поги́бнуть 'to perish'	поги́б, поги́бла, поги́бло; поги́бли
привы́кнуть 'to get used to'	привы́к, привы́кла, привы́кло, привы́кли
прони́кнуть 'to penetrate'	прони́к, прони́кла, прони́кло; прони́кли

Note: irregular Past tenses:

ошиби́ться 'to make a mistake'	оши́бся, оши́блась; оши́блись
тере́ть 'to rub'	тёр, тёрла, тёрло; тёрли
умере́ть 'to die'	у́мер, умерла́, у́мерло; у́мерли

EXERCISES

(i)   *Translate into Russian:*

I shall, you will and they will (perfectively) . . .
sit down on the sofa; save the forest; fall into the river; lie down in the road; start to sing; take these books; go and stand in the queue; support the ladder.

(ii) a.   *Give the 1st person singular, the 3rd person singular and the 3rd person plural*

(*я* . . . , *он/она́* . . . , *они́* . . .) *of the present tense of the following verbs:*
бежа́ть ('to run'); бере́чь ('to save'); бить ('to hit'); боро́ться ('to struggle'); боя́ться ('to fear'); верте́ть ('to twirl'); вести́ ('to lead'); висе́ть ('to hang, be suspended'); воева́ть ('to make war'); вреди́ть ('to harm'); гляде́ть ('to gaze'); горе́ть ('to burn, be on fire'); дыша́ть ('to breathe'); е́здить ('to travel'); есть ('to eat'); жале́ть ('to pity'); ждать ('to wait'); жечь ('to burn'); жить ('to live'); забо́титься ('to be concerned'); звать ('to call'); знако́миться ('to get to know'); иска́ть ('to seek'); класть ('to put'); колеба́ться ('to hesitate, oscillate'); лежа́ть ('to lie [flat]'); лете́ть ('to fly'); лить (to pour'); лови́ть ('to

catch'); молча́ть ('to be silent'); мыть ('to wash'); наде́яться ('to hope, rely'); нра́виться ('to please'); носи́ть ('to carry'); отдава́ть ('to give away'); отсу́тствовать ('to be absent'); перестава́ть ('to cease'); петь ('to sing'); пла́кать ('to weep'); плати́ть ('to pay'); плыть ('to swim'); пресле́довать ('to pursue'); принадлежа́ть ('to belong'); пря́таться ('to hide'); расти́ ('to grow'); ре́зать ('to cut'); реша́ть ('to decide'); роди́ться ('to be born'); сади́ться ('to sit down'); сиде́ть ('to sit'); сле́довать ('to follow'); смея́ться ('to laugh'); содержа́ть ('to contain'); сомнева́ться ('to doubt'); состоя́ть ('to consist'); спать ('to sleep'); станови́ться ('to become'); стуча́ть ('to knock'); суди́ть ('to judge'); терпе́ть ('to put up with'); тра́тить ('to spend'); труди́ться ('to labour'); учи́ться ('to learn'); чи́стить ('to clean'); шуме́ть ('to make a noise').

b. *Give the masc. and fem. forms of their past tense.*

c. *Do the same for the perfective future and past tenses of these verbs:*
бро́сить ('to throw'); взять ('to take'); возни́кнуть ('to occur, crop up'); воспо́льзоваться ('to make use of'); войти́ ('to go in'); встре́тить ('to meet'); вы́брать ('to choose'); вы́звать ('to challenge, evoke'); вы́разить ('to express'); дать ('to give'); доби́ться ('to get'); доказа́ть ('to prove'); доста́ть ('to get'); забы́ть ('to forget'); заинтересова́ться ('to become interested'); закры́ть ('to close'); заня́ть ('to occupy'); запрети́ть ('to forbid'); заста́вить ('to force'); захвати́ть ('to seize'); защити́ть ('to defend'); избе́гнуть ('to avoid'); избра́ть ('to elect'); испра́вить ('to correct'); исче́знуть ('to disappear'); лечь ('to lie down'); наде́ть ('to put on'); напа́сть ('to attack'); нача́ть ('to begin'); обрати́ться ('to address'); объяви́ть ('to declare'); оказа́ться ('to turn out, emerge as'); освети́ть ('to illuminate'); освободи́ть ('to free'); останови́ться ('to stop'); оста́ться ('to stay'); ошиби́ться ('to make a mistake'); победи́ть ('to be victorious'); пове́сить ('to hang'); повлия́ть ('to influence'); поддержа́ть ('to support'); подня́ть ('to lift'); поня́ть ('to understand'); посети́ть ('to visit'); посла́ть ('to send'); предложи́ть ('to suggest'); предпоче́сть ('to prefer'); предупреди́ть ('to warn'); прибли́зиться ('to approach'); привле́чь ('to attract'); прие́хать ('to arrive'); приня́ть ('to accept'); прода́ть ('to sell'); произвести́ ('to produce'); пропа́сть ('to go missing'); разви́ть ('to develop'); сесть ('to sit down'); снять ('to remove'); согласи́ться ('to agree'); сократи́ться ('to contract'); спасти́ ('to save'); уви́деть ('to catch sight of'); увле́чься ('to become keen on'); умере́ть ('to die'); упа́сть ('to fall'); услы́шать ('to hear'); успе́ть ('to manage'); уста́ть ('to get tired')

(iii) a. *Translate into Russian:*
1 My heart belongs to Olga.
2 She is taking a book from the library.
3 Boris is rowing on the Volga.
4 We shall save the cathedral.
5 Birch trees are growing in the square.
6 They're burning old newspapers.
7 She's putting the spoons in the box.
8 Why are you giving her only one plate?
9 I press his hand.
10 You may all decide as you like.

b. *Now put them in the past tense, perfective where possible.*

(iv) a.   *Translate into Russian:*

1   Who among you decides?
2   Who's holding the flag?
3   They're always silent.
4   We're depriving her of meat and butter.
5   He's knocking his head against the wall.
6   These books contain the works of all the great poets.
7   Some of their names sound very strange.
8   Who does this horse belong to?
9   Why don't you answer?
10 Who's that lying in the middle of the room?
11 He never informs me of his time of arrival.
12 Do you hear the sound of the bells from here?
13 She thinks he is turning into a frog.
14 She forbids them to go to the stadium.
15 The music is ending.
16 This poem expresses the poet's love of nature.
17 He is dedicating this novel to his wife.
18 The boys are smashing the old gate.
19 Why are you shouting? No one ever answers.
20 She's always looking for her glasses.

     b.   *Now put them in the imperfective past tense.*

(v) *Give the present or future perfective tense from each of the following infinitives, indicate whether they are imperfective or perfective and translate the 1st person plural:*

     пить; откры́ть; брить; звать; пожа́ть; отнести́; мочь; привести́.

10 ASPECT OF THE VERB

10.1 Formation of the perfective

The perfective is usually formed from the basic imperfective verb in one of
two ways:

either by changing Conjugation from 1st to 2nd:

Imperfective	Perfective	
конча́ть	ко́нчить	'to finish, end'
освобожда́ть	освободи́ть	'to free, liberate'
оставля́ть	оста́вить	'to leave'
покупа́ть	купи́ть	'to buy'
получа́ть	получи́ть	'to receive'

or by adding a prefix:

писа́ть	написа́ть	'to write'
чита́ть	прочита́ть	'to read'

Note: Adding a prefix may simply change a verb from imperfective to straightforward
perfective, often without much consideration for meaning, e.g.

(по-)	стро́ить/постро́ить	'to build'
(с-)	де́лать/сде́лать	'to do, to make'
(вы-)	мыть/вы́мыть	'to wash'

10.2 Secondary imperfectives

While the prefix used to form the straightforward perfective does *not* change
the basic meaning of the verb, another prefix with the same verb can have a
significant effect on meaning: but replacing the prefix creates another
perfective verb so a new imperfective verb, a secondary imperfective, has to
be developed from it (see also pp. 83, 85).

10.2.1 So, from basic стро́ить/постро́ить 'to build' a change of prefix gives,
e.g. перестро́ить (*perf.*) – 'to rebuild' from which a new, secondary
imperfective has to be formed: перестра́ивать. Similarly:

достра́ивать/достро́ить	'to finish off (building)'
застра́ивать/застро́ить	'to build all over, to develop'

надстра́ивать/надстро́ить	'to build on top of, to add (*eg.* a floor)'
настра́ивать/настро́ить	'to tune'
пристра́ивать/пристро́ить	'to build onto, to add (a garage)'
расстра́иваться/расстро́иться	'to become upset'
устра́ивать/устро́ить	'to arrange'
	etc.

and from **чита́ть/прочита́ть**	'to read':
вычи́тывать/вы́читать	'to subtract'
дочи́тывать/дочита́ть	'to finish off (reading)'
отчи́тывать/отчита́ть	'to reprimand'
перечи́тывать/перечита́ть	'to reread'
почи́тывать/почита́ть	'to do a bit of reading, to have a read'
	etc.

and from **писа́ть/написа́ть**	'to write, to paint':
впи́сывать/вписа́ть	'to inscribe'
выпи́сывать/вы́писать	'to write out, to subscribe, to order'
запи́сывать/записа́ть	'to note, to jot down, to record'
опи́сывать/описа́ть	'to describe'
перепи́сывать/переписа́ть	'to rewrite, to copy'
припи́сывать/приписа́ть	'to ascribe, to add (a note, words)'
подпи́сывать/подписа́ть	'to sign'
распи́сывать/расписа́ть	'to fresco, paint (pictures on walls)'
спи́сывать/списа́ть	'to write down, to copy from'
	etc.

and from **ста́вить/поста́вить**	'to put, to stand':
вставля́ть/вста́вить	'to insert'
выставля́ть/вы́ставить	'to exhibit'
доставля́ть/доста́вить	'to deliver'
заставля́ть/заста́вить	'to force, make (s.one do s.thing)'
обставля́ть/обста́вить	'to surround, furnish, clutter up'
оставля́ть/оста́вить	'to leave'
переставля́ть/переста́вить	'to move, to shift'
подставля́ть/подста́вить	'to place under, to sneak under'
поставля́ть/поста́вить	'to supply, deliver'
предоставля́ть/предоста́вить	'to leave, put at disposal of'
представля́ть/предста́вить	'to present, to imagine'
приставля́ть/приста́вить	'to place next to, lean against'
противопоставля́ть/противопоста́вить	'to contrast'
расставля́ть/расста́вить	'to place around'
составля́ть/соста́вить	'to compile; to comprise, constitute'
уставля́ться/уста́виться	'to stare'
	etc.

and from класть/положи́ть	'to put, to lay down':
вкла́дывать *or* влага́ть/вложи́ть	'to insert, to invest'
закла́дывать/заложи́ть	'to put behind, to guarantee'
накла́дывать/наложи́ть	'to put onto'
откла́дывать/отложи́ть	'to put off, to postpone'
перекла́дывать/переложи́ть	'to move, to put elsewhere'
прикла́дывать/приложи́ть	'to apply, to attach (to letter)'
прокла́дывать/проложи́ть	'to lay down, to build (a road)'
раскла́дывать/разложи́ть	'to spread out'
скла́дывать/сложи́ть	'to put together, to add, to pile, to fold'
укла́дывать/уложи́ть	'to pack'
	etc.

10.2.2 Prefixes may be added to verbs which form their perfective by changing conjugation. From basic **пуска́ть/пусти́ть** 'to let go, to release, to allow' can be formed:

впуска́ть/впусти́ть	'to let in, to admit'
выпуска́ть/вы́пустить	'to let out, to release'
допуска́ть/допусти́ть	'to allow, to assume'
запуска́ть/запусти́ть	'to launch'
опуска́ть/опусти́ть	'to lower, let down onto'
отпуска́ть/отпусти́ть	'to release, to free'
подпуска́ть/подпусти́ть	'to allow to approach'
пропуска́ть/пропусти́ть	'to let through, allow to pass, miss'
распуска́ться/распусти́ться	'to let oneself go, to blossom'
спуска́ть/спусти́ть	'to lower, to let down from, to release'
упуска́ть/упусти́ть	'to let slip, to omit'
	etc.

and from ступа́ть/ступи́ть	'to step':
вступа́ть/вступи́ть	'to enter, to join'
выступа́ть/вы́ступить	'to step out, to speak publicly'
заступа́ться/заступи́ться	'to plead, to intercede'
наступа́ть/наступи́ть	'to tread on, to begin'
наступа́ть (Impf only)	'to advance'
отступа́ть/отступи́ть	'to retreat'
переступа́ть/переступи́ть	'to step across, to overstep'
подступа́ть/подступи́ть	'to approach, to come up close to'
поступа́ть/поступи́ть	'to act, to enter, to join'
приступа́ть/приступи́ть	'to get down to'
уступа́ть/уступи́ть	'to yield, to cede'
	etc.

10.2.3 Some of these verb 'families' are not as tidy as the preceding ones, employing either conjugation change, secondary imperfectivization, or both:

from **меня́ть/поменя́ть** 'to change':

заменя́ть/замени́ть	'to replace, to exchange'
изменя́ть/измени́ть	'to alter; to betray'
отменя́ть/отмени́ть	'to cancel'
применя́ть/примени́ть	'to employ, to apply'
сменя́ть/смени́ть	'to replace, to take over from'
обме́нивать/обменя́ть	'to exchange, to swap'
обме́нивать/обмени́ть	'to swap by mistake'
подме́нивать *or* **подменя́ть/подмени́ть**	'to switch (slyly)'
разме́нивать/разменя́ть	'to change (into small change)'
(no *impf*) **/перемени́ть**	'to change'
	etc.

10.3 Use of aspect

10.3.1 Although the basic difference between the aspects is clear, the choice of aspect has been known to present English-speaking students of Russian with some difficulties. This is partly because English itself is a poor indicator of which aspect to use; if you ask someone 'Have you read *Anna Karenina*?' you might be asking (a) whether they are familiar with it, whether they've ever read it, i.e. has the action of reading *Anna Karenina* ever taken place on their part? – to which the answer might be 'yes, five times' or 'yes, many years ago' or 'yes, but only in parts'. In both question and answer the imperfective would be used:

– Ты чита́ла *А́нну Каре́нину*? – Да, чита́ла. 'Yes, I've read it'.
All you are interested in is whether the action ever took place.

Or (b) you might be asking whether they've now finished it – you know they were supposed to read it or that they were intending to, and you are interested in the completion of the action resulting in the book now being free for you to borrow or in your both being able to go off and do something else. In both the perfective would be used:

– Ты прочита́ла *А́нну Каре́нину*? – Да, прочита́ла 'Yes, I've finished it'.

'Have you read it?' and 'Yes, I have' can be ambiguous in English. The Russian perfective and imperfective aspects differentiate clearly.

Similarly, depending on context, 'она́ убира́ла ко́мнату' can be translated as 'she tidied the room', 'she was tidying . . . ', 'she used to tidy . . . ', 'she would (often) tidy . . . ', 'she has (often) tidied . . . ', 'she had tidied . . . ', 'she had been tidying . . . ', etc. As an imperfective verb 'она́ убира́ла' is merely a statement of the fact that she did spend some time tidying the room: there is no inference as to whether she actually completed the job or of any result from her efforts; simply, – the action took place. 'Она убрала комнату', however, tells us that the job was done and that the room could now be used.

If a friend wished to inform you that someone had rung while you were out you would be told: кто-то звонил 'someone rang', a statement of the mere fact of the action – imperfective. If the perfective were used: кто-то позвонил, it would mean that you were expecting a call and the anticipated action was in fact completed: 'someone did ring', and an outcome achieved.

Likewise, if the three bears had each asked: кто ел мою кашу? 'who's been eating my porridge?' – they would have been using the imperfective to emphasize the fact of the action and some curiosity as to the identity of the culprit; if, on the other hand, they had used the perfective: кто съел мою кашу? 'who's eaten up my porridge?' the focus would shift to the completion of the action, to the fact that as a result there was no porridge left – away from the crime itself and towards the outcome of the action: their plight of being deprived of porridge and their need to get even.

10.3.2 As with the other tenses of the verb, aspect of the **infinitive** may depend on where the emphasis lies – on the action itself or on the result:

я хочу учить польский язык	I want to learn Polish, i.e. to do Polish, to be a student of Polish, to enjoy the process of learning
я хочу выучить польский язык	I want to learn Polish, i.e. to learn it properly in order to be able to do something with it

Here the choice between imperfective **учить** and perfective **выучить** depends on the meaning of the infinitive, not on the introductory verb: do you want to be doing it or do you want to get it done?

10.3.3 The same may be said of other introductory verbs as of **хотеть**, e.g. **обещать** 'to promise', **просить** 'to ask, request', **пытаться** 'to attempt', **советовать** 'to advise', **стараться** 'to try', **уговаривать** 'to persuade' and the modal words: **надо, нужно, необходимо, должен (должна, должно; должны)** 'it is necessary, one must, ought', i.e. actions repeated or of indefinite duration are conveyed by the imperfective infinitive; single completed actions of short duration require a perfective infinitive:

я хочу смотреть телевизор	I want to watch telly
я хочу посмотреть новости	I want to see the news

он обещáл приходи́ть кáждый день he promised to come every day
он обещáл прийти́ в полови́не
   восьмóго   he promised to come at half past seven

нам нáдо вставáть в семь   we (always) have to get up at seven
нам нáдо встать в семь   we have to get up at seven (today)

мы старáлись стрóить домá на рóвном мéсте
we tried to build the houses on level ground
мы старáлись пострóить дом на рóвном мéсте
we tried (were trying) to build the house on level ground
мы постарáлись пострóить дом на рóвном мéсте
we tried (made an attempt) to build the house on level ground

Note: the perfective is possible even for repeated action if you want to emphasize its completion each time:
   кáждый день тебé нáдо бýдет выходи́ть *or* вы́йти порáньше, чтóбы успéть на автóбус
   you'll have to go out a bit earlier every day to catch the bus

10.3.4 After some introductory verbs, however, there is no choice for the infinitive:

• after verbs of **beginning**, **continuing** and **finishing** only the imperfective is used:
   мы начинáли понимáть язы́к   we were beginning to understand
                                     the language
   мы нáчали обсуждáть положéние   we began discussing the situation
   они́ продолжáли говори́ть всю ночь they went on talking all night

   он перестáл изучáть матемáтику и стал занимáться мýзыкой
   he stopped studying maths and began to do music

   онá принялáсь крáсить окнó   she set to painting the window
   я обязáтельно брóшу кури́ть   I'll definitely give up smoking

Note: the verbs of beginning, continuing and finishing may themselves be either imperfective or perfective, depending on their meaning

• after verbs of **learning**, **avoiding** becoming **accustomed**, **unaccustomed** or **bored** and after **полюби́ть** and **понрáвиться** the imperfective infinitive is used:
   они́ привы́кли зáвтракать пóздно they've got used to having breakfast late

когда́ ты нау́чишься гото́вить омле́т?
when are you going to learn to make an omelette?

она́ избега́ет проси́ть нас о по́мощи   she's avoiding asking us for help
как я уста́ла слу́шать его́ расска́зы   how tired I am of hearing his
                                        stories

ей стра́шно понра́вилось рисова́ть Са́шин портре́т
she really loved drawing Sasha's portrait

- after the perfectives **забы́ть, успе́ть** and **уда́ться** only the perfective
  infinitive is used:
     он обяза́тельно забу́дет почи́стить зу́бы
     he's bound to forget to clean his teeth

     ты успе́ешь позвони́ть нам ве́чером?
     will you have time to ring us this evening?

     мне удало́сь уви́деть Нуре́ева   I managed to see Nureyev

Note: after the imperfectives of these verbs either aspect of the infinitive is possible:
     он всегда́ забыва́ет чи́стить *or* почи́стить зу́бы
     he always forgets to clean his teeth

10.4 Actions which take time

With expressions of **time** while the imperfective is normally used if the
emphasis is on the duration of an action, the perfective may be used if the
emphasis is on completion:
     я бу́ду спать весь день   I'll sleep all day
     всю ночь она́ рабо́тала   all night she worked
but:
     по́езд ме́дленно ушёл   the train slowly left
     он постепе́нно прочита́л весь текст   he gradually read the whole text

With expressions of duration the distinction is normally clear:

- with the imperfective you visualize the **action**:
  она́ три часа́ убира́ла ко́мнату
  she was tidying the room for three hours (i.e. she spent three hours at it,
  but you are still not sure whether the room is any tidier now; you just
  know she worked at it for three whole hours)

- with the perfective you are made aware of the **result**:
  она́ убрала́ ко́мнату за три часа́
  she tidied the room in three hours (i.e. got it done, the room is now fit to
  live in)

Note: the prefix про- may be used on some perfective verbs to express a completed
action lasting a given time:

  он прорабо́тал год во Фра́нции
  he worked a year in France, spent a year working in France

  я бою́сь, что он проспи́т весь уикэ́нд
  I'm afraid he'll sleep through the whole weekend

Note: the prefix по- may be used to form a perfective expressing an action performed
for a limited time, a 'semi-perfective':

  они́ посиде́ли за столо́м о́коло ча́са и пото́м пошли́ в кино́
  they sat at the table for about an hour and then went to the cinema

10.5 Simultaneous actions are conveyed by the imperfective

  мы сиде́ли и обсужда́ли план разви́тия
  we sat and discussed the development plan

  весь день мы бу́дем ходи́ть, собира́ть грибы́, наслажда́ться све́жим
  во́здухом
  we'll walk all day, pick mushrooms and enjoy the fresh air

10.6 Continuous (imperfective) actions may culminate in a completed (perfective) action

  стро́или, стро́или и в про́шлом году́, наконе́ц, постро́или гара́ж
  they were building and building and last year finally got the garage built

  они иска́ли, иска́ли и, наконе́ц, нашли́ его́
  they searched and searched and finally found him

  мы до́лго добира́лись до верши́ны и к ве́черу добрали́сь
  we spent a long time making our way to the summit and reached it by
  evening

10.7 Continuous (imperfective) actions may be interrupted by a single completed (perfective) action

  они́ спа́ли, когда́ он пришёл   they were sleeping when he arrived

  мы шли по доро́ге, когда́ уви́дели во́лка
  we were walking along the road when we saw a wolf

10.8 Aspect of negated verb

In the negative the distinction between imperfective and perfective is very sharp

- the imperfective verb with не negates the action in its entirety, i.e. it does not take place at all and is not even begun:

  она́ не е́ла ка́шу — she didn't eat (didn't touch) the porridge

  он не объясня́л мне схе́му — he didn't explain the diagram to me (i.e. perhaps was not expected to, didn't even try: total denial of the action in any form)

- the perfective verb negates only the completion of the action:

  она́ не съе́ла ка́шу — she hasn't finished her porridge (but was intending to, maybe even began it)

  он не объясни́л мне схе́му — he didn't explain the diagram to me (i.e. didn't manage to make it clear; although he tried, I still don't understand it)

'Пиза́нская ба́шня па́дает уже́ шестьсо́т лет, но ещё не упа́ла' (press) the (leaning) tower of Pisa has been falling (and is still in the process of falling, therefore present tense, imperfective), but hasn't (actually finally, perfectively) fallen yet

In negating an action in its entirety, the **imperfective** verb may negate also the very idea or intention of performing the **action:**

  он не покупа́л уче́бника — he didn't buy the textbook (and never tried or even intended to)

In negating only the completion of an action, the perfective verb allows the possibility that the action was intended or attempted:

  он не купи́л уче́бника — he didn't get the textbook (didn't manage to get it, though he tried)

10.9 Negated infinitives

With the negative infinitive there is a preference for the imperfective where the question of completion is not crucial:

  они́ всё проси́ли меня́ оста́ться — they kept asking me to stay

  они́ проси́ли меня́ не остава́ться — they asked me not to stay

  мы обеща́ем прийти́ по́сле обе́да — we promise to come after dinner

  мы обеща́ем не приходи́ть по́сле обе́да

  we promise not to come after dinner

я постара́юсь успе́ть на по́езд	I'll try to be in time for the train

я постара́юсь не опа́здывать на по́езд
I'll try not to be late for the train

он реши́л помо́чь им	he decided to help them
он реши́л не помога́ть им	he decided not to help them

10.10 After не на́до, не ну́жно 'one mustn't', не сле́дует 'one shouldn't' and не сто́ит 'it isn't worth it' only the imperfective infinitive is used

на́до встать сего́дня в семь часо́в   we've got to get up at seven today
не на́до встава́ть сего́дня в семь часо́в
we don't have to get up at seven today
не сле́дует вам поднима́ть таки́е тя́жести
you shouldn't lift such weights
не сто́ит нам чита́ть э́ту кни́гу   it's not worth our reading this book

10.11 нельзя́

With the imperfective infinitive **нельзя́** means *either* 'you can't' in the sense of 'it is forbidden to':

нельзя́ кури́ть   it is forbidden to smoke

or 'you can't' in the sense of 'it is not possible to':

нельзя́ бы́ло спать там   it was impossible to sleep there

нельзя́ with the perfective infinitive can only mean 'it is not possible to':

нельзя́ бу́дет найти́ доро́гу в темноте́
it'll be impossible to find the way in the dark

*   **нельзя́ не** means 'it is impossible not to', i.e. 'one can only . . .', 'one can't help . . .', and may be used with either the imperfective or perfective infinitive:

нельзя́ не соглаша́ться   one can but agree
нельзя́ не согласи́ться   one can but agree

10.12 The imperative

In the **imperative** the general principles concerning aspects apply, with the perfective used to order completion of an action, but with some invitation ('*do* write') while the imperfective is more categorical. The choice of aspect in the imperative is covered in chapter 16.

Жемчу́жины наро́дной му́дрости

не говори́, что де́лал, говори́, что сде́лал	don't say what you've been doing, say what you've done

EXERCISES

(i) *Translate into English; comment on the use of aspects:*

'Ки́ти ста́ла умоля́ть мать позво́лить ей познако́миться с Ва́ренькой' (Tolstoy).

'Свия́жский был, несомне́нно, че́стный, до́брый, у́мный челове́к, кото́рый ве́село де́лал де́ло, и уже́, наве́рное, никогда́ не де́лал и не мог сде́лать ничего́ дурно́го. Ле́вин стара́лся поня́ть и не понима́л и всегда́, как на живу́ю зага́дку, смотре́л на него́ и на его́ жизнь' (Tolstoy).

'– Бо́же мой! На́до бежа́ть! – пробормота́л он и бро́сился в пере́днюю. Но здесь ожида́л его́ тако́й у́жас, како́го, коне́чно, он ещё ни ра́зу не испы́тывал. Он стоя́л, смотре́л и не ве́рил глаза́м свои́м' (Dostoevsky).

'Таранта́с тро́нулся и помча́лся. В душе́ путеше́ственника бы́ло сму́тно, но он жа́дно гляде́л круго́м на поля́, на холмы́ . . . И вдруг ему́ ста́ло так хорошо́. Он попро́бовал заговори́ть с изво́зчиком, и его́ ужа́сно что-то заинтересова́ло из того́, что отве́тил ему́ мужи́к, но чрез мину́ту сообрази́л, что всё ми́мо уше́й пролете́ло и что он, по пра́вде, не по́нял того́, что мужи́к отве́тил' (Dostoevsky).

'Окружено́ село́ наво́зом, кото́рый здесь на поля́ не выво́зят, а броса́ют пря́мо за село́м, так что для того́, что́бы вы́йти из села́, на́до всегда́ пройти́ че́рез не́которое коли́чество наво́за' (Lenin).

'В до́ме, где ра́ньше находи́лась городска́я упра́ва, а по́сле револю́ции помеща́лся Сове́т наро́дных депута́тов, размести́лась неме́цкая комендату́ра' (N. Ostrovsky).

'Он боя́лся, что все ля́гут спать, а он оди́н оста́нется тоскова́ть и трево́житься в э́ту втору́ю коммунисти́ческую ночь' (Platonov).

'Ива́ну Никола́евичу всё изве́стно, он всё зна́ет и понима́ет. Он зна́ет, что в мо́лодости он стал же́ртвой престу́пных гипнотизёров, лечи́лся по́сле э́того и вы́лечился' (Bulgakov).

'Шопе́н е́здил, концерти́ровал, полжи́зни про́жил в Пари́же' (Pasternak).

'Рома́н [*Воскресе́ние*] по ме́ре оконча́тельной отде́лки глава́ за главо́й печа́тался в журна́ле «Ни́ва», у петербу́ргского изда́теля Ма́ркса . . . Номера́ журна́ла выходи́ли регуля́рно, без опозда́ния. На́до бы́ло поспе́ть к сро́ку ка́ждого' (Pasternak).

'К деньга́м Кузьма́ всю жизнь относи́лся о́чень про́сто: есть – хорошо́, нет – ну и ла́дно . . . Кузьма́ не понима́л и не стара́лся поня́ть, как у люде́й остаётся сверх того́, что ухо́дит на жизнь' (V. Rasputin).

'Жела́ние уе́хать из США созре́ло у 72-ле́тнего Брандо́ постепе́нно' (press).

'Брандо́ заяви́л журнали́стам: «Я хоте́л бы оста́ться здесь до конца́ мои́х дней»' (press).

(ii) *Translate into Russian:*

1   What did you do today?
2   What were you doing today?
3   What have you been doing today?
4   What have you done today?
5   She found the present when she got up.
6   I didn't notice that I'd lost my glasses.
7   We spent three days painting the house.
8   She waited for three hours to buy some meat.
9   She thought she'd forgotten how to make borshch.
10 Have you read *War and Peace*? Yes, but I've never finished it.
11 She spent two hours choosing a hat, and finally chose a yellow one.
12 I always used to like Yalta, but this time I preferred Sochi.
13 This artist hasn't painted a single portrait in five years.
14 We tidied up the kitchen for a whole hour.
15 He sewed himself a suit in five hours.
16 They gradually worked out a plan that everyone could accept.
17 We spent the whole day selling apples; we sold them all by evening.
18 Who's taken my umbrella? – I can't find it.
19 Who took my umbrella? – it's broken.
20 He slowly sat down and began reading the paper.
21 What are you going to do this morning? I'm going to buy a hat.
22 I haven't been late for a lecture in three years.
23 I haven't been late for a lecture once.
24 He would write to his mother every week.
25 He will write to his mother every month.

11 VERBS OF MOTION

11.1 Definite and indefinite verbs of motion

The following verbs describing motion form a distinct group having two imperfective forms, the definite and indefinite (or *determinate* and *indeterminate*), as well as a perfective. The definite verb describes motion in one direction, often with a destination stated or expected from the context: 'I'm going home', 'he's flying to New York tomorrow', 'we were taking them to the shops' and even the question 'where are you going?'; the indefinite verb describes the activity generally, motion there and back or in no one, specified direction: 'I walk every day', 'he always flies to New York (and back)', 'we used to take our dog to help look for mushrooms'. Russian distinguishes clearly between these two categories of motion:

11.1.1 *Definite* (in one direction)   *Indefinite* (there and back)

идти́	ходи́ть	'to go' (on foot)
éхать	éздить	'to go' (by any form of transport)
бежа́ть	бéгать	'to run'
везти́	вози́ть	'to transport, carry by vehicle'
вести́	води́ть	'to lead, drive, take (on foot)'
летéть	летáть	'to fly'
нести́	носи́ть	'to carry' (on foot)
нести́сь	носи́ться	'to rush; to float, drift (in the air)'
брести́ ('to shuffle along')	броди́ть	'to roam, amble'
гнать	гоня́ть	'to drive'
гна́ться	гоня́ться	'to pursue'
кати́ть	катáть	'to roll'
кати́ться	катáться	'to roll'
лезть	лáзить	'to climb'
плыть	плáвать	'to swim, float, sail'
ползти́	пóлзать	'to crawl'
тащи́ть	таскáть	'to pull, drag'
тащи́ться	таскáться	'to drag oneself along'

11.1.2 The perfectives of these verbs are formed from the definite form with the prefix по- . Thus the normal perfective of идти́ is **пойти́**, which often means 'to set off' as well as 'to go (and get there)'. The perfective of éхать is **поéхать** 'to go' (by transport and either to have gone, set off or to have got there); of лете́ть – **полете́ть** 'to fly' (set off or to have got there by air – in either case the *result* is that the person is not here).

EXERCISE

Translate into Russian:
1 He walks to work every day, but travels home by tram.
2 I'm flying to St Petersburg tomorrow; I often fly there on business.
3 She was swimming in the lake when he was running to the station.
4 They were carrying their suitcases towards the hotel.
5 I'm taking you to the post-office, but then I'm going to the library.

11.2 Prefixed verbs of motion

11.2.1 With other prefixes, as well as with по-, the definite verbs form perfectives, e.g.

прийти́ 'to arrive'; **уе́хать** 'to leave'; **вы́бежать** 'to rush out'; **ввезти́** 'to import'; **перевести́** 'to translate'; **пролете́ть** 'to fly past'; **разнести́** 'to distribute'; **отнести́сь** 'to treat, relate to'; **побрести́** 'to plod'; **обогна́ть** 'to overtake'; **докати́ться** 'to roll up to'; **вы́лезть** 'to crawl out'; **перепль́ть** 'to swim across'; **сползти́** 'to climb down'; **утащи́ть** 'to drag away'; etc.

11.2.2 These compound verbs of motion (the verbs of motion with prefixes such as при-, у-, вы-, etc.) have straightforward perfective and imperfective aspects – there are no distinct definite and indefinite forms, e.g.

Imperfective	Perfective	
перелета́ть	перелете́ть	'to fly across'
уноси́ть	унести́	'to carry away'

• With compounds of идти́, везти́, вести́, гнать, лете́ть, нести́ the imperfectives are formed from the corresponding indefinite infinitive, e.g.

Imperfective	Perfective	
приходи́ть	прийти́	'to come [on foot]'
приводи́ть	привести́	'to bring [a person]'
привози́ть	привезти́	'to bring [by transport]'
пригоня́ть	пригна́ть	'to drive, herd home'
прилета́ть	прилете́ть	'to arrive [by air]'
приноси́ть	принести́	'to bring [on foot]'.

Similar pairs may be formed with other prefixes:
заходи́ть/зайти́ 'to call, drop in on'; **развози́ть/развезти́** 'to deliver';
выводи́ть/вы́вести 'to lead out', etc.

- With the other verbs secondary imperfectivization (see pp. 83, 85, 95–7)
  takes place, e.g.

Imperfective	Perfective	
уезжа́ть	уе́хать	'to leave'
зата́скивать	затащи́ть	'to drag in'
влеза́ть	влезть	'to creep in'
переплыва́ть	переплы́ть	'to swim across'
забреда́ть	забрести́	'to wander off'

Note also:

пробега́ть	пробежа́ть	'to run past'
дополза́ть	доползти́	'to crawl as far as', etc.

with a change of stress from the basic **бе́гать** and **по́лзать**.

11.2.3 As an illustration of the range of meanings which can extend from a single verb of motion here is a list of the common compounds of **ходи́ть** : **идти́** 'to go (on foot)':

Imperfective	Perfective		Typical construction
входи́ть	войти́	'to enter'	в + *acc.*
всходи́ть			
(*or* восходи́ть)	взойти́	'to ascend'	на + *acc.*
выходи́ть	вы́йти	'to go out'	из + *gen.*
доходи́ть	дойти́	'to reach'	до + *gen.*
заходи́ть	зайти́	'to call on'	к + *dat.*, в + *acc.*
исходи́ть	(изойти́)	'to emanate'	из + *gen.*
находи́ть	найти́	'to find'	+ *acc.*
находи́ться	найти́сь	'to be situated'	в, на + *acc.*, у + *gen.*
обходи́ть	обойти́	'to avoid'	+ *acc.*
обходи́ться	обойти́сь	'to do without'	без + *gen.*
отходи́ть	отойти́	'to move away'	от + *gen.*
переходи́ть	перейти́	'to cross'	че́рез + *acc.*
подходи́ть	подойти́	'to approach; to suit'	к + *dat.* + *dat.*
превосходи́ть	превзойти́	'to surpass'	+ *acc.*
приходи́ть	прийти́	'to arrive'	в + *acc.*
проходи́ть	пройти́	'to pass'	ми́мо + *gen.*
происходи́ть	произойти́	'to occur'	где, когда́, с кем
расходи́ться	разойти́сь	'to part'	с + *inst.*
сходи́ть	сойти́	'to descend'	с + *gen.*
сходи́ться	сойти́сь	'to agree'	с + *inst.*
уходи́ть	уйти́	'to leave'	из, с, от + *gen.*

Жемчу́жины наро́дной му́дрости

язы́к до Ки́ева доведёт	(your) tongue will get (you) to Kiev

11.2.4 A few perfective verbs are formed from indefinite verbs of motion; these do not normally have corresponding imperfectives. They include:

сходи́ть	'to go and fetch' за + *inst.*
сбе́гать	'to run to fetch' за + *inst.*
съе́здить	'to travel' (once there & back)
слета́ть	'to fly' (once there & back)
своди́ть	'to take' (once to theatre, *etc.* on foot)
свози́ть	'to take' (once to theatre, *etc.* by transport)
заходи́ть	'to start walking'
забе́гать	'to start running'
забе́гаться	'to run oneself to a standstill'
исходи́ть	'to walk all over' (something)
изъе́здить (*impf.* изъе́зживать)	'to travel all over' (somewhere)
износи́ть (*impf.* изна́шивать)	'to wear (something) out'
налета́ть	'to fly' (so many hours, miles)
находи́ться	'to tire oneself walking'
набе́гаться	'to exhaust oneself running'
вы́ездить ло́шадь	'to break in a horse'
обла́зить	'to climb all over'
проводи́ть (*impf.* провожа́ть)	'to accompany, see someone off'
прое́здиться	'to spend all one's money travelling'
уходи́ть	'to wear out; do someone in'
(*impf.* уха́живать	'to look after; to woo' за + *inst.*)

* A 'semi-perfective' form **походи́ть** exists, meaning 'to have a walk, do a bit of walking'.

EXERCISES

(i)   *Note and translate these common compound verbs of motion; make up sentences using the typical constructions provided:*

Imperfective	Perfective	Typical construction
влеза́ть	влезть	в окно́; на де́рево
воспроизводи́ть	воспроизвести́	стиль; атмосфе́ру
входи́ть	войти́	в дом
въезжа́ть	въе́хать	в го́род; на маши́не
выбега́ть	вы́бежать	из кварти́ры

вывози́ть	вы́везти	что́-то из Росси́и; за грани́цу
вылета́ть	вы́лететь	из шка́фа; в окно́
выноси́ть	вы́нести	что́-то из до́ма; на площа́дку; боль
выходи́ть	вы́йти	из спа́льни; на у́лицу; за́муж
доезжа́ть	дое́хать	до конца́; до це́нтра
доноси́ть	донести́	до до́ма; власта́м
доноси́ться	донести́сь	до уше́й, издалека́
доходи́ть	дойти́	до угла́; до неё
загоня́ть	загна́ть	кого́-то в у́гол
залеза́ть	зале́зть	в во́ду
залета́ть	залете́ть	в окно́; в Берли́н
заходи́ть	зайти́	к подру́ге; в буфе́т; на мину́тку
избега́ть	избежа́ть	
	or избе́гнуть	встре́чи; поли́ции; тру́дностей
налета́ть	налете́ть	на жу́ликов; на грузови́к
находи́ть	найти́	де́ньги; в лесу́; на пла́же
находи́ться	найти́сь	в це́нтре; о́коло собо́ра
		в па́рке; под дива́ном
обводи́ть	обвести́	кого́-то вокру́г па́льца
обзаводи́ться	обзавести́сь	семе́йством; жено́й
обходи́ть	обойти́	весь го́род; зако́н
обходи́ться	обойти́сь	без по́мощи
относи́ться	отнести́сь	к де́лу; к сы́ну; к XV ве́ку
отходи́ть	отойти́	от меня́; от окна́
переводи́ть	перевести́	с ру́сского; на неме́цкий
переходи́ть	перейти́	че́рез мост; на э́ту сто́рону
подводи́ть	подвести́	кого́-то; ито́ги
подходи́ть	подойти́	к две́ри; к нача́льнику; мне
превосходи́ть	превзойти́	ожида́ния; свои́х сопе́рников
преподноси́ть	преподнести́	кому́-то пода́рок
прибега́ть	прибежа́ть	в теа́тр; на ле́кцию
прибега́ть	прибе́гнуть	к стро́гим ме́рам; к хи́трости
привози́ть	привезти́	что́-то в страну́; из А́нглии; на
		вокза́л; с ры́нка; на по́езде
приезжа́ть	прие́хать	в Ло́ндон; в го́сти; из Ми́нска
прилета́ть	прилете́ть	в Москву́; из Пари́жа; в час
приноси́ть	принести́	что́-то де́тям; из магази́на
приходи́ть	прийти́	в зал; из шко́лы; в себя́; на рабо́ту;
		со ста́нции; к себе́ домо́й
прогоня́ть	прогна́ть	из аудито́рии
проезжа́ть	прое́хать	ми́мо вокза́ла; че́рез Ки́ев
производи́ть	произвести́	впечатле́ние; эффе́кт
произноси́ть	произнести́	иностра́нные слова́
пролета́ть	пролете́ть	ми́мо окна́; над голово́й
проплыва́ть	проплы́ть	че́рез Ла-Ма́нш
проходи́ть	пройти́	че́рез парк; ми́мо па́мятника

разноси́ть	разнести́	пи́сьма; в ра́зные сто́роны
расходи́ться	разойти́сь	с партнёрами; с му́жем; по дома́м
сгоня́ть	согна́ть	со сце́ны; в ста́до
слеза́ть	слезть	с де́рева
слета́ть	слете́ть	с кры́ши
сноси́ть	снести́	дом; что-то с ле́стницы; невзго́ды
сходи́ть	сойти́	с ле́стницы
сходи́ться	сойти́сь	с на́ми; в подро́бностях; умо́м
убега́ть	убежа́ть	от него́; от опа́сности
уезжа́ть	уе́хать	из А́нглии; в Аме́рику
улета́ть	улете́ть	на юг; в А́фрику
уходи́ть	уйти́	из до́ма; из жи́зни; от меня́; в отста́вку; на пе́нсию

(ii) a. *Using the appropriate prefixed compounds of* ходи́ть/идти́ (i.e. *with* в-, вы-, до-, за-, от-, пере-, под-, при-, про-, с-, у-) *give the forms required to replace the dots . . . on the 'map' to express:* 'he is . . . '; 'he will . . . '; 'he used to . . . '; *and* 'he has . . .'

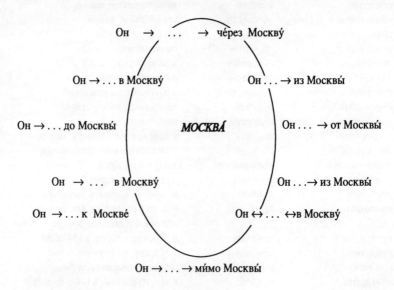

Он → . . . → че́рез Москву́

Он → . . . в Москву́   Он . . . → из Москвы́

Он → . . . до Москвы́   *МОСКВА́*   Он . . . → от Москвы́

Он → . . . в Москву́   Он . . . → из Москвы́

Он → . . . к Москве́   Он ↔ . . . ↔в Москву́

Он → . . . → ми́мо Москвы́

b. *Do the same with the prefixed forms of* -езжа́ть/-е́хать *and* -лета́ть/- лете́ть.

(iii) *Translate into Russian:*

1   Whenever I call on Boris he's always working in his garden.
2   When I call on Boris I'll ask him about his garden.
3   Whenever I go to London I always pop into the British Museum.
4   He went to London yesterday and brought her a present.
5   She ran past me as I was coming out of the house.
6   We brought him a ticket and took him to the stadium.
7   The child was found behind the sofa; it had crawled there and fallen asleep.
8   When he comes down off the roof I'll chase him out of the park.
9   This surpassed all my expectations: now we'll do without the car.
10 The author approached the theme subtly and reproduced the conversational style of the end of the last century exactly.
11 What happened after the train left?
12 What happened as the train was leaving?
13 He was thinking of her as he walked to the station.
14 The rain started when we were sitting on the river bank.
15 As she was walking to work she noticed a strange bird.

12   PARTICIPLES

Russian has four possible participle forms of the verb:

(a)	the present active participle
(b)	the past active participle (imperfective and perfective)
(c)	the present passive participle
(d)	the past passive participle (imperfective and perfective)

• A participle is a verbal adjective, a word used to describe a noun in terms of an action; as an adjective it agrees with the noun which it describes in gender, number and case. Thus, in the sentence 'the student reading the book understands Russian', the word 'reading' is a participle – it identifies the student as distinct from any others present in terms of the action (s)he is performing.

12.1 Present active participle

12.1.1 The present active participle refers to an action which takes place at the same time as the action of the main verb. It is formed from the third person plural of the present tense by removing the final -т and adding the adjectival endings -щий, -щая, -щее; -щие, etc. (see p. 31)

читáть	читáю[т]	читáющий, читáющая, читáющее; читáющие, etc. 'reading'
писáть	пи́шу[т]	пи́шущий, etc. 'writing'
рисовáть	рису́ю[т]	рису́ющий, etc. 'drawing'
нести́	несу́[т]	несу́щий, etc. 'carrying'
говори́ть	говоря́[т]	говоря́щий, etc. 'speaking'
кричáть	кричá[т]	кричáщий, etc. 'shouting'

12.1.2 Participles from reflexive verbs always end in -ся (not -сь):

казáться	кáжу[т]ся	кáжущийся, кáжущаяся, кáжущееся; кáжущиеся, etc. 'seeming'
находи́ться	нахóдя[т]ся	находя́щийся, находя́щаяся, находя́щееся; находя́щиеся, etc. 'situated'

12.1.3 In 1st Conjugation verbs the stress on a present active participle is on the same syllable as the third person plural of the present tense, and in 2nd Conjugation verbs it is on the same syllable as in the infinitive:

требовать	требую[т]	**требующий**, etc. 'demanding'
вязать	вяжу[т]	**вяжущий**, etc. 'tying up, knitting'
учиться	уча[т]ся	**учащийся**, etc. 'learning; student'

Note: the exceptions:

любить	любя[т]	**любящий**, etc. 'loving'
служить	служа[т]	**служащий**, etc. 'serving'

Жемчужины народной мудрости

лающая собака реже кусает	a barking dog bites more rarely

12.1.4 The present active participle may be replaced by a relative clause; in the example

студе́нт, чита́ющий кни́гу, понима́ет по-ру́сски

or студе́нтка, чита́ющая кни́гу, понима́ет по-ру́сски

the student reading the book understands Russian

чита́ющий 'reading' could be replaced by кото́рый чита́ет 'who is reading' and чита́ющая by кото́рая чита́ет:

студе́нтка, кото́рая чита́ет кни́гу, понима́ет по-ру́сски

the student who is reading the book understands Russian

The relative clause (see pp. 68–9) is more common than the participles in spoken Russian.

12.1.5 Present participles refer to actions contemporary with the main verb, i.e. not necessarily referring to the present:

мы спроси́ли де́вушку, стоя́щую на остано́вке

we asked the girl standing at the bus stop

EXERCISES

(i) a. *Give the meaning of each infinitive below:*
   b. *Give the present active participle of:*

де́лать; бе́гать; бежа́ть; бить; благодари́ть; боле́ть [to be ill]; боле́ть [to ache]; боро́ться; боя́ться; брать; вести́; ви́деть; висе́ть; владе́ть; воева́ть; возвраща́ться; встава́ть; встреча́ть; вы́глядеть; горди́ться; горе́ть; дава́ть; держа́ть; достига́ть; е́здить; е́хать; жела́ть; зави́сеть; идти́; име́ть; класть; каса́ться; лета́ть; освеща́ть; остава́ться; относи́ться; отсу́тствовать; покупа́ть; проводи́ть; проси́ть; пря́таться; развива́ть; расти́; ре́зать; свети́ть; содержа́ть; состоя́ть; существова́ть; терпе́ть; течь; чу́вствовать.

(ii) a. *Translate into English; and*

b. *Replace the participles italicized in the sentences below with relative clauses introduced by* который *in the appropriate case:*

'Суда́, *стоя́щие* на при́стани, бы́ли все – и́ли сторожевы́е, и́ли купе́ческие' (Lermontov).

'Вдруг на я́ркой полосе́, *пересека́ющей* пол, промелькну́ла тень' (Lermontov).

'Я так привы́кла к тому́, что мы всегда́ говори́ли то́лько о веща́х, *каса́ющихся* меня́, что уже́ находи́ла э́то есте́ственным' (Tolstoy).

'Среди́ тишины́ раздаётся глухо́й стук топора́, *звуча́щий* одино́ко и гру́стно' (Chekhov).

'То́ня (. . .) смотре́ла на знако́мый, родно́й ей сад, на *окружа́ющие* его́ стро́йные тополя́, *вздра́гивающие* от лёгкого ветерка́' (N. Ostrovsky).

Номенклату́ра – э́то 'лю́ди, *уме́ющие* осуществля́ть директи́вы, *могу́щие* поня́ть директи́вы, *могу́щие* приня́ть директи́вы, как свои́ родны́е, и *уме́ющие* проводи́ть их в жизнь' (Stalin).

'Б. Е́льцин, по́сле того́ как уви́дел во вре́мя предвы́борных пое́здок *встреча́ющие* его́ ра́достные то́лпы, заяви́л, что победи́т в пе́рвом ту́ре' (press).

12.2 Past active participle

12.2.1 The past active participle qualifies a noun in terms of an action performed by it some time in the past: 'the man *who used to read* poetry', 'in the bus *which had* just *arrived*'. It is formed from the past tense of the verb, imperfective or perfective depending on meaning, by removing the final -л and adding -вший, -вшая, -вшее; -вшие, etc.

Imperfective:

де́лать	де́ла[л]	де́лавший, де́лавшая, де́лавшее; де́лавшие, etc. 'who was doing', 'used to do', 'had been doing'
смотре́ть	смотре́[л]	смотре́вший, etc. 'who looked'
люби́ть	люби́[л]	люби́вший, etc. 'who loved'
занима́ться	занима́[л]ся	занима́вшийся, занима́вшаяся, занима́вшееся; занима́вшиеся, etc. 'who was engaged in'

Perfective:

сде́лать	сде́ла[л]	сде́лавший, etc. 'who did', 'has done', 'had done'
посмотре́ть	посмотре́[л]	посмотре́вший, etc. 'who looked'
полюби́ть	полюби́[л]	полюби́вший, etc. 'who fell for'
заня́ться	заня[л]ся́	заня́вшийся, etc. 'who took up'

- Not all verbs form their past tense regularly:

Note:

нести́	нёс	нёсший, etc. 'who carried'
везти́	вёз	вёзший, etc. 'who transported'
жечь	жёг	жёгший, etc. 'who burned'
лечь	лёг	лёгший, etc. 'who lay'
па́хнуть	пах	па́хший, etc. *or* па́хнувший, etc. 'which smelled'
привы́кнуть	привы́к	привы́кший, etc. *or* привы́кнувший, etc. 'who got used to'
исче́знуть	исче́з	исче́знувший, etc. 'who vanished'
прони́кнуть	прони́к	прони́кший, etc. *or* прони́кнувший, etc. 'who penetrated'
спасти́	спас	спа́сший, etc. 'who saved'

So, too, all their compounds, e.g.

унести́	унёс	унёсший, etc. 'who carried away'
привезти́	привёз	привёзший, etc. 'who brought'
заже́чь	зажёг	зажёгший, etc. 'who set light to'

Note, too:

вести́	вёл	ве́дший, etc. 'who led'
идти́	шёл	ше́дший, etc. 'who walked'
пасть	пал	па́дший, etc. 'who fell'

And all their compounds, e.g.

прийти́	пришёл	прише́дший, etc. 'who arrived'
произойти́	произошёл	происше́дший, etc. 'that occurred'

12.2.2 The past active participle, like the present active participle, may be replaced by a relative clause:

студе́нт, чита́вший кни́гу, тепе́рь пи́шет курсову́ю рабо́ту

or: студе́нт, кото́рый чита́л кни́гу, тепе́рь пи́шет курсову́ю рабо́ту

the student who was reading the book is now writing a project

студе́нтка, написа́вшая э́то сочине́ние, второку́рсница

or: студе́нтка, кото́рая написа́ла э́то сочине́ние, второку́рсница

the student who wrote this essay is a second-year

The past active, like the other participles, is commoner in literary Russian than in conversational speech.

12.2.3 Though the past active participle usually refers to actions performed before the action of the main verb, it is often used for simultaneous actions in the past:

'Она́ не реша́лась войти́ в гости́ную, пока́ в ней раздава́лись голоса́ спо́ривших' (Turgenev).

she couldn't bring herself to go into the drawing room while the voices of those who were quarrelling were still ringing out

Жемчу́жины наро́дной му́дрости

проголода́вшемуся не до вку́са	for one who has become hungry taste doesn't matter

---

EXERCISES

(i) a. *Give the meaning of each infinitive below:*
    b. *Give the past active participle of:*

брать, взять; ве́шать, пове́сить; дви́гаться, дви́нуться; забыва́ть, забы́ть; заходи́ть, зайти́; корми́ть, покорми́ть; ложи́ться, лечь; объясня́ть, объясни́ть; остава́ться, оста́ться; оставля́ть, оста́вить; открыва́ть, откры́ть; поднима́ть, подня́ть; посыла́ть, посла́ть; проводи́ть, провести́; приглаша́ть, пригласи́ть; просыпа́ться, просну́ться; сади́ться, сесть; смея́ться, засмея́ться; удивля́ться, удиви́ться.

(ii) *Replace the relative pronouns and verbs italicized in the sentences below with a past active participle:*

Мой друг, *кото́рый изуча́л* неме́цкий язы́к, рабо́тает тепе́рь в Берли́не.
Моя́ подру́га, *кото́рая изуча́ла* кита́йский язы́к, за́втра лети́т в Гонг Конг.
Она́ чита́ет газе́ту, *кото́рая лежа́ла* на столе́.
Ма́льчики, *кото́рые игра́ли* в футбо́л, уста́ли.
Мно́го молоды́х ру́сских специали́стов, *кото́рые око́нчили* ву́зы, вы́ехали на За́пад.
Он говори́л с же́нщиной, *кото́рая то́лько что прие́хала* из Москвы́.
Они́ обсужда́ли пробле́му, *кото́рая неда́вно возни́кла*.
Говори́ли об экспеди́ции, *кото́рая отпра́вилась* на Да́льний Восто́к.

(iii) a. *Give the infinitives from which the participles italicized in the sentences below derive; and*
    b. *Translate the sentences:*

'(Он) огляну́лся и уви́дел же́нщину высо́кого ро́ста в чёрном пла́тье, *останови́вшуюся* в дверя́х' (Turgenev).

'Фéничка подняла́ на База́рова свои́ глаза́, *каза́вшиеся* ещё темне́е от белова́того о́тблеска, *па́давшего* на ве́рхнюю часть её лица́' (Turgenev).

'Отва́жен был плове́ц, *реши́вшийся* в таку́ю ночь пусти́ться че́рез проли́в на расстоя́ние 20 вёрст, и ва́жная должна́ быть причи́на, его́ к тому́ *побуди́вшая*' (Lermontov).

'Слы́шится звук *ло́пнувшей* струны́, замира́ющий, печа́льный' (Chekhov).

Господи́н из Сан Франци́ско всё погля́дывал на *стоя́вшую* во́зле него́ знамени́тую краса́вицу' (Bunin).

'Пéрвый день прошёл благополу́чно, и Па́вка шага́л домо́й с чу́вством челове́ка, че́стно *зарабо́тавшего* свой о́тдых' (N. Ostrovsky).

'Я име́л слу́чай и сча́стье знать мно́гих ста́рших поэ́тов, *жи́вших* в Москве́' (Pasternak).

'В э́то чуде́сное у́тро все, *прие́хавшие* на Капри́, ещё спа́ли' (Bunin).

'Лай, *доноси́вшийся* с противополо́жного бе́рега, был чист, слаб и далёк' (Kazakov).

'Вы́шел из тюрьмы́ Кругло́в други́м челове́ком: *похуде́вшим*, темноли́цым, сми́рным, просты́м с ви́ду, но ещё бо́лее *ожесточи́вшимся* в душе́' (Kazakov).

'Похо́д Ермака́, *положи́вший* нача́ло присоедине́нию Сиби́ри к Росси́и, стал одни́м из са́мых значи́тельных собы́тий в ру́сской исто́рии пери́ода феодали́зма' (R. G. Skrynnikov).

'Сюже́т «Сабри́ны» стар как мир и с криста́льной чистото́й воспроизво́дит ска́зку о Зо́лушке – шофёрской до́чке, *преврати́вшейся* в принце́ссу и *покори́вшей* двух бра́тьев-миллиарде́ров' (press).

(iv) *Translate into Russian, using participles where possible:*

1 The paper receives many letters from people working in the Far East.
2 The paper used to receive many letters from people working in the Far East.
3 The paper receives many letters from people who used to work in the Far East.
4 The paper used to receive many letters from people who had worked in the Far East.

12.3 Present passive participle

The present passive participle is less common than the other participles. It describes a noun in terms of an action being done to it in the present or simultaneously to the main verb:

журна́л, чита́емый студе́нткой, сто́ит два до́ллара
the magazine being read by the student costs two dollars

12.3.1 The present passive participle is formed from the 1st person plural of the present tense of the verb by adding the hard adjectival endings -ый, -ая, -ое; -ые, etc.

чита́ть	чита́ем	**чита́емый, чита́емая, чита́емое; чита́емые,** etc. '(which is) being read'
люби́ть	лю́бим	**люби́мый, люби́мая, люби́мое; люби́мые,** etc. '(who, which is) loved'

12.3.2 The present passive participle is, however, formed only from transitive verbs in the following categories:

* Regular verbs of the 1st Conjugation, like чита́ть, e.g.
  встреча́ть   встреча́ем   **встреча́емый,** etc.   'being met'

[but *not*, for example, from писа́ть (пишу́, пи́шешь . . .) 'to write' *or* пить (пью, пьёшь . . .) 'to drink']

* 1st Conjugation verbs with the infinitive ending in -овать, e.g.
  атакова́ть   атаку́ем   **атаку́емый,** etc.   'being attacked'
  дати́ровать   дати́руем   **дати́руемый,** etc.   'being dated, ascribed'

* The 2nd Conjugation verbs води́ть, вози́ть, носи́ть and their prefixed compounds:

  вози́ть   во́зим   **вози́мый,** *etc.*   'being conveyed'
  носи́ть   но́сим   **носи́мый,** *etc.*   'being carried; being worn'
  переводи́ть   перево́дим   **переводи́мый,** etc.   'being translated'

* Some other 2nd Conjugation verbs, like люби́ть e.g.
  храни́ть   храни́м   **храни́мый,** etc.   'being preserved'
  цени́ть   це́ним   **цени́мый,** etc.   'valued'
  терпе́ть   те́рпим   **терпи́мый,** etc.   'tolerated'

[but not, for example, from говори́ть 'to say' *or* стро́ить 'to build']

Note: давáть and its prefixed compounds form their present passive participle from the infinitive:

давáть	даём	*but*	**давáемый**, etc.	'being given'
продавáть	продаём	*but*	**продавáемый**, etc.	'being sold'

So, too: узнавáть узнаём *but* **узнавáемый**, etc. 'recognized'

• The present passive participle may be formed from some verbs which do not take a direct object in the accusative case:

угрожáть (+ *dat*)	*but*	**угрожáемый**, etc.	'threatened'
предшéствовать (+ *dat*)	*but*	**предшéствуемый**, etc. 'preceded'	
комáндовать (+ *inst*)	*but*	**комáндуемый**, etc.	'commanded'

12.3.3 From the present passive participle are formed adjectives whose English equivalent ends in -able or -ible, many of them negative, e.g.

забывáть 'to forget'	**незабывáемый**, etc. 'unforgettable'
выносúть 'to bear, tolerate'	**невыносúмый**, etc. 'unbearable'
исчерпáть 'to drain'	**неисчерпáемый**, etc. 'inexhaustible'
называ́ть 'to call'	**так называ́емый**, etc. 'so called'
реализовáть 'to put into practice'	**реализýемый**, etc. 'practicable'

Some of these adjectives are formed from the perfective verb, i.e. from the perfective future tense:

выражáть/вы́разить 'to express'	**невырази́мый**, etc. 'inexpressible'
объясня́ть/объясни́ть 'to explain'	**необъясни́мый**, etc. 'inexplicable'
ощущáть/ощути́ть 'to sense'	**ощути́мый**, etc. 'perceptible'
совмещáть/совмести́ть 'to combine'	**совмести́мый**, etc. 'compatible'
срáвнивать/сравни́ть 'to compare'	**несравни́мый**, etc. 'incomparable'

EXERCISES

(i) a. *Give the meaning of each infinitive below:*
     b. *Give the present passive participle of:*

бросáть; води́ть; давáть; докáзывать; допускáть; запи́сывать; изображáть; испóльзовать; носи́ть; отдавáть; повторя́ть; поддéрживать; получáть; проводи́ть; развивáть; снимáть; собирáть; терпéть; устрáивать; цени́ть

(ii) *Replace the relative clauses in the sentences below with present passive participles*:

Грамма́тика, кото́рую мы изуча́ем, не интересу́ет меня́.

Литерату́ра, кото́рую студе́нты изуча́ют, не интересу́ет их.

Грибы́, кото́рые они́ собира́ют, несъедо́бные.

Джи́нсы, кото́рые здесь продаю́т, о́чень старомо́дные.

В кварти́ре, кото́рую он покупа́ет, нет ме́бели.

В отры́вке, кото́рый мы перево́дим, мно́го тру́дностей.

Мы ви́дели свои́ми глаза́ми траги́ческую сце́ну, кото́рую а́втор изобража́ет.

(iii) a.   *Give the infinitive from which the italicized participles are derived: and*
      b.   *Translate:*

'Я сел у забо́ра на ка́мень; предо мной тяну́лось мо́ре, и однообра́зный шум его́, подо́бный ро́поту засыпа́ющего го́рода, напо́мнил мне ста́рые го́ды ... *Волну́емый* воспомина́ниями, я забы́лся ...' (Lermontov).

'Степа́н Арка́дьич, *провожа́емый* почти́тельным швейца́ром, с портфе́лем прошёл в свой ма́ленький кабине́т' (Tolstoy).

'Что́бы быть *люби́мым* то́ю любо́вью, како́ю он сам люби́л Ки́ти, ну́жно бы́ло быть краса́вцем, а гла́вное - осо́бенным челове́ком' (Tolstoy).

'Лёвин подошёл к гора́м, на кото́рых греме́ли це́пи *спуска́емых* и *поднима́емых* сала́зок, грохота́ли кати́вшиеся сала́зки и звуча́ли весёлые голоса́' (Tolstoy).

'Сто́рож (. . .) не слы́шал *отодвига́емого* за́дом по́езда, и его́ раздави́ли' (Tolstoy).

'Вро́нский испыта́л неприя́тное чу́вство, како́е испыта́л бы челове́к, *му́чимый* жа́ждою и добра́вшийся до исто́чника и находя́щий в э́том исто́чнике соба́ку, овцу́ и́ли свинью́, кото́рая и вы́пила и возмути́ла во́ду' (Tolstoy).

'Расскажи́те нам что-нибу́дь заба́вное, но не зло́е, – сказа́ла жена́ посла́нника, вели́кая мастери́ца изя́щного разгово́ра, *называ́емого* по-англи́йски small talk' (Tolstoy).

'Эффе́кт, *производи́мый* реча́ми княги́ни Мягко́й, всегда́ был одина́ков, и секре́т *производи́мого* е́ю эффе́кта состоя́л в том, что она́ говори́ла хоть и не совсе́м кста́ти, как тепе́рь, но просты́е ве́щи, име́ющие смысл' (Tolstoy).

'И господи́н из Сан-Франци́ско (. . .) уже́ с тоско́й и зло́бой ду́мал об э́тих жа́дных, воня́ющих чесноко́м людишках, *называ́емых* италья́нцами' (Bunin).

'Пе́рвый был не кто ино́й, как Михаи́л Алекса́ндрович Берлио́з, председа́тель одно́й из крупне́йших моско́вских литерату́рных ассоциа́ций, сокращённо *имену́емой* МАССОЛИТ' (Bulgakov).

'Вокру́г бы́ло ти́хо. Стоя́ла в лесу́ засто́йная духота́, хотя́ *обдува́емый* летя́щим от недалёкого Бе́лого мо́ря ве́тром лес шелесте́л в вышине́, пока́чивал кро́нами стро́йных со́сен' (D. Eremin).

'Она́ ду́мала о своём му́же, неве́домо где *носи́мом* ве́трами войны́' (Polevoy).

'*Охраня́емый* На́стей бага́ж лежа́л у скамьи́' (Antonov).

12.4 Past passive participle

The past passive participle qualifies a noun with reference to an action performed on it in the past – 'the picture (which was) painted by his father', 'the person (who has been) arrested'. The past passive participle, like the other participles, may be replaced by a relative clause. Although the past passive participle may be formed from imperfective verbs (e.g. чи́танный '[having been] read' – regularly or continuously), in practice the perfective form is more common.

Additionally, the short, or predicative, form of the past passive participle is used to form the passive voice of perfective verbs, e.g.

> э́то письмо́ бы́ло напи́сано вчера́
> this letter was written yesterday

This usage of the past passive participle will be explained later (see pp. 126–7).

12.4.1 Formation of the past passive participle

Regular 1st Conjugation verbs whose infinitive ends in -ать or -ять form the past passive participle by removing the -ть and adding -нный, -нная, -нное; -нные, *etc.* (-нн- and the hard adjectival endings):

прочита́ть 'to read'	**прочи́танный, прочи́танная, прочи́танное; прочи́танные**, etc. '(which has been) read'
написа́ть 'to write'	**напи́санный**, etc. 'written'
потеря́ть 'to lose'	**поте́рянный**, etc. 'lost'
заинтересова́ть 'to interest, intrigue'	**заинтересо́ванный**, etc. 'interested'

Жемчу́жины наро́дной му́дрости

поте́рянного вре́мени не дого́нишь	you can't catch up lost time

- 2nd Conjugation verbs in -ать do the same:
  сдержа́ть 'to restrain'   сде́ржанный, etc. 'held back'
  услы́шать 'to hear'   услы́шанный, etc. 'heard'

The stress on these participles is on the stem of the verb, except for those in -ировать which are all 1st Conjugation:
  изоли́ровать 'to isolate, insulate'
  изоли́рованный, etc. 'isolated, insulated'

- 1st Conjugation verbs with their infinitive in -ти, -зть, -сть and -чь form their past passive participle in -ённый:
  принести́ 'to bring'   принесённый, etc. 'brought'
  увезти́ 'to carry away'   увезённый, etc. 'carried off'
  перевести́ 'to translate'   переведённый, etc. 'translated'
  спасти́ 'to save'   спасённый, etc. 'rescued'
  уче́сть 'to consider'   учтённый, etc. 'taken into account'
  испе́чь 'to bake'   испечённый, etc. 'baked'

Note: the prefix вы- with perfective verbs is always stressed, so:
  вы́нести 'to take out [on foot]'   вы́несенный, etc. 'brought out '
  вы́везти 'to export'   вы́везенный, etc. 'exported'

Note: укра́сть 'to steal'   укра́денный, etc. 'stolen'
  найти 'to find'   на́йденный, etc. 'found'
  прогры́зть 'to gnaw through'   прогры́зенный, etc. 'gnawed through'

12.4.2 Many 1st Conjugation verbs with monosyllabic infinitives, including бить 'to hit'; брить 'to shave'; вить 'to twist'; лить 'to pour'; пить 'to drink'; шить 'to sew'; петь 'to sing' and their prefixed compounds form their past passive participle in -тый, -тая, -тое; -тые, etc. Thus, for example:

  бить 'to hit, strike'   би́тый, etc. 'struck, damaged'
  разби́ть 'to break, smash'   разби́тый, etc. 'smashed'
  уби́ть 'to kill'   уби́тый, etc. 'killed, murdered'
  свить 'to weave'   сви́тый, etc. 'twined'
  разви́ть 'to develop'   разви́тый, etc. 'developed'
  проли́ть 'to spill'   проли́тый, etc. 'spilled'
  вы́пить 'to drink'   вы́питый, etc. 'drunk, consumed'
  сшить 'to sew'   сши́тый, etc. 'sewn'
  спеть 'to sing'   спе́тый, etc. 'sung'

Жемчу́жины наро́дной му́дрости

би́тая посу́да два ве́ка живёт	cracked crockery lives two centuries

- 1st Conjugation verbs which in the perfective future tense introduce -м- or -н-, and their prefixed compounds also form their past passive participle in -тый, -тая, -тое; -тые, etc.:

взять 'to take' (возьму́, возьмёшь . . .)　　**взя́тый**, etc. 'taken'
заня́ть 'to engage' (займу́, займёшь . . .)　　**за́нятый**, etc. 'occupied'
поня́ть 'to understand' (пойму́, поймёшь . . .)　　**по́нятый**, etc. 'understood'

(and all other prefixed compounds from the same root, e.g. наня́ть, обня́ть, отня́ть, подня́ть, предприня́ть, приня́ть, снять)

сжать 'to squeeze' (сожму́, сожмёшь. . .)　　**сжа́тый**, etc. 'compressed'
нача́ть 'to start' (начну́, начнёшь. . .)　　**на́чатый**, etc. 'begun'
оде́ть 'to dress' (оде́ну, оде́нешь. . .)　　**оде́тый**, etc. 'dressed'

- Verbs in -ыть (all 1st Conjugation) form their past passive participle in -тый, -тая, -тое; -тые, etc.:
забы́ть 'to forget'　　**забы́тый**, etc. 'forgotten'
откры́ть 'to open'　　**откры́тый**, etc. 'open[ed]'

- Verbs in -уть (all 1st Conjugation) form their past passive participle in -тый, -тая, -тое; -тые, etc.:
вы́нуть 'to take out'　　**вы́нутый**, etc. 'taken out, extracted'
протяну́ть 'to stretch'　　**протя́нутый**, etc. 'extended'

- Verbs in -ереть (all 1st Conjugation) form their past passive participle in -тый, -тая, -тое; -тые, etc.:
запере́ть 'to lock up'　　**за́пертый**, etc. 'locked'
стере́ть 'to wipe off'　　**стёртый**, etc. 'wiped off, erased'

- Verbs in -оть (all 1st Conjugation) form their past passive participle in -тый, -тая, -тое; -тые, etc.:
коло́ть 'to chop; prick'　　**ко́лотый**, etc. 'chopped'
распоро́ть 'to unpick'　　**распо́ротый**, etc. 'unstitched'

12.4.3 2nd Conjugation verbs form their past passive participle from the 1st person singular of the perfective future tense (or present tense for imperfectives) by removing the final -ю or -у and adding -енный or -ённый, etc.; it ends in -ённый only if the stress is on the ending *throughout* the tense:

заме́тить (заме́чу, заме́тишь . . .)　　**заме́ченный**, etc. 'noticed'
назна́чить (назна́чу, назна́чишь . . .)　　**назна́ченный**, etc. 'appointed'
осмотре́ть (осмотрю́, осмо́тришь　　**осмо́тренный**, etc. 'inspected'
посади́ть (посажу́, поса́дишь . . .)　　**поса́женный**, etc. 'seated; set'

постро́ить (постро́ю, постро́ишь . . .)	**постро́енный**, etc. 'built'
свари́ть (сварю́, сва́ришь . . .)	**сва́ренный**, etc. 'boiled'
соедини́ть (соединю́, соедини́шь . . .)	**соединённый**, etc. 'united'
удиви́ть (удивлю́, удиви́шь . . .)	**удивлённый**, etc. 'surprised'

Note: if a consonant change occurs in the 1st person singular of the verb it also occurs in the past passive participle. The rules for these consonant changes were provided on pp. 76–7, and examples of common 2nd Conjugation verbs with end stress throughout their present and perfective future tenses were given on pp. 80–1.

• There is, however some apparent inconsistency in the formation of the past passive participle of 2nd Conjugation verbs in -дить and -деть: as such verbs change -д- to -ж- in the 1st person singular, the same consonant change would be expected in the past passive participle; this is not always so:

разбуди́ть 'to wake' (разбужу́, разбу́дишь . . .)	**разбу́женный**, etc. 'woken'
пробуди́ть 'to arouse' (пробужу́, пробуди́шь . . .)	**пробуждённый**, etc. 'aroused'
возбуди́ть 'to excite' (возбужу́, возбуди́шь . . .)	**возбуждённый**, etc. 'excited'
освободи́ть 'to free' (освобожу́, освободи́шь . . .)	**освобождённый**, etc. 'freed'
обсуди́ть (обсужу́, обсу́дишь . . .)	**обсуждённый**, etc. 'discussed'
уви́деть (уви́жу, уви́дишь . . .)	**уви́денный**, etc. 'seen'

12.5 Uses of the past passive participle

12.5.1 In the long form, past passive participles agree, like adjectives, with the nouns which they qualify in gender, number and case:

на холме́ стои́т собо́р, постро́енный в оди́ннадцатом ве́ке
on the hill stands a cathedral built in the eleventh century
(постро́енный is *nom. masc. sing.* agreeing with собо́р, the subject of стои́т)

за́мок о́коло собо́ра, постро́енного в оди́ннадцатом ве́ке
the castle near the cathedral built in the eleventh century
(постро́енного is *gen. masc. sing.* agreeing with собо́ра which is in the gen. after о́коло)

мы чита́ли статью́, напи́санную профе́ссором Ивано́вым
we were reading an article written by Professor Ivanov
(напи́санную is *acc. fem. sing.* agreeing with статью́, the direct object of чита́ли)

12.5.2 These participles may be replaced by relative clauses – 'a cathedral which was built in the eleventh century', 'an article which was written by Prof. Ivanov'

Note: the participial phrase may sometimes stand before the noun:

на холмé стои́т постро́енный в оди́ннадцатом вéке собóр

12.5.3 The short form of the past passive participle like the short-form adjective is used only as a complement to the verb 'to be' and has only *masc.,* *fem., neut.* and a *plur.* form. But those ending in -нный lose one -н-:

напи́санный	**напи́сан, напи́сана, напи́сано; напи́саны** 'written'
окóнченный	**окóнчен, окóнчена, окóнчено; окóнчены** 'finished'
освещённый	**освещён, освещенá, освещенó; освещены́** 'lit up'
закры́тый	**закры́т, закры́та, закры́то; закры́ты** 'closed'

12.5.4 The short form of the past passive participle is used to convey the passive voice of the verb in all tenses – present, past and future:

письмó напи́сано по-рýсски
the letter is written in Russian

письмó бы́ло напи́сано по-рýсски
the letter was written in Russian

письмó бýдет напи́сано по-рýсски
the letter will be written in Russian

зáмок освещён
the castle is lit up

зáмок был освещён
the castle was lit up

зáмок бýдет освещён
the castle will be lit up

Жемчýжины нарóдной мýдрости

скáзано – сдéлано	(no sooner was it) said – (than it was) done

Remember: the short-form past passive participle may *only* be used as a complement of the verb 'to be', so forming a complete sentence; when the participle merely qualifies a noun, even in the nominative case, the long form must be used:

письмó, напи́санное по-рýсски, пришлó сегóдня ýтром
a letter written in Russian arrived this morning

за́мок, освещённый вчера́ ве́чером, был постро́ен в XI в.

the castle lit up last night was built in the eleventh century

(The main clause, a complete sentence, is 'the castle was built in the eleventh century', therefore был   постро́ен – short form; 'lit up last night' merely qualifies or describes 'castle', it identifies which castle we are talking about, therefore: освещённый – long form)

12.5.5   Imperfective past passive participles are not common but may be encountered; they tend to sound dated or colloquial:

он вспо́мнил кни́ги, чи́танные в де́тстве

he remembered books read (which used to be read) in childhood

EXERCISES

(i)   *Give the past passive participle of the following verbs and their meaning:*

адресова́ть; взять; вы́пить; дать; добы́ть; доказа́ть; дости́гнуть; забы́ть; заня́ть; записа́ть; испыта́ть; наде́ть; обеща́ть; помы́ть; посла́ть; потяну́ть; призва́ть; принести́; провести́; разви́ть; сде́лать; слома́ть; собра́ть; спасти́; спря́тать; увезти́; бро́сить; встре́тить; вы́лечить; допусти́ть; заме́тить; запрети́ть; купи́ть; обрати́ть; освети́ть; освободи́ть; отличи́ть; отпра́вить; победи́ть; поздра́вить; пробуди́ть; разбуди́ть; соедини́ть; удиви́ть; уси́лить; утверди́ть.

(ii)   *Replace the relative clauses with past passive participles:*

Статья́, кото́рую мы прочита́ли, неинтере́сная.

Грибы́, кото́рые мы собра́ли, несъедо́бные.

В кварти́ре, кото́рую они́ купи́ли, нет ме́бели.

В отры́вке, кото́рый мы перевели́, мно́го тру́дностей.

Она́ потеря́ла письмо́, кото́рое она́ получи́ла вчера́.

Я потеря́л кни́гу, кото́рую я взял в библиоте́ке у́тром.

Мы осмотре́ли заво́д, кото́рый постро́или там в про́шлом году́.

(iii) *Translate into Russian:*

1   The flat had been bought.
2   The mushrooms were gathered.
3   The play was translated by Pasternak.
4   The letter has been received.
5   The money has been lost.
6   The factory was built last year.

(iv) *Translate and comment on the use of the italicized participles:*

'Воспомина́ния Алексе́я Елисе́евича Кручёных «Наш вы́ход» о нача́льной эпо́хе ру́сского футури́зма, *напи́санные* 64 го́да наза́д, наконе́ц *напеча́таны* по́лностью' (press).

'Си́мволы президе́нтской вла́сти.

Пе́рвый си́мвол – Штанда́рт Президе́нта. Э́то квадра́тный флаг цвето́в росси́йского триколо́ра с госуда́рственным ге́рбом – двугла́вым орло́м – посереди́не.

Второ́й си́мвол – специа́льно *и́зданный* в еди́нственном экземпля́ре текст Конститу́ции.

А тре́тий – Знак Президе́нта Росси́и. Э́то крест из серебра́, *покры́тый* руби́новой эма́лью, с золоты́м орло́м.

Есть ещё и звезда́, *позоло́ченная*, из серебра́, *покры́тая* эма́лью, с деви́зом «По́льза, честь и сла́ва». Э́тот о́рден – «За заслу́ги пе́ред Оте́чеством» I сте́пени. Он вме́сте с други́ми президе́нтскими зна́ками *изгото́влен* в Яросла́вле в це́нтре «Ру́сские ремёсла»' (press).

'Соглаше́ние об осно́вах взаимоотноше́ний ме́жду Росси́йской Федера́цией и Чече́нской Респу́бликой, *определённое* в соотве́тствии с общепри́знанными при́нципами и но́рмами междунаро́дного пра́ва, должно́ быть *дости́гнуто* до 31 декабря́ 2001 го́да' (press).

12.6 Participles used as adjectives and nouns

Participles properly envisage an action being performed – 'a light shining in the forest', 'the houses surrounding the factory', 'a potato baked by Aunt Vera last weekend'. However, some participles, used commonly, may lose their reference to an actual action and be used as adjectives to describe a state of affairs or condition – 'a shining light', 'the surrounding houses', 'a baked potato'.

12.6.1 Adjectivalized present active participles, e.g.
блесте́ть 'to shine', present active participle **блестя́щий** 'shining' and adjective 'brilliant':

> э́то блестя́щая карти́на   this is a brilliant picture

окружа́ть 'to surround', present active participle **окружа́ющий** 'surrounding' and adjective 'surrounding'

загрязне́ние окружа́ющей среды́
pollution of the environment (of the surrounding milieu)

So, also:
веду́щий 'leading'; реша́ющий 'decisive'; сле́дующий 'next, following'
and compounds such as нефтеперераба́тывающий 'oil-refining'

12.6.2 Some adjectivalized participles are used as nouns (but decline as
adjectives):
     веду́щий 'presenter' (on television)
     заве́дующий 'manager'
     куря́щие 'smokers'
     настоя́щее 'the present'
     слу́жащий 'office worker, employee'
     трудя́щийся 'worker'
     уча́щиеся 'students, pupils'
     бу́дущее 'the future' – (derived from the future tense of быть)

Note: the compounds: главнокома́ндующий 'commander-in-chief';
        млекопита́ющее 'mammal'; пресмыка́ющееся 'reptile'

12.6.3 Adjectivalized past active participles
     бы́вший 'former, ex-'
     сумасше́дший 'mad' (from с ума́ сойти́ – to go out of one's mind) *or*
     'madman'

12.6.4 Adjectivalized present passive participles
     люби́мый 'beloved, favourite'
     необита́емый 'uninhabited'
     терпи́мый 'tolerable'

12.6.5 Adjectivalized past passive participles
     образо́ванный 'educated'
     озабо́ченный 'worried, preoccupied'
     определённый 'definite, certain'
     отдалённый 'remote, distant'
     сде́ржанный 'restrained'
     уединённый 'secluded, isolated' (and many others)
     'По у́лицам ходи́ли каки́е-то взволно́ванные, расте́рянные лю́ди'
     (A. Sakharov).
     excited and confused people were walking along the streets

Note: Unlike participles, adjectives like these retain the double -нн- in the *fem.*, *neut.* and *plur.* short form, and in the adverb:

Participle: **образо́ван, образо́вана, образо́вано; образо́ваны** 'formed (by . . .)'
Adjective: **образо́ван, образо́ванна, образо́ванно; образо́ванны** 'educated'

Participle: **озабо́чен, озабо́чена,** (*neut.* not used); **озабо́чены** 'worried (by . . .)'
Adjective: **озабо́чен, озабо́ченна, озабо́ченно; озабо́ченны** 'anxious'

Participle: **определён, определена́, определено́; определены́** 'defined'
Adjective: **определёнен, определённа, определённо; определённы** 'definite'

12.6.6 Some adjectives derived from past passive participles in double -нн- have lost one -н- in their full, long form:

Participle: **сва́ренный** '(which has been) boiled'
капу́ста, сва́ренная тётей Ма́шей   'the cabbage boiled by Aunt Masha'
Adjective: **варёный** 'boiled': варёная капу́ста 'boiled cabbage' (any boiled cabbage)

Participle: **зажа́ренный** 'fried, roasted' | Participle: **вы́сушенный** 'dried'
Adjective: **жа́реная** рыба 'fried fish' | Adjective: **сушёные** грибы 'dried mushrooms'

Participle: **заморо́женный** 'frozen' | Participle: **засо́ленный** 'salted'
Adjective: **моро́женый** 'frozen' | Adjective: **солёные** огурцы́ 'gherkins'
neut. моро́женое 'ice cream' declines as an adjective.

Participle: **покра́шенный** 'painted, dyed' | Participle: **ра́ненный** 'wounded'
Adjective: **кра́шеная** стена́ 'painted wall' | Adjective: **ра́неный** солда́т 'wounded
кра́шеные во́лосы 'dyed hair' | soldier'

Жемчу́жины наро́дной му́дрости

| пу́ганая воро́на куста́ бои́тся | the frightened crow fears the bush |
| незва́ный гость ху́же тата́рина | an uninvited guest is worse than a Tartar |

Note: **да́нные**, plural of **да́нное** – the *neut. sing.* of the past passive participle of **дать**, is used as a noun, 'data', and decline as a plural adjective.

Note: the noun **учёный** 'scientist' is likewise related to a past passive participle, in this case from **учить** 'to teach'.

12.7 Adverbs from participles

- Adverbs may be formed from the present active participle:
    зна́ющий 'knowing': **зна́юще** 'knowingly'
    блестя́щий 'shining': **блестя́ще** 'brilliantly' (see also p. 55)

- from the present passive participle:

  неузнава́емый 'unrecognizable': **неузнава́емо** 'unrecognizably'
  необъясни́мый 'inexplicable': **необъясни́мо** 'inexplicably' (see also p. 55)

- and from the past passive participle:

  взволно́ванный 'agitated': **взволно́ванно** 'agitatedly'
  образо́ванный 'educated': **образо́ванно** 'educatedly, in an educated manner'
  озабо́ченный 'anxious': **озабо́ченно** 'anxiously'
  определённый 'defined': **определённо** 'definitely'
  неопределённо 'indeterminately, vaguely'

EXERCISES

(i) *Translate into Russian:*

1 The Republic was formed after the war.
2 She was prepared to work.
3 The plans were definite and clear.
4 The plans were defined by a committee.
5 Soldiers wounded during the battle were lying on the ground.
6 The wounded soldiers were lying on the ground.
7 She arrived with dyed hair.
8 She arrived with hair dyed red (to [в + *acc.*] a red colour).
9 We had no data about unemployment.
10 We received the data from the scientists.

(ii) *Form adverbs from the following:*

пуга́ющий; потряса́ющий; раздража́ющий; вызыва́ющий; устраша́ющий; ужаса́ющий; нагнета́ющий; леденя́щий; воодушевля́ющий; давя́щий; томя́щий; пленя́ющий; освежа́ющий; утеша́ющий; оглуша́ющий; изнемога́ющий; незабыва́емый; неузнава́емый; зри́мый; терпи́мый; неисправи́мый; невообрази́мый; неповтори́мый; испу́ганный; смущённый; откры́тый; удивлённый; оби́женный; серди́тый; припо́днятый; возбуждённый; сде́ржанный; обра́дованный; раздражённый; воодушевлённый.

(iii) *Form adverbs from the past passive participles of the following verbs:*

заслужи́ть (*pf.*) 'to deserve'; 'deservedly' =
оживи́ть (*pf.*) 'to enliven'; 'animatedly' =
уве́рить (*pf.*) 'to assure'; 'confidently' =

определи́ть (*pf.*) 'to define, determine'; 'indeterminately' =

оби́деть (*pf.*) 'to offend'; 'aggrievedly' =

возмути́ть (*pf.*) 'to outrage'; 'upset, indignantly' =

напря́чь (*pf.*) 'to strain'; 'tense, strained' =

удиви́ть (*pf.*) 'to surprise'; 'in surprise' =

цивилизова́ть (*impf.* and *pf.*) 'to civilize'; 'in a civilized way' =

оправда́ть (*pf.*) 'to justify'; 'unjustifiedly' =

13 GERUNDS

Not to be confused with participles, which are adjectival, gerunds in Russian are verbal adverbs: that is, they refine the meaning of a verb by qualifying it with a gerund formed from another verb, e.g. 'we talked, *sitting* on the grass', '*opening* the door, she found a letter'. Generally the gerund describes how or when an action takes (or took, or will take) place; less commonly it may be used to describe why: '*loving Boris*, she always trusts him'.

There are two basic forms of the gerund in Russian: the present gerund, formed from the imperfective verb, and the past gerund, usually formed from the perfective.

• Like adverbs, and unlike participles, gerunds are indeclinable.
Like verbs, gerunds may be negated: '*not noticing* the rain, she walked to the station', 'he just sat there, *without moving* (*not moving*)'.

13.1 The present gerund

13.1.1 The present gerund is formed from the 3rd person plural of the present tense by removing the last two letters and adding -я (or, if the rules of spelling don't allow this, -a):

игра́ть	игра́[ют]	**игра́я**	'playing'
суди́ть	су́д[ят]	**судя́**	'judging'
держа́ть	де́рж[ат]	**держа́**	'holding'
рисова́ть	рису́[ют]	**рису́я**	'drawing'

Note: лежа́ть   леж[а́т] *but* **лёжа**   'lying'

• The present gerund of быть is **бу́дучи** 'being'

• With reflexive verbs the reflexive ending is reduced to -сь
смея́ться   сме[ю́т]ся   **смея́сь**   'laughing'

13.1.2 Verbs in -авать form their present gerund from their infinitive:

встава́ть	встаю́т] *but*	**встава́я**	'getting up'
продава́ть	прода[ю́т] *but*	**продава́я**	'selling'
признава́ться	призна[ю́т]ся *but*	**признава́ясь**	'admitting'

13.1.3 Not all verbs form a present gerund; these include many with monosyllabic infinitives, such as пить, бить, спать, мочь, and also бежа́ть, е́хать.

13.1.4 Some former gerunds are in common use as straightforward adverbs, without reference to a particular action, e.g.
зря 'in vain'; **мо́лча** 'silently, without a word'; **спустя́** 'later'; **хотя́** 'although'

Note: ме́жду на́ми говоря́ 'between ourselves'
не говоря́ уже́ 'not to mention'   не перестава́я 'ceaselessly'
не спеша́ 'unhurriedly'   не устава́я 'tirelessly'
не счита́я 'not counting'
втора́я остано́вка, не счита́я э́ту   the second stop, not counting this one

Note: gerunds used as prepositions: благодаря́ (+ *dat.*) 'thanks to'; несмотря́ (на + *acc.*) 'despite, in spite of'

Жемчу́жины наро́дной му́дрости

ло́дырь си́дя спит, лёжа рабо́тает	the layabout sleeps sitting, and works lying down

EXERCISE

Form present gerunds from the following verbs:

возвраща́ться; говори́ть; дава́ть; жа́ловаться; знать; молча́ть; стоя́ть; остава́ться; перепи́сываться; повторя́ть; прислу́шиваться; пря́тать; слу́шать; слы́шать; собира́ться; теря́ть

13.2 The past gerund

13.2.1 The past (usually perfective) gerund is formed from the past tense by removing the final -л of the masculine form and adding -в:
сде́лать   сде́ла[л]   **сде́лав**   'having made, after making'
отве́тить   отве́ти[л]   **отве́тив**   'having answered, after answering'

- An alternative ending in -вши is rarer in modern Russian, but must be used with reflexive verbs:
вы́пить   вы́пи[л]   **вы́пив** (*or* **вы́пивши**) 'having drunk'
заня́ться   заня́[л]ся   **заня́вшись** 'having engaged in, studied, occupied oneself'

13.2.2 The past gerund of verbs whose masculine past tense does not end in -л is formed by adding -ши to the final consonant:

вы́расти	вы́рос	**вы́росши**	'having grown up'
заже́чь	зажёг	**зажёгши**	'having lit, set fire to'
постри́чься	постри́гся	**постри́гшись**	'having cut one's hair'
привле́чь	привлёк	**привлёкши**	'having attracted'
привы́кнуть	привы́к	**привы́кши**	'having got used to'
спасти́	спас	**спа́сши**	'having rescued'
умере́ть	у́мер	**у́мерши**	'having died'

Note: исче́знуть   исчё́з *but*   **исче́знув**   'having disappeared'

- Compounds of идти́, везти́, вести́, нести́ form their past gerund from the perfective future in the same way as the present gerund:

    зайти́   зайду́т   **зайдя́**   'having called on';

So, also: **войдя́** 'having entered', **вы́йдя** 'having gone out', etc.

вы́везти	вы́везут	**вы́везя**	'having exported'
перевести́	переведу́т	**переведя́**	'having translated'
принести́	принесу́т	**принеся́**	'having brought', etc.

Alternative forms in -ши exist for compounds of идти́:

    зайти́   зашёл   **заше́дши**   'having called on'

and: **прише́дши** 'having arrived', **вы́шедши** 'having gone out', **уше́дши** 'having left', etc.

Жемчу́жины наро́дной му́дрости

не изме́рив бро́ду, не су́йся в во́ду	don't shove yourself into the water without having measured the ford (look before you leap)

EXERCISE

Form past gerunds from the following verbs:

ввезти́; вы́вести; заинтересова́ть; закры́ть; испуга́ть; испуга́ться; получи́ть; постро́ить; прийти́; приня́ть; пры́гнуть; уви́деть; унести́; уста́ть; устро́иться

13.3 Use of the gerund

• The gerund functions like an adverb qualifying the action of a verb; it
  may be replaced by an adverbial clause (just as a participle may be
  replaced by a relative clause): 'opening the door she found a letter' may be
  paraphrased as 'when she opened the door. . .' or 'as she opened the door
  . . .' or 'after she opened the door . . .'

But the gerund may only be used when the subject is the same in both clauses:
'when *she* opened the door, *she* found a letter'; it cannot be used when the
subjects are different: 'when he opened the door, she noticed a letter'.

13.3.1 Gerunds may be used to replace adverbial clauses of time (i.e. clauses
which in English begin with 'when', 'while', 'as', 'after', etc.). Note that the
present gerund denotes an action simultaneous to the action of the main verb:

   убирáя кóмнату, мы нашлú часы́
   tidying up the room we found a watch ('as, when or while we were
   tidying . . .')

   въезжáя в гóрод, он всегдá крéстится
   driving into town he always crosses himself

   въезжáя в гóрод, онá не вúдела ни одногó человéка
   driving into town she didn't see a single person

   въезжáя в гóрод, онú обязáтельно замéтят нóвый мост
   driving into town they're bound to notice the new bridge

Note: the past gerund denotes an action previous to that of the main verb:

   сказáв э́то, Борúс встал и вы́шел
   saying this ('having said', 'after saying') Boris got up and went out

   откры́в óкна, мы покрáсим все стéны
   after opening the windows we'll paint all the walls

   откры́в óкна, нáши сосéди обязáтельно включáют рáдио
   having opened the windows our neighbours invariably switch on the
   radio

   найдя́ дéньги, бáбушка пошлá к свящéннику
   on finding the money my grandmother went to see the priest

Жемчу́жины наро́дной му́дрости

не разби́вши яи́ц, не сде́лаешь яи́чницы	you won't make an omelette without having broken some eggs

Compare:

Present gerund: говоря́ э́то, он встал и вы́шел 'saying this ('as he said this') he got up and went out'

Past gerund: сказа́в э́то, он встал и вы́шел 'having said this he got up and went out'.

13.3.2 Gerunds may also be used to replace adverbial clauses of cause (i.e. clauses which in English begin with 'because', 'since', 'as', etc.):

ду́мая о кани́кулах, она́ забы́ла отпра́вить письмо́
thinking about the holidays (because she was thinking ...) she forgot to post the letter

опозда́в на электри́чку, он взял такси́
having missed the train (since, as he'd missed ...) he took a cab

13.3.3 The past gerund may be formed from the imperfective verb when it denotes a continuous action in the past or when it is being negated:

'служи́в отли́чно-благоро́дно, долга́ми жил его́ оте́ц' (Pushkin).
having served most honourably, his father lived in debt

це́лый день ничего́ не е́вши, Бори́с зашёл к нам пообе́дать
having eaten nothing all day Boris came to have dinner with us

Жемчу́жины наро́дной му́дрости

не у́жинавши – ле́гче, а поу́жинавши – кре́пче	not having had supper, one feels lighter, but having had supper – stronger

13.3.4 The gerund may sometimes be used to replace a clause introduced by 'and' if the subject is the same and the actions in both clauses are linked:

она́ лежа́ла на траве́, ду́мая о Никола́е
she was lying on the grass thinking about Nikolai
(= она́ лежа́ла на траве́ и ду́мала ... – she lay ... and thought ...)

встав, он вы́шел   he got up and went out

Note: the gerund is, like the participle, separated from the main clause by a comma.

Remember: the gerund may *only* be used when the subjects of both clauses are the same; it cannot be used, for example, in a sentence such as: 'the train arriving late, she bought an evening paper' because 'the train' and 'she' are different subjects.

Likewise a gerund is impossible in translating 'our friends having gone to Moscow, we were able to use their car'. 'Our friends' and 'we' are different subjects.

Жемчу́жины наро́дной му́дрости

не ра́дуйся нашёдши, не плачь потеря́вши	don't rejoice having found something, don't grieve having lost something

EXERCISES

(i) *Translate into Russian using present gerunds:*

1   We talked, sitting on the grass.
2   Opening the door, she found a letter.
3   Loving Boris, she always believes him.
4   Not noticing the rain, she walked to the station.
5   He simply sat there, without moving.

(ii) *Translate, using past gerunds:*

1   After opening the cupboard he chose a book.
2   Having arranged matters she returned to the office.
3   On finding the letter Natasha ran into the kitchen.
4   When he hears the news he'll be amazed.
5   Since we didn't hear the bell we continued talking.

(iii) *Translate, using a gerund if possible:*

1   On opening the window we saw a bear.
2   Having finished her essay she began to sing.
3   Having got used to it, the climate began to seem normal to us.
4   Since he'd just washed the car he didn't want to drive across the field.
5   He ran across the square without noticing the rain.
6   When we get home we'll switch on the radio.
7   We paid for the meal and went out into the street.
8   When the bus arrives, we'll ask the driver.
9   I've read War and Peace, not to mention the shorter works.
10 Judging by the clouds I think it's going to snow.

13.4 Participle or gerund?

Confusion between these two parts of speech is possible for English speakers since the English equivalents in '-ing' are identical.

Remember: the participle is adjectival and qualifies a person or thing;
the gerund is adverbial and qualifies the action of a verb.

- So in the sentence: 'the tickets are under the book lying on the table' the word 'lying' qualifies 'the book' and distinguishes it from any other books – hence in Russian this is a participle: биле́ты под кни́гой, лежа́щей на столе́

- And in the sentence: 'he was drinking coffee, lying on the sofa' the word 'lying' qualifies his drinking, tells us when he was drinking, i.e. 'while lying on the sofa' (it clearly wasn't the coffee which was lying on the sofa) – hence in Russian this is a gerund: он пил ко́фе, лёжа на дива́не.

13.4.1 Sometimes only the word order in English provides the clue:

A bird singing by the lake woke me up (participle)
A bird woke me up, singing by the lake (gerund)

The man sitting on the bench looked lonely (participle)
The man looked lonely, sitting on the bench (gerund)

He noticed a cat listening to his radio (participle)
Listening to his radio, he noticed a cat (gerund)

13.4.2 There are occasions when either a participle or a gerund could be used, but where the distinction between adjectival and adverbial use is maintained:

'Мину́т че́рез де́сять, умы́тый и причёсанный и чу́вствующий смуще́ние всем свои́м те́лом, Алексе́й входи́л в столо́вую' (Chayanov).

about ten minutes later, washed, combed and feeling thoroughly embarrassed, Alexei was entering the canteen.

It would not have been impossible to have used gerunds: . . . умы́вшись и причеса́вшись и чу́вствуя . . . ; but these would have drawn attention to the actions of washing and shaving and combing, whereas with the participle we focus on Alexei's appearance and state of mind 'now', as he entered: 'Alexei who was now washed and combed and who felt thoroughly embarrassed . . .'

• Participles and gerunds are not mutually exclusive:

'Пётр, изнеможённый, заму́ченный тоско́й и трево́гой, не вы́спавшийся, предчу́вствуя, что вот-вот на земле́ произойдёт что-то ужа́сное, шёл вслед' (Chekhov).

Peter, (who was) exhausted, racked by anguish and alarm, not having (and who had not) slept properly, followed behind (while) sensing that something terrible was about to happen on earth

---

EXERCISE

(i) *Decide which is which before you translate into Russian:*

1 The girl was reading a newspaper lying on the floor.
  ('which was lying' or 'while she was lying'?)
2 I found the dog walking along the river bank.
  ('which was walking' or 'while I was walking'?)
3 What student reading Tolstoy does not sleep soundly?
4 They finished building the roof protecting the ruins from the rain.
5 I always pick up the papers remaining on the bus when the other passengers have got out.

(ii) *Note:* further confusion may occasionally be caused by ungrammatical English, such as: 'reading the book, a brick fell on his head' (bricks don't read books) or 'on opening the door the dog attacked us' (dogs don't normally open doors). Such solecisms should be corrected in translation:

когда́ он чита́л кни́гу, кирпи́ч упа́л ему́ на́ голову
while he was reading the book, a brick fell on his head
в тот моме́нт, когда́ мы откры́ли дверь, соба́ка бро́силась на нас
the moment we opened the door the dog attacked us

Translate into Russian:

1 Having built a garage our car will be out of danger.
2 After flowering we'll cut down the lilac.
3 Listening to the news the phone rang.

14 THE SUBJUNCTIVE

The subjunctive mood expresses an action as desired, advised or hypothesized. It adds a note of obligation or advisability to the statement of an action: 'they would like to go', 'I should write', etc.

14.1 Formation of the subjunctive (or conditional)

To form the subjunctive add the particle **бы** to the past tense of the verb; the usual distinctions between imperfective and perfective are in force, so it is still necessary to be aware of the difference between, for instance, 'I (you, he, etc.) would give' in a general or regular sense and 'I (you, he, etc.) would give' on a specific occasion. Only one tense is used for the subjunctive to cover present, past and future meanings:

Imperfective дава́ть 'to give'	Perfective дать
я, ты, он **дава́л бы** (*or:* **бы дава́л**)	я, ты, он **дал бы** (*or:* **бы дал**)
я, ты, она́ **дава́ла бы** (*or:* **бы дава́ла**)	я, ты, она́ **дала́ бы** (*or:* **бы дала́**)
оно́ **дава́ло бы** (*or:* **бы дава́ло**)	оно́ **да́ло бы** (*or:* **бы да́ло**)
мы, вы, они́ **дава́ли бы** (*or:* **бы дава́ли**)	мы, вы, они́ **да́ли бы** (*or:* **бы да́ли**)

'I, etc., would give, should give, would have given, should have given'

Note: the particle **бы** cannot be combined with any other tense of the verb.

Note: the particle бы may be contracted to **б: я б сказа́л** 'I'd have said'.

14.2 Uses of the subjunctive

14.2.1 On its own the subjunctive may express *advisability*:

> вы чита́ли бы газе́ты   you should (have) read the papers
> вы прочита́ли бы газе́ту   you should (have) read the paper

14.2.2 The subjunctive is used with the conjunction что́бы 'in order that' to express *purpose*; the particle бы of the subjunctive is subsumed into что́бы:

> мы говори́ли гро́мко, что́бы все слы́шали
> we spoke loudly so that everyone would hear

мы бу́дем говори́ть гро́мко, что́бы все слы́шали
we'll speak loudly in order for everyone to hear

Note: что́бы is often preceded by phrases, such as для того́, с тем, etc.:
я пишу́ для того́, что́бы чита́ли   I write so that people should read

Note: If the subject of both verbs is the same что́бы is followed by the infinitive:
мы говори́ли ти́хо, что́бы не меша́ть други́м
we spoke quietly in order not to disturb the others (. . . so that we would
not . . .)

14.2.3 The subjunctive is used with the conjunction что́бы after verbs of
wanting or *wishing* if the subjects are different:

я хочу́, что́бы он пошёл домо́й   I want him to go home
('I want that he should go home')
мы хоте́ли, что́бы вы э́то сде́лали за́втра
we wanted you to do this tomorrow
('we wanted that you should do . . .')

When no other subject is referred to, the infinitive is used – without что́бы:
я хочу́ пойти́ домо́й   I want to go home
мы хоте́ли э́то сде́лать за́втра   we wanted to do that tomorrow

Note: the verb of wanting may itself be in the subjunctive, though this is not
necessary:
мы хоте́ли бы, что́бы вы сде́лали э́то за́втра
we would like *or* we would have liked you to do this tomorrow
('. . . that you would do . . .' *or* '. . . that you would have done . . .')

она́ жела́ла бы, что́бы они́ бы́ли сча́стливы
she would wish them to be happy ('. . . that they should be . . .')

and, when no other subject is referred to, with the infinitive:
я хоте́л бы пойти́ домо́й   I'd like to go home

14.2.4 The subjunctive is used with the conjunction что́бы after verbs of
demanding:

они́ тре́буют, что́бы мы уе́хали неме́дленно
they are demanding that we leave immediately

я наста́иваю на том, что́бы он заплати́л за ча́йник
I insist that he pay for the kettle ('. . . on his paying . . .')

14.2.5 The subjunctive may be used with the conjunction чтобы after verbs of *advising*, *suggesting*, *requesting* and *ordering*, although the infinitive is just as good:

> я советую, чтобы вы сходили сейчас за молоком
>
or: я советую вам сходить сейчас за молоком
>
> I advise you to go and get the milk now

> они предложили, чтобы мы заехали к ним по дороге домой
>
or: они предложили нам заехать к ним по дороге домой
>
> they suggested that we call in on them on the way home

> приказали, чтобы водитель открыл багажник
>
or: приказали водителю открыть багажник
>
> the driver was ordered to open the boot

> попроси, чтобы он закрыл ворота!
>
or: попроси его закрыть ворота!
>
> ask him to close the gate

14.2.6 The subjunctive may be used with the conjunction чтобы instead of the perfective future after verbs of *thinking* and *expecting*, especially if they are negative:

> я думаю, что она придёт завтра
>
> I think she'll come tomorrow

> я не думаю, чтобы она пришла завтра
>
> I don't think she'll come tomorrow

> мы не ожидали, что он пришлёт нам свою книгу
>
or: мы не ожидали, чтобы он прислал нам свою книгу
>
> we didn't expect that he'd send us his book

14.2.7 The subjunctive is used for categorical assertions expressing *urgency* or *necessity*:

> нужно, чтобы они понимали технологию
>
> it is necessary that they understand the technology

> важно было, чтобы она не потеряла деньги
>
> it was important that she didn't lose the money

> он всегда заботится о том, чтобы закрывали ворота
>
> he always bothers to make sure that the gate is closed

14.2.8 The subjunctive is used for negative hypotheses:

невозмо́жно, что́бы она́ сказа́ла э́то
it's impossible that she would have said that ('for her to have said')

невероя́тно, что́бы он э́то сде́лал
it's inconceivable that he would do ('for him to have done') this

14.2.9   The subjunctive is used with the particle ни in hypothetical generalizations introduced by pronouns or adverbs of the type *whoever, whatever, whenever, wherever, however*:

кто бы ни приходи́л, они́ обяза́тельно пока́жут им свои́ сла́йды
whoever comes, they're bound to show them their slides

кого́ бы они́ ни посла́ли, мы гото́вы рабо́тать с ни́ми
whoever they send, we're prepared to work with them

что бы она́ ни сказа́ла, он не оби́дится
whatever she says, he won't be offended

где бы мы ни сиде́ли, мы не могли́ ви́деть сце́ну
wherever we sat we couldn't see the stage

куда́ бы он ни пошёл, он не найдёт её
wherever he goes he won't find her

когда́ бы я ни ви́дела его́, он всегда́ в се́ром костю́ме
whenever I see him he's always wearing a grey suit

Note: Generalizations of this sort may be expressed without the subjunctive:

кто ни придёт, она́ ничего́ не ска́жет
whoever comes she won't say anything

кого́ они́ ни пошлю́т, мы бу́дем гото́вы рабо́тать с ни́ми
whoever they send we'll be prepared to work with them

что она́ ни ска́жет, я не пойду́
whatever she says I won't go

EXERCISES

(i) *Give the masculine, feminine and plural subjunctive of the following verbs:*

писа́ть, написа́ть; приходи́ть, прийти́; отвеча́ть, отве́тить; выезжа́ть, вы́ехать; собира́ть, собра́ть; люби́ть, полюби́ть; интересова́ться, заинтересова́ться; переводи́ть, перевести́; мочь, смочь; класть, положи́ть

(ii) *Translate into Russian:*

1   She put the book there so that they would see it.
2   I shall tell him so that he knows my opinion.
3   They are sending her to Moscow so that she can finish her book.
4   I shall write them a note so that they don't forget.
5   He wants to find his dog.
6   He wants us to find his dog.
7   He wants to help her.
8   She wants him to help her.
9   The students want to go home.
10   We don't want the students to go home.
11   I wanted her to open the door.
12   I asked her to open the door.
13   I suggested that she open the door.
14   I advised her to open the door.
15   I demanded that she open the door.
16   I insisted that she open the door.
17   I ordered her to open the door.
18   It was necessary for her to open the door.
19   It was important for her to open the door.
20   She should have opened the door.
21   Boris was always expecting us to invite him to Windsor.
22   She is always telling them to be quiet.
23   We often wait for hours for them to open the gates.
24   The tourists sometimes ask her to sing one more song.
25   Why do they always insist that we sit here.
26   It is important for him to meet us on Thursday.
27   I would like you to hear this.
28   She didn't want us to find the body.
29   I don't remember that he ever said that.
30   It is inconceivable that she should have left so early.
31   Whatever you say, nothing changes.
32   Wherever they worked, they were always happy.
33   Whenever he thinks about her, he always closes his eyes.
34   Wherever my sisters go, they always ring me up.
35   She always complained, whatever he wore.
36   However difficult this is, we must finish it by six.

15 CONDITIONAL CLAUSES

Conditional clauses are introduced typically, but not always, in Russian by
если 'if'. There are two kinds of condition: **real** and **hypothetical**.

15.1 Real conditions

These are normal, straightforward propositions that if one set of conditions
prevails, something definitely ensues:

если брат свободен, он приезжает к нам обедать
if my brother is free he comes to have dinner with us

если дождь пойдёт, мы не поедем
if it rains we won't go

Note: in these clauses the tense of the verb is logical, though it may differ from
English: present tense 'rains' in this example really means 'will rain', as the Russian
says.

Note: impersonal conditional clauses may be expressed with the infinitive:

если оставить этот вопрос в стороне, то можно будет согласиться
if one leaves this question to one side it will be possible to agree

Жемчужины народной мудрости

если хочешь мира, готовься к войне	if you want peace, prepare for war

EXERCISES

(i) *Translate into English:*

1 Если русские военные отсюда уйдут, этот режим не продержится и недели.
2 Люди всегда недовольны своей жизнью, даже если они живут в Швейцарии.
3 Если мы возьмём список пятидесяти самых богатых людей России и
посмотрим их налоговые декларации, то увидим, что 'официальные' доходы
этих людей не превышают 50 миллионов рублей в год.
4 Если отправить посылку сегодня, то она получит её ко дню рождения.

5 Да́же е́сли игнори́ровать экономи́ческое положе́ние, жизнь в Украи́не ста́ла
   значи́тельно сложне́е для большинства́ наро́да.

(ii) *Translate into Russian:*

1 If it rained we usually went to the cinema.
2 If you like we can have dinner in town.
3 If they arrive tomorrow we'll have to leave.
4 I'll show her my slides if it rains.
5 We can start work if you're ready.

15.2 Hypothetical conditions

Hypothetical conditions are unreal and either have not come about or may
not come about; they state that if one set of conditions were to prevail or
were to have prevailed, something would or would have happened. They are
expressed by the subjunctive, or conditional as it is called when used for this
purpose:

> е́сли бы я был бога́тым челове́ком, я купи́л бы э́ту карти́ну
> if I were a rich man I'd buy this picture

or: if I'd been a rich man I'd have bought this picture

Note: the conjunction е́сли may, as in English, be omitted; this requires inversion of
word order and adds a wistful note:

> был бы я бога́тым челове́ком, я купи́л бы э́ту карти́ну
> were I a rich man I'd buy this picture

or: had I been a rich man I'd have bought this picture

Note: it is possible to find the imperative being used to introduce a conditional clause:

> живи́ он у нас, я бы показа́ла ему́, как гото́вить борщ
> were he to live at our place, I'd show him how to make borshch

Note: a rather colloquial alternative to е́сли is е́жели, which is used sparingly.

EXERCISES

(i) *Translate into English:*

1 'Ма́рия Алекса́ндровна (мать Ле́нина) о́чень люби́ла своего́ сы́на, и поэ́тому
   она́ реши́ла сде́лать как-нибу́дь, что́бы он бро́сил кури́ть. И вот одна́жды
   она́ ему́ сказа́ла:

– Мы живём на пéнсию . . . И хотя́ твои́ папирóсы недóрого стóят, но всё-таки бы́ло бы лу́чше для хозя́йства, éсли бы ты не кури́л' (Zoshchenko).

2   Éсли бы нас призна́ли «развива́ющейся» странóй, мы сра́зу получи́ли бы мнóжество льгот.

3   'Éсли бы мои́ роди́тели взду́мали учи́ть меня́ игра́ть, допу́стим, на бараба́не, я стал бы игра́ть на бараба́не' (Rostropovich).

4   'Порабóтай на́ши арти́сты так, как рабóтает Са́ра Берна́р, знай стóлько, скóлько она́ зна́ет, они́ далекó бы пошли́!' (Chekhov).

(ii) *Replace the present and future tenses by the conditional:*

Éсли бу́дет теплó, они́ бу́дут проводи́ть весь день на пля́же.
Éсли у нас бу́дет врéмя, мы пойдём на концéрт.
Éсли у негó бу́дут дéньги, он ку́пит ей цветы́.
Éсли она́ узна́ет об э́том, она́ всё объясни́т нам.
Мы прости́м ему́ всё, éсли он извини́тся.
Мы кóнчим э́то у́тром, éсли сосéди не помеша́ют нам.
Éсли я свобóдна, я обы́чно сплю до оди́ннадцати.
Éсли вы не бу́дете шумéть, я прочита́ю кни́гу сегóдня.
Я пойду́ с тобóй на вечери́нку, éсли меня́ пригласят.
Éсли нас попрóсят, мы помóжем им.

(iii) *Translate into Russian:*

1   It would be nice if he said 'thank you' sometimes.
2   He would have gone to London if he'd had the money.
3   He'll go to London if he has the money.
4   I'd like the flat more if it were on the first floor.
5   I think she would have killed him if she'd seen him.

16 THE IMPERATIVE

Imperatives are commands or exhortations. They may be imperfective or perfective. Usually they refer to the 2nd person, singular or plural: 'do this (you)!'

16.1 Formation of the imperative

16.1.1 To form the imperative remove the last two letters of the 3rd person plural of the present or perfective future tense and if the remaining stem ends in a vowel add -й (*sing.*) *or* -йте (*plur.*):

де́лать	де́ла[ют]	де́лай! де́лайте! 'do'
посове́товать	посове́ту[ют]	посове́туй! посове́туйте! 'advise'
стоя́ть	сто[я́т]	стой! сто́йте! 'stand', 'stop'
занима́ться	занима́[ют]ся	занима́йся! занима́йтесь!
		'get on with your work'

16.1.2 If, after removal of the last two letters of the 3rd person plural, the stem ends in a consonant and the stress in the 1st person singular is on the ending add -и́ *or* -и́те:

писа́ть	пиш[ут] (пишу́)	пиши́! пиши́те! 'write'
снять	сним[ут] (сниму́)	сними́! сними́те! 'take (it) off'
говори́ть	говор[я́т] (говорю́)	говори́! говори́те! 'say, speak'
заплати́ть	запла́т[ят] (заплачу́)	заплати́! заплати́те! 'pay'

Жемчу́жины наро́дной му́дрости

где щи, тут и нас ищи́	where there is cabbage soup, seek us here, too

16.1.3 If the stress is on the stem throughout a verb's conjugation, and after removal of the last two letters of the 3rd person plural the stem ends in a consonant add -ь *or* -ьте:

пла́кать	пла́чут (пла́чу)	не плачь! не пла́чьте! 'don't cry'
бро́сить	брос[ят] (бро́шу)	брось! бро́сьте! 'throw'
прове́рить	провер[ят] (прове́рю)	прове́рь! прове́рьте! 'check'
отста́ть	отста́н[ут] (отста́ну)	отста́нь! отста́ньте! 'get away from me'
оде́ться	оде́н[ут]ся (оде́нусь)	оде́нься! оде́ньтесь! 'get dressed'
гото́виться	гото́в[ят]ся (гото́влюсь)	гото́вься! гото́вьтесь! 'get ready'

Note: However, if the stem ends in two consonants which would be difficult to pronounce with only a soft sign, the imperative ends in unstressed -и, -ите:

отвы́кнуть	отвы́кн[ут]	**отвы́кни! отвы́кните!**	'break the habit'
исчéзнуть	исчéзн[ут]	**исчéзни! исчéзните!**	'disappear'

Note: perfective verbs with the prefix вы- which is always stressed add endings appropriate to the verb's root, they do not end in -ь, -ьте even though the stem is stressed throughout:

вы́пустить　　　вы́пуст[ят] *but* **вы́пусти! вы́пустите!** 'release, let go'
(*cf.* **пусти́! пусти́те!**)

Жемчу́жины наро́дной му́дрости

век живи́, век учи́сь	(if you) live for a century, (you) learn for a century
семь раз отмéрь, оди́н раз отрéжь	measure out seven times, cut once

16.1.4 Some irregular or awkward imperatives:

быть	**будь! бу́дьте!** 'be'
(and забы́ть	не **забу́дь!** не **забу́дьте!** 'don't forget')
бежáть	**беги́! беги́те!** 'run'
(and compounds, e.g. убежáть	**убеги́! убеги́те!** 'run away')
брать	**бери́! бери́те!** 'take'
(and compounds, e.g. вы́брать	**вы́бери! вы́берите!** 'choose')
вставáть	**вставáй! вставáйте!** 'get up'
(and other verbs in -авать which contract in conjugation:	
признавáться	**признавáйся! признавáйтесь!** 'confess')
давáть	**давáй! давáйте!** 'give'
(and compounds, e.g. раздавáть	**раздавáй! раздавáйте!** 'hand out')
дать	**дай! дáйте!** 'give' (*pf.*)
(and compounds, e.g. передáть	**передáй! передáйте!** 'pass', 'hand me')
есть	**ешь! éшьте!** 'eat'
лечь	**ляг! ля́гте!** 'lie down'
помóчь	**помоги́! помоги́те!** 'help'
понять	**пойми́! пойми́те!** 'realise'
(so too: занять	**займи́! займи́те!** 'borrow'
приня́ть	**прими́! прими́те!** 'accept', *etc.*)
сесть	**сядь! ся́дьте!** 'sit down'
снять	**сними́! сними́те!** 'take (it) off; take the photo'
пить	**пей! пéйте!** 'drink'
(and compounds, e.g. допи́ть	**допéй! допéйте!** 'drink up')

(so too: бить: **бей! бéйте!** 'hit'; лить: **лей! лéйте!** 'pour'; вить: **вей! вéйте!** 'wind' and their compounds)

16.1.5 Some common verbs do not form imperatives: there is no imperative form of ви́деть 'to see' or of слы́шать 'to hear'; the form **поезжа́й! поезжа́йте!** is used as the imperative of е́хать.

EXERCISE

Form imperatives from the following verbs:

чита́ть; рисова́ть; включи́ть; поста́вить; знако́миться; суди́ть; молча́ть; спать; убра́ть; встать; поддви́нуться; взять; вы́пить; нача́ть; продава́ть.

16.2 Aspect in the imperative

16.2.1 The basic distinction between imperfective and perfective aspects of the verb is preserved in the imperative.

- The imperfective is used for continuous or repeated actions:
  всегда́ посыла́й ей цветы́!   always send her flowers
  сиди́ здесь и рису́й цветы́!   sit here and draw the flowers

- The perfective is used to denote the attainment of a result:
  пошли́ ей цветы́ сейча́с же!   send her the flowers at once
  посиди́ здесь и нарису́й мне э́ти цветы́!   sit here and draw me these flowers

16.2.2 On top of the basic distinction between imperfective and perfective, the aspects have expressive uses in the imperative.

- The imperfective denotes the action itself with the sense of 'just do it, get on with it!':
  вот, чита́й!   here, read this (i.e. sit down and keep quiet)

- The perfective imperative expresses greater urgency than the imperfective: the perfective focuses on completing the action with the sense of 'get it done, I want to see a result!':
  ся́дьте! sit down   войди́те! come in
  вот, прочита́й!   here, read this (i.e. read it and tell me what you make of it)

They need not be peremptory and both imperfective and perfective may be moderated by пожа́луйста 'please'.

16.2.3 While the perfective imperative is less comprehensive, more restricted in its meaning than the imperfective (it is concerned only with completion of the action), it is often used for requests or invitations:

дай хлеб, пожáлуйста! pass me the bread, please

But since drawing attention to the completion and the need for a result might be too impertinent, the imperfective is sometimes preferred:

садúтесь! sit down (*but:* сáдьте! – sit!)
передавáй им привéт! give them my best wishes
приходúте к нам! come and see us (*but:* придúте в семь! come at seven)

- the imperfective imperative is used for requests which are qualified by adverbs:

говорúте грóмче! talk louder
слýшайте внимáтельно! listen carefully

16.2.4 With the negative, however, the imperfective is used for prohibition:

открóйте окнó, пожáлуйста! open the window, please
but: не открывáйте окнó, пожáлуйста! please don't open the window
не говорú э́то Борúсу! don't tell Boris this (you mustn't)
не опáздывайте на лéкции! don't be late for lectures
не давáй ему дéнег! don't give him any money
не обращáй внимáния! don't pay any attention

16.2.5 With the negative, the perfective is used for warning:

не скажú э́того Борúсу! don't tell Boris this (be careful not to)
не опоздáйте на пóезд! don't miss the train
не упадú! mind you don't fall
не уронúте чáшку! don't drop the cup
не забýдьте отпрáвить письмó! don't forget to post the letter

- The note of warning may be intensified by prefixing the imperative (perfective or imperfective) with the imperfective imperative of смотрéть: смотрú! смотрúте!:

смотрú, не упадú! watch out you don't fall
смотрúте, не опáздывайте! mind you aren't late

16.3 Other forms of the imperative with specific registers

- the infinitive can be used in a rather military tone:

молчáть! silence! встать! (get) up! on your feet!
не курúть! no smoking! не сметь! don't even think of it!

- The subjunctive has a plaintive tone:

  сходи́ли бы вы за молоко́м!   I wish you'd go and get the milk, be a good chap and fetch the milk

- The past tense of some verbs is sometimes used as an imperative:

  пошёл!   be off, get out!

- Certain words can be used as imperatives:

стоп!	stop!	марш!	get going!
вон!	out!	за́навес!	curtain!
вас к телефо́ну!	phone! It's for you!	скоре́й за мной!	quick, after me!

Жемчу́жины наро́дной му́дрости

ешь калачи́, пока́ горячи́!	eat the rolls while they are hot

EXERCISES

(i) *Translate into English and give the infinitive from which these imperatives are derived:*

подожди́те мину́тку!
не волну́йтесь!
предста́вь себе́, как там краси́во!
разреши́те мне пройти́, пожа́луйста!
отда́й ему́ де́ньги!
извини́те за шум! У нас идёт ремо́нт

(ii) *Translate into Russian:*

1 Make (use убира́ть/убра́ть) your bed (i.e. you can't possibly go on living in this mess).
2 Make your bed (i.e. Aunt Nina will be here in half an hour).
3 Send them photographs (i.e. from time to time).
4 Send them the photographs (i.e. so they can see what you look like).
5 Don't lose your documents (ie. you must always have your passport with you).
6 Don't lose your documents (i.e. careful you don't drop any).
7 Mind you don't forget to put on the fur hat (i.e. it's part of the uniform).
8 Mind you don't forget to put on a fur hat (i.e. it's going to be very cold).

(iii) *Translate into English:*

'– О́льга, я об одно́м прошу́ вас, – сказа́л худо́жник умоля́юще и приложи́в ру́ку к се́рдцу, – об одно́м: не му́чьте меня́! Бо́льше мне от вас ничего́ не ну́жно!

– Но покляни́тесь, что вы меня́ всё ещё лю́бите!
– Э́то мучи́тельно! – процеди́л сквозь зу́бы худо́жник и вскочи́л. – Ко́нчится тем, что я бро́шусь в Во́лгу и́ли сойду́ с ума́! Оста́вьте меня́!' (Chekhov).

16.4 Forms of 1st- and 3rd-person imperative

Various forms of 1st- and 3rd-person imperative are possible, including:
1st-person - сде́лаем э́то *or* дава́й сде́лаем э́то *or* дава́й де́лать э́то 'let's do this'.
3rd-person - пуска́й де́лает э́то *or* пусть сде́лает э́то 'let him do this'

(i) 1st-person imperative: 'let's . . .'

The 1st person plural of the perfective future (without the pronoun мы) can be used to convey the imperative; it is used on its own to cover я + ты, and with the suffix -те to cover я + вы (either plural or polite singular):

пойдём! пойдёмте!	let's go!
возьмём сыр!	let's take the cheese
посмо́трим вы́ставку!	let's have a look at the exhibition
пообе́даем сего́дня в рестора́не!	let's have dinner in the restaurant today

Note: the imperfective идём may be used colloquially in the same way:

идёмте в кино́!   let's go to the cinema

The simple first-person plural forms of the imperative may be supplemented by the imperatives of дава́ть:

дава́й помо́жем! дава́йте помо́жем! 'let's help'

Note: дава́й! and дава́йте! may be used with the infinitive to express an invitation:

дава́й петь! let's sing   дава́йте реша́ть! let's decide

Note: there is an analogous construction with the imperatives of дать:

дай посмотрю́! *or* дай посмотре́ть!   let me have a look!

- The plural form of the past tense is sometimes used as a 1st person imperative:

пошли́! пое́хали! let's be off!

(ii) Third-person imperative: 'may he . . . , let them . . .'

This is formed with the Imperative forms пуска́й *or* пусть followed by the third person of the Present tense or Perfective Future of the Verb; пусть is more peremptory than пуска́й:

пуска́й чита́ет	let him/her read (let him if he wants to)
пусть чита́ет	let him/her read (let him get on with it)
пуска́й он э́то ду́мает	let him think that
пусть сде́лают	let them do it

Note: the archaic construction Да здра́вствует . . . ! 'long live . . . !'
да здра́вствует на́ша побе́да!   long live our victory!

EXERCISE

Translate into Russian:

1   Let's go to Moscow!
2   Let her go to Moscow if she likes.
3   Let her go to Moscow to fetch the picture.
4   Let's help him to look for his dog.
5   Let them look for his dog.

---

17   VERB PREFIXES

Many basic Russian words can take a range of prefixes which refine or alter their meanings. Similar ranges exist in English: 'admit', 'commit', 'emit', 'omit', 'permit', 'remit', 'submit'; 'tend': 'attend', 'contend', 'intend', 'pretend', 'subtend'; 'announce', 'denounce', 'pronounce', 'renounce', and so on. Prefixes, very often of Latin origin, have meanings and can be used with a number of words: a quick check in a dictionary will show how many words begin with, say, 'sub' (= 'under'). In Russian the prefixes are usually Slavonic in origin. Note that from some prefixed Russian verbs, nouns and other parts of speech may be derived.

(You will see that some of the prefixes have alternative forms: в- *or* во-, вз- *or* вс-. The reasons for these are phonetic: о- *may* be added to the prefix for euphony if the prefix ends in a consonant and if the verb root begins with a *group* of consonants or with the vowel о:

вгоня́ть, but (*pf.*) **вогна́ть**	'to drive in' (from гоня́ть)
вооружа́ть, (*pf.*) **вооружи́ть**	'to arm' (from the same root as ору́дие 'tool');

and if the prefix ends in -з while the root begins with a *voiceless* consonant, regressive assimilation takes place devoicing the з to с which is reflected in the spelling:

взбега́ть 'to run up(wards)'	*but*	**всходи́ть** 'to go up' (on foot)
избира́ть 'to elect'	*but*	**исключа́ть** 'to exclude'
раздава́ть 'to distribute'	*but*	**рассказа́ть** 'to recount')

17.1 В-

в- (*or* во-) corresponds to the preposition в; the verb (or noun) is usually complemented by в (+ *acc.*) It denotes:

- movement or action 'into'

вбега́ть/вбежа́ть в дом	to run into the house
вкла́дывать/вложи́ть в я́щик	to put into a drawer, box
включа́ть/включи́ть в спи́сок	to include in a list
вта́скивать/втащи́ть в ко́мнату	to drag into the room

- movement or action 'up', 'upwards'

вбега́ть/вбежа́ть на́ гору	to run up the hill
влеза́ть/влезть на де́рево	to climb a tree

- Some reflexive forms with the prefix в- denote intense involvement

вду́мываться/вду́маться в де́ло	to consider it deeply
вчи́тываться/вчита́ться в но́вую поэ́зию	to become absorbed in reading recent poetry

17.2 Вз-

вз- *or* вс- (*or* взо-) is close to the adverb вверх 'upwards'. It denotes:

- movement 'up', 'upwards', not necessarily literally

взбега́ть/взбежа́ть на́ гору	to run up the hill
взбега́ть/взбежа́ть по ле́стнице	to run up the stairs
вскрыва́ть/вскрыть письмо́	to unseal a letter
вспомина́ть/вспо́мнить на́шу встре́чу	to recall our meeting
всходи́ть/взойти́ на трибу́ну	to mount the rostrum

- Some perfective verbs with this prefix denote an intense action

вскрича́ть	to exclaim, cry (with stronger emotion than закрича́ть)
взреве́ть	to roar, howl

- This prefix is also used to form the straight perfective of some verbs

волнова́ть/взволнова́ть	to agitate, disturb, stir (up)
кипяти́ть/вскипяти́ть	to boil

17.3 Воз-

воз- *or* вос- is closely related to вз- , вс-

возбужда́ть/возбуди́ть	to arouse, excite
возвраща́ться/возврати́ться *or* верну́ться	to return
возобновля́ть/возобнови́ть заня́тия	to resume studies
возража́ть/возрази́ть про́тив его́ пла́на	to object to his plan
воспи́тывать/воспита́ть	to bring up, educate
восстана́вливать/восстанови́ть произво́дство	to restore production

17.4 Вы-

вы- corresponds to and is often used with the preposition из (+ *gen.*)
It is the opposite of в-. It denotes:

* movement from inside to outside

выбега́ть/вы́бежать из до́ма	to run out of the house
выгоня́ть/вы́гнать из шко́лы	to expel from school
выска́кивать/вы́скочить из окна́	to jump out of the window
выта́скивать/вы́тащить ме́бель из кварти́ры	to drag furniture out of the apartment
выходи́ть/вы́йти из ко́мнаты	to go out of the room

* removal, excision of an object or part of an object

выбива́ть/вы́бить	to knock out, dislodge
выбира́ть/вы́брать	to choose
выпи́сывать/вы́писать слова́ из газе́ты	to write out, extract, copy the words out of the paper
вырыва́ть/вы́рвать страни́цу из кни́ги	to tear a page out of a book

* attainment of a goal, obtaining by persistent effort

выраба́тывать/вы́работать	to work out; produce
выстра́ивать/вы́строить	to build

* a sense of satisfactory completion, rather similar to above, but reflexive

выпла́киваться/вы́плакаться	to have a good cry
высыпа́ться/вы́спаться	to have a good sleep

* This prefix is also used to form the straight perfective of some verbs, though often with the sense of particular fullness, completeness

лечи́ть/вы́лечить	to cure
пить/вы́пить	to drink
стира́ть/вы́стирать	to wash (clothes), launder
суши́ть/вы́сушить	to dry

17.5 До-

до- corresponds to the preposition до (+ *gen.*) and is often used with it. It denotes:

* reaching a destination or goal which may be spatial or temporal

доезжа́ть/дое́хать до Москвы́	to reach Moscow
дожива́ть/дожи́ть до глубо́кой ста́рости	to live to a ripe old age

* performing an action up to a certain point or limit

дочи́тывать/дочита́ть кни́гу до середи́ны	to read a book up to the middle

- completion of the final stage of an action
  допи́сывать/дописа́ть главу́   to finish writing the chapter
  достра́ивать/достро́ить зал   to finish building the hall

- additional performance of an action to reach a required objective
  допла́чивать/доплати́ть   to pay off
  остаётся доплати́ть ты́сячу рублей   there are still 1000 r. to pay

- Some reflexive forms with the prefix до- denote eventual attainment of a result
  дожида́ться/дожда́ться   to wait until desired outcome
  дозва́ниваться/дозвони́ться   to get through on the phone

17.6 За-

за- corresponds to the preposition за (+ *acc.*) It denotes:

- movement behind an object
  забега́ть/забежа́ть за у́гол   to run round the corner
  забра́сывать/забро́сить му́сор за сте́ну to throw the rubbish over (beyond) the wall
  заходи́ть/зайти́ за де́рево   to go behind a tree

- movement or action taken beyond a desired limit
  забега́ть/забежа́ть далеко́ в лес   to run off far into the woods
  запуска́ть/запусти́ть   to neglect, let decay

- covering, screening, obscuring
  заве́шивать/заве́шать сте́ну плака́тами   to cover a wall with posters
  or: /заве́сить
  закрыва́ть/закры́ть   to close; to cover
  он закры́л лицо́ рука́ми   he buried his face in his hands
  застра́ивать/застро́ить уча́сток дома́ми to develop an area, build over it

- calling in on
  заезжа́ть/зае́хать в посо́льство   to call in on the embassy
  залета́ть/залете́ть   to fly in to see
  заходи́ть/зайти́ к дру́гу   to drop in to see a friend

- earning
  завоёвывать/завоева́ть   to win, get by conquest
  зараба́тывать/зарабо́тать   to earn
  заслу́живать/заслужи́ть   to deserve, earn, win

- recording, fixing
  запечатлева́ть/запечатле́ть   to imprint, fix
  запи́сывать/записа́ть   to record

- a few perfective verbs with this prefix denote the start of an action:
  замолча́ть (*pf.*)   to fall silent
  запла́кать (*pf.*)   to burst into tears
  засмея́ться (*pf.*)   to burst out laughing

- some colloquial reflexive verbs with this prefix denote overdoing the action:
  загова́риваться/заговори́ться   to get carried away in talking
  заси́живаться/засиде́ться   to sit too long

- this prefix is also used to form the straight perfective of some verbs:
  плати́ть/заплати́ть   to pay
  интересова́ть/заинтересова́ть   to interest

17.7   Из- (ис-)

из- *or* ис- (*or* изо-) corresponds to the preposition из (+ *gen.*). It denotes:

- motion outwards, mainly in an abstract sense (less concrete than вы-)
  избира́ть/избра́ть   to elect
  извиня́ть/извини́ть   to excuse
  издава́ть/изда́ть   to publish
  исключа́ть/исключи́ть   to exclude
  исходи́ть   to derive, originate from

- exhaustiveness, totality of an action
  изна́шивать/износи́ть ту́фли   to wear out one's shoes
  испи́сывать/исписа́ть всю бума́гу   to use up all the paper
  исче́рпывать/исчерпа́ть запа́сы   to exhaust reserves

- из- (ис-) is also used to form the straight perfective of some verbs:
  по́ртить/испо́ртить   to spoil, ruin
  пуга́ть/испуга́ть   to frighten

17.8   На-

На- corresponds to the preposition на (+ *acc.*) It denotes:

- movement onto a surface or colliding with an object, the verb often being complemented by the preposition на (+ *acc*.)

наезжа́ть/нае́хать на сте́ну	to drive into a wall
накла́дывать/наложи́ть повя́зку на ра́ну	to lay, put a bandage on a wound
накле́ивать/накле́ить ма́рку на конве́рт	to stick a stamp on an envelope
наступа́ть/наступи́ть ему́ на́ ноги	to tread on his toes

- action performed on an indefinite quantity of something which is put in the genitive case

набира́ть/набра́ть я́год	to pick a lot of berries
накупа́ть/накупи́ть книг	to buy a number of books

- some reflexive verbs with this prefix denote satiety: they are usually found in the perfective:

наговори́ться (*pf.*)	to have a good long talk
(наеда́ться)/**нае́сться**	to eat one's fill
(напива́ться)/**напи́ться** (*pf.*)	to have a lot to drink
насмотре́ться (*pf.*)	to feast one's eyes on

- this prefix is also used to form the straight perfective of some verbs:

писа́ть/написа́ть	to write
смеши́ть/насмеши́ть	to amuse, make laugh
учи́ть/научи́ть	to teach

17.9 Над- (надо-)

над- (or надо-) corresponds to the preposition над (+ *inst*.). It denotes:

- action involving enlargement of an object, generally by adding on top

надкле́ивать/надкле́ить поло́ску бума́ги	to glue on a strip of paper
надстра́ивать/надстро́ить эта́ж	to add on a storey

17.10 Недо-

недо- negates до- , i.e. it denotes the failure to finish off an action completely:

недове́шивать/недове́сить	to give short measure
недовыполня́ть/недовы́полнить	to underfulfil
недооце́нивать/недооцени́ть	to underestimate, undervalue

17.11   Низ- (нис-)

низ- *or* нис- (*or* низо-) denotes movement downwards and is bookish:

низверга́ть/низве́ргнуть	to cast down, overthrow
низводи́ть/низвести́	to bring down, reduce
нисходи́ть/низойти́	to descend

17.12   О- (Об-)

о- *or* об- (*or* обо-) does not correspond to a preposition; it denotes:

* movement round an object

обводи́ть/обвести́ его́ вокру́г па́льца	to twist him round your finger
обходи́ть/обойти́ фа́брику	to walk round a factory

* movement round in order to avoid

обходи́ть/обойти́ лу́жу	to walk round a puddle
объезжа́ть/объе́хать го́род	to avoid the town

* action around an object

обводи́ть/обвести́ сад забо́ром	to fence round the garden
обступа́ть/обступи́ть	to crowd round
окружа́ть/окружи́ть	to surround

* enveloping or covering all over

обвива́ть/обви́ть	to wind round, entwine
обива́ть/оби́ть	to upholster
обсыпа́ть/обсы́пать	to sprinkle
оку́тывать/оку́тать	to wrap up, cloak

* outdoing or overtaking

обгоня́ть/обогна́ть	to overtake

* action done to excess

обка́рмливать/обкорми́ть	to overfeed
объеда́ться/объе́сться	to overeat, gorge oneself

* deliberately deceitful action

обве́шивать/обве́сить	to cheat by giving short weight
обма́нывать/обману́ть	to deceive
обме́ривать/обме́рить	to give short measure to
обсчи́тывать/обсчита́ть меня́ на 1000р.	to cheat me out of, short change me by 1000 roubles

- creation of a state or condition corresponding to an adjectival root

обогаща́ть/обогати́ть	to enrich
осложня́ть/осложни́ть	to complicate

- this prefix is also used to form the straight Perfective of some Verbs:

ра́доваться/обра́доваться	to be glad, rejoice
слѐпнуть/ослѐпнуть	to go blind

17.13 Обез-

обез- (*or* обес-) is used to form verbs from noun roots meaning deprivation of the object denoted by the noun:

обезгла́вливать/обезгла́вить	to behead
обезуме́ть (*Perf.*)	to go mad

17.14 От-

от- (*or* ото-) corresponds to the preposition от (+ *gen*). It denotes:

- movement away from

отбра́сывать/отбро́сить	to throw away, discard
отклоня́ть/отклони́ть про́сьбу	to decline, turn away a request
отпуска́ть/отпусти́ть	to let go, release
отходи́ть/отойти́	to walk away

- removal of part of an object

отку́сывать/откуси́ть кусо́к от но́жки	to bite a piece off the leg
отпи́ливать/отпили́ть но́гу	to saw off the leg
отрыва́ть/оторва́ть	to tear, rip off

- dissuading

отвлека́ть/отвлѐчь	to distract, divert
отгова́ривать/отговори́ть	to dissuade

- repaying

отзыва́ться/отозва́ться	to respond, react
отпла́чивать/отплати́ть ему́ той же моне́той	to pay him back in his own coin

- completion of a term of duty

отси́живать/отсиде́ть в тюрьме́	to do one's time in prison
отслу́живать/отслужи́ть	to serve out one's time

17.15 Пере-

пере- corresponds to the preposition че́рез (+ *acc.*). It denotes:

* movement across

перебра́сывать/перебро́сить мяч че́рез забо́р	to throw the ball over the fence
перелета́ть/перелете́ть (че́рез) грани́цу	to cross a border by air
переса́живаться/пересе́сть на друго́й по́езд	to change trains
переходи́ть/перейти́ у́лицу (*or* че́рез у́лицу)	to cross the street

* outdoing someone, excess

перекри́кивать/перекрича́ть всех	to outshout everyone
переси́ливать/переси́лить	to overcome

* overdoing an action, excess

перева́ривать/перевари́ть	to overcook
переоце́нивать/переоцени́ть	to overestimate
переполня́ть/перепо́лнить	to overfill

* repetition

перепи́сывать/переписа́ть	to rewrite, copy
перестра́ивать/перестро́ить	to rebuild
перечи́тывать/перечита́ть	to reread

* spending a period of time

перезимова́ть (*pf.*)	to overwinter
переночёвывать/переночева́ть	to spend the night

* dividing an object

перепи́ливать/перепили́ть	to saw in two
пересека́ть/пересе́чь	to cut in half; to intersect

* action embracing a large number of objects

перела́мывать/переломи́ть	to break all of something
перели́стывать/перелиста́ть кни́гу	to flip through a book

* some reflexive forms with the prefix пере- denote mutual actions (reactions):

перегля́дываться/перегляну́ться	to glance at each other
перепи́сываться (*impf.*)	to write to one another

17.16 Пре-

пре- is close to пере-, but is bookish and comparatively rare. It denotes:

- change, transformation

превраща́ть/преврати́ть	to change, convert, transform
превраща́ться/преврати́ться	to turn into, be transformed into
в идеа́льного му́жа	an ideal husband

- limitation, curtailment

прегражда́ть/прегради́ть	to bar, block
прекраща́ть/прекрати́ть	to cease, stop

- excessive action

преувели́чивать/преувели́чить	to exaggerate
преуменьша́ть/преуме́ньшить	to underestimate
or /преуменьши́ть	

17.17 По-

по- is the most commonly used prefix in forming the straight perfective of unprefixed imperfective verbs. In doing so it focuses attention on:

- achievement of a result, thereby limiting the meaning to that aspect of the action

мыть/помы́ть	to wash/to have washed
стро́ить/постро́ить	to build/get the thing built

- limitation of action to a short period of time (sometimes known as 'semi-perfectives')

бесе́довать/побесе́довать	to chat/to have a short chat
гуля́ть/погуля́ть	to stroll/to have a little stroll
сиде́ть/посиде́ть	to sit/to sit for a while
спать/поспа́ть	to sleep/to have a snooze

- beginning of motion or emotion

е́хать/пое́хать	to travel/to drive off
идти́/пойти́	to go/to set off, get going
люби́ть/полюби́ть	to love, like/to take to, fall for
чу́вствовать/почу́вствовать	to feel/to start to feel, feel suddenly

17.18 Под-

под- corresponds to the preposition под 'under' (+ *acc.*). It denotes:

* movement or action under

подкла́дывать/подложи́ть	to put, lay under
подпи́сывать/подписа́ть	to sign
подставля́ть/подста́вить ведро́ под кран	to stand the bucket under the tap

* approach

подставля́ть/подста́вить ле́стницу к окну́	to put a ladder up to the window
подходи́ть/подойти́ к две́ри	to approach the door (on foot)
подъезжа́ть/подъе́хать к воро́там	to drive up towards the gates

* movement or action directed upwards from below

подбра́сывать/подбро́сить мяч	to throw the ball up
подде́рживать/поддержа́ть	to support

* supporting, backing

подда́кивать/подда́кнуть	to back, assent, say yes to
подпева́ть/подпе́ть под орке́стр	to sing along with the orchestra

* addition, supplementary action

подбра́сывать/подбро́сить дров в печь	to throw more wood in the stove
подлива́ть/подли́ть вина́ в бока́л	to top up a glass with wine

* surreptitious action

подслу́шивать/подслу́шать	to eavesdrop
подсма́тривать/подсмотре́ть	to spy, keep a crafty eye on

17.19 Пред-

пред- (*or* предо-) corresponds to the preposition пе́ред (пред) (+ *inst.*) 'before, in front of'. It denotes:

* action of setting something before a person or object

предлага́ть/предложи́ть	to put forward, suggest, offer
предпочита́ть/предпоче́сть	to prefer
представля́ть/предста́вить	to present, introduce, represent

* anticipation, prevention

предви́деть (*impf.*)	to foresee
предостерега́ть/предостере́чь	to warn

предотвраща́ть/предотврати́ть	to prevent
предска́зывать/предсказа́ть	to foretell
предупрежда́ть/предупреди́ть	to warn, give notice
предусма́тривать/предусмотре́ть	to foresee, provide for

17.20 При-

при- corresponds to the preposition при (+ *pr.*) 'attached to, in the presence of', but is often used with other prepositions. It denotes:

* presence

| прису́тствовать (*impf.*) при встре́че | to be present at the meeting |

* arrival, movement into the presence of someone

прибега́ть/прибежа́ть	to come running
привози́ть/привезти́ на база́р	to bring to market (by some form of transport)
приземля́ться/приземли́ться	to land (of an aircraft)
приходи́ть/прийти́ в гости́ницу	to arrive, come to the hotel (on foot)

* attaching, adding

прибавля́ть/приба́вить	to add
привя́зывать/привяза́ть ло́шадь к забо́ру	to tie the horse to a fence
прикла́дывать/приложи́ть си́лу	to apply force
прикле́ивать/прикле́ить ма́рку к конве́рту	to stick a stamp on an envelope
прикрепля́ть/прикрепи́ть к стене́	to fasten, fix to the wall
применя́ть/примени́ть	to apply, employ
прислу́шиваться/прислу́шаться	to bend your ear to

* tentative, incomplete action

| привстава́ть/привста́ть | to raise oneself a little |
| приоткрыва́ть/приоткры́ть дверь | to half open the door |

17.21 Про-

про- is close in meaning to the prepositions че́рез and сквозь (+ *acc.*) 'through'. It denotes:

* movement or action through an object

пробива́ть/проби́ть	to break through
проку́сывать/прокуси́ть	to bite through
проника́ть/прони́кнуть	to penetrate
проруба́ть/проруби́ть окно́ в Евро́пу	to hack a window through to Europe

• movement past an object

проезжа́ть/прое́хать ми́мо дворца́	to drive past the palace
проплыва́ть/проплы́ть ми́мо маяка́	to sail *or* swim past the lighthouse
проходи́ть/пройти́ ми́мо воро́т	to walk past the gate

• thoroughness of the action

проду́мывать/проду́мать пробле́му	to think a problem through
прожа́ривать/прожа́рить	to bake right through
промока́ть/промо́кнуть	to get thoroughly wet, soaked
прослу́шивать/прослу́шать се́рдце	to listen to someone's heart

• action continued for a specified time, usually perfective

(пролёживать)/пролежа́ть весь день в посте́ли	to lie in all day
(проси́живать)/просиде́ть це́лый фильм	to sit through the whole film
(просыпа́ть)/проспа́ть ле́кцию	to sleep through the lecture

• errors of omission and commission

проба́лтываться/проболта́ться	to blab
прогова́риваться/проговори́ться	to let the cat out of the bag
прои́грывать/проигра́ть	to lose
прослу́шивать/прослу́шать	to miss, fail to hear
(просма́тривать)/просмотре́ть	to overlook

• this prefix is also used to form the straight perfective of some verbs:

комменти́ровать/прокомменти́ровать	to comment on
слу́шать/прослу́шать	to listen
чита́ть/прочита́ть	to read

17.22 Раз- (рас-)

раз- or рас- (or разо-) suggests dispersal, separation and movement apart. It denotes:

• scattering, spreading, distributing

разбра́сывать/разбро́сить	to scatter, throw in all directions
раздава́ть/разда́ть	to give out, distribute
раздава́ться/разда́ться	to resound
разлива́ть/разли́ть чай	to pour out the tea

• dispersal

расходи́ться/разойти́сь	to disperse
разъезжа́ться/разъе́хаться по дома́м	to break up and go home

- undoing, untying, opening up

развя́зывать/развяза́ть	to untie, undo
разговори́ться (*pf.*)	to strike up a conversation
раздева́ть(ся)/разде́ть(ся)	to undress (get undressed)
разоружа́ть/разоружи́ть	to disarm
раскрыва́ть/раскры́ть	to open wide; expose

- division

разбива́ть/разби́ть	to smash to pieces
разреза́ть/разре́зать	to cut up
разрыва́ть/разорва́ть	to blow up; tear up
распада́ться/распа́сться	to fall apart, disintegrate

- all-round thoroughness of an action

рассле́довать (*impf.* and *pf.*)	to investigate
рассма́тривать/рассмотре́ть	to examine thoroughly
расспра́шивать/расспроси́ть	to question
расцелова́ть (*pf.*)	to smother in kisses

17. 23 C- (co-)

c- or co- corresponds to the preposition c (+ *gen.* and + *inst.*). It denotes:

- movement or action downwards from the top of an object

спи́сывать/списа́ть	to copy down
спуска́ть/спусти́ть	to lower, let down
ссыла́ть/сосла́ть	to banish, exile
стира́ть/стере́ть	to wipe off
сходи́ть/сойти́ с ле́стницы	to come downstairs

- joining, concentrating

скле́ивать/скле́ить	to stick together, glue
соединя́ть/соедини́ть	to unite, combine
сосредото́чивать/сосредото́чить	to concentrate, focus
составля́ть/соста́вить	to put together, compile
сходи́ться/сойти́сь	to meet, come together

- harmonious action

| соглаша́ться/согласи́ться | to agree |
| созва́ниваться/созвони́ться | to phone one another |

- accompaniment, support, sympathy

сопровожда́ть/сопроводи́ть	to accompany
сотру́дничать (*impf.*) с ни́ми	to co-operate with them
сочу́вствовать (*impf.*) ему́	to sympathize with him

- comparison

сопоставля́ть/сопоста́вить	to compare, juxtapose
сра́внивать/сравни́ть	to compare

- when added to some indeterminate or reiterative verbs of motion c-forms a perfective verb meaning a single journey there and back

свози́ть дете́й к врачу́	to take the children to the doctor's
сходи́ть в магази́н за фру́ктами	to go to the shop for fruit

- this prefix is also used to form the straight perfective of some verbs:

де́лать/сде́лать	to do, make
фотографи́ровать/сфотографи́ровать	to photograph

17.24 У-

у- denotes:

- movement away, removal of whole or part of an object

убира́ть/убра́ть	to remove, tidy up
увольня́ть/уво́лить	to dismiss, sack
уезжа́ть/уе́хать из го́рода	to leave town
уноси́ть/унести́ из шко́лы	to carry away from school
устраня́ть/устрани́ть	to remove, eliminate
уходи́ть/уйти́ от жены́, из до́ма	to leave one's wife, one's home

- restraining, retaining

уберега́ть/убере́чь от моро́за	to keep safe from frost
уде́рживать/удержа́ть	to hold back

- putting away

укла́дывать/уложи́ть	to pack, put away
умеща́ть/умести́ть	to find room for

- perseverance, keeping going

уде́рживать/удержа́ть	to withstand
устоя́ть (*pf.*)	to hold one's position

- creation of a state or condition corresponding to an adjectival root

увели́чивать/увели́чить	to enlarge
уменьша́ть/уме́ньшить *or* уменьши́ть	to lessen, decrease
упроща́ть/упрости́ть	to simplify
усложня́ть/усложни́ть	to complicate

- y- is sometimes used to strengthen the meaning of the unprefixed verb:

from жить: ужива́ться/ужи́ться с ним	to settle down with him
from ложи́ться/лечь: укла́дываться/уле́чься	to settle down for the night
from сади́ться/сесть: уса́живаться/усе́сться	to make oneself comfy
from ве́шать/пове́сить карти́ну на сте́ну	to hang a picture on the wall
уве́шивать/уве́шать сте́ну карти́нами	to cover a wall with pictures

Жемчу́жины наро́дной му́дрости

не обду́мавши, не реша́й, а реши́вши, не переду́мывай	without thinking it over, don't decide, but having decided, don't rethink

---

EXERCISES

(i) *Translate the following passages and comment on the italicized prefixes:*

'Я *во*шёл в ха́ту: две ла́вки и стол, да огро́мный сунду́к во́зле пе́чи составля́ли всю её ме́бель. На стене́ ни одного́ о́браза – дурно́й знак! В *раз*би́тое стекло́ *в*рыва́лся морско́й ве́тер. Я *вы*тащил из чемода́на восково́й ога́рок и, *за*свети́в его́, стал *рас*кла́дывать ве́щи, поста́вил в у́гол ша́шку и ружьё, пистоле́ты положи́л на стол, *раз*остла́л бу́рку на ла́вке, каза́к свою́ на друго́й; че́рез де́сять мину́т он *за*храпе́л, но я не мог засну́ть.

Так *про*шло́ о́коло ча́са. Ме́сяц свети́л в окно́, и луч его́ игра́л по земляно́му по́лу ха́ты. Вдруг на я́ркой полосе́, *пере*сека́ющей пол, *про*мелькну́ла тень. Я *при*встал и взгляну́л в окно́: кто-то втори́чно *про*бежа́л ми́мо него́ и скры́лся Бог зна́ет куда́. Я не мог полага́ть, чтоб э́то существо́ *с*бежа́ло по отве́су бе́рега; одна́ко ина́че ему́ не́куда бы́ло дева́ться. Я встал, *на*ки́нул бешме́т, опоя́сал кинжа́л и ти́хо-ти́хо *вы*шел из ха́ты; навстре́чу мне слепо́й ма́льчик. Я *при*таи́лся у забо́ра, и он ве́рной, но осторо́жной по́ступью *про*шёл ми́мо меня́' (Lermontov).

'– Кто там? *Вой*ди́те, – *раз*да́лся го́лос Фе́нички.

– Э́то я, – проговори́л Па́вел Петро́вич и *от*вори́л дверь.

Фе́ничка *вс*кочи́ла со сту́ла, на кото́ром она́ *у*се́лась со свои́м ребёнком, и, *пере*да́в его́ на́ руки де́вушки, кото́рая тотча́с же *вы*несла его́ вон из ко́мнаты, торопли́во попра́вила свою́ косы́нку.

– *Из*вини́те, е́сли я помеша́л, – на́чал Па́вел Петро́вич' (Turgenev).

'Он стал *обнима́ть* сы́на . . . «Еню́ша, Еню́ша», *разда́лся* трепещу́щий же́нский го́лос. Дверь *распахну́лась*, и на поро́ге показа́лась кру́гленькая, ни́зенькая стару́шка в бе́лом чепце́ и коро́ткой пёстрой ко́фточке. Она́ а́хнула, пошатну́лась и наве́рно бы *упа́ла*, е́сли бы Ба́заров не *поддержа́л* её. Пу́хлые её ру́чки мгнове́нно *обви́лись* вокру́г его́ ше́и, голова́ *прижа́лась* к его́ груди́, и всё *замо́лкло*. То́лько слы́шались её преры́вистые всхли́пыванья' (Turgenev).

'Ми́стер Дью́ли уже́ *переходи́л* че́рез у́лицу к своему́ до́му, когда́ вдруг из-за угла́ *вы́вернулся* кра́сный автомоби́ль' (E. Zamyatin).

'– Мы – производи́тели цеме́нта. А цеме́нт – э́то кре́пкая связь. Цеме́нт – э́то мы, това́рищи, рабо́чий класс. Пора́ *перейти́* к на́шему прямо́му де́лу – к произво́дству цеме́нта для строи́тельства социали́зма.

После́дние слова́ Гле́ба *взволнова́ли* рабо́чих. Мно́гие *вскочи́ли* с ме́ста и ста́ли тре́бовать сло́ва. Глеб *по́днял* ру́ку, тре́буя внима́ния. Да́ша *зазвони́ла* колоко́льчиком' (F. Gladkov).

'Па́вка незаме́тно *вы́скользнул* в дверь, *пробежа́л* че́рез сад, *переле́з* че́рез забо́р и *вы́брался* на доро́гу, веду́щую к ле́су' (N. Ostrovsky).

'В ко́мнате Корча́гина, на столе́ у окна́, гру́ды *принесённых* из парти́йной библиоте́ки книг, стопа́ газе́т; не́сколько *испи́санных* блокно́тов' (N. Ostrovsky).

(ii) *Translate into Russian:*

1 They were letting the people through.
2 They let the children out.
3 They're letting us have the day off.
4 She let them come up to the door.
5 They launch the sputniks from here.
6 They'll change the timetable in the spring.
7 We'll change the colour of the walls next time.
8 He's changed completely since she left.
9 Her face changed when he came in.
10 I wish someone would change the bulb.
11 They changed the sheets today.
12 I want to change dollars into roubles.
13 I want to change this note.
14 We exchange students every year.
15 I think we've swopped umbrellas by mistake.
16 They shortchanged her while she was in a hurry.
17 I'll definitely include him in the list.
18 The mushrooms weren't fried properly.
19 Let's take the picture down off the wall.
20 This arouses my curiosity.
21 She's made enough pancakes to sink a battleship.

22 We overlooked his mistake.
23 I want to keep on working here till (I get my) pension.
24 They moved slowly away from one another.
25 He ripped a page out of the book.
26 She became totally engrossed reading the text.
27 They cheated him when they cut him out a length of fabric.
28 It only remained to finish writing the last three pages.
29 Did you sleep well?
30 He was looking closely into my face.

18 THE VERB 'TO BE' AND THOSE OF 'BECOMING', 'APPEARING', *ETC.*

Russian generally requires the instrumental case after verbs meaning 'to be', 'to appear', 'to become', 'to seem', 'to look', 'to turn out as'.

18.1 Instrumental or nominative after быть

18.1.1 When, in the present tense, no form of the verb быть appears, the noun complement remains in the nominative:

она́ прекра́сный инжене́р	she is an excellent engineer

18.1.2 nouns as complement to the verb **быть** in the infinitive, future, conditional, imperative or gerund generally go into the instrumental:

она́ всегда́ хоте́ла **быть инжене́ром**	she always wanted to be an engineer
он, наве́рное, бу́дет инжене́ром	he probably will be an engineer

я был(а́) бы инжене́ром, е́сли бы была́ возмо́жность
I would be an engineer if there were an opportunity
or: I would have been an engineer if there had been an opportunity

Будь мужчи́ной! Будь хоро́шим челове́ком! Не будь дурако́м!
Be a man! Be a good chap! Don't be an idiot!

бу́дучи инжене́ром, он сра́зу по́нял, в чём де́ло
being an engineer, he realized at once what the matter was

18.1.3 With the past tense of быть the noun complement may be in *either* the nominative *or* the instrumental case; normally the nominative is used to indicate a permanent, fundamental condition, whereas the instrumental indicates a temporary state:

	он был настоя́щий поэ́т	he was a real poet
cf.	он был хоро́шим поэ́том	he was a good poet
	она́ была́ ру́сская	she was Russian
cf.	она́ была́ мое́й подру́гой	she was my friend
	мой де́душка был майо́ром	my grandfather was a major

(It has to be pointed out, however, that the above is not a hard-and-fast rule and the nominative can be used to express a temporary condition:

он был архитектор   he was an architect

and the instrumental can be used to express a permanent condition:

мать царя́ была́ сестро́й англи́йской короле́вы

the Tsar's mother was the sister of the Queen of England.

'Вообще́ Арбу́зов был неожи́данным челове́ком. Вот вы, наприме́р, зна́ете, что он дружи́л с Ю́рием Три́фоновым? Арбу́зов и Три́фонов сошли́сь на по́чве спо́рта – о́ба бы́ли зая́длые футбо́льные и хокке́йные боле́льщики' (Yu. Ellis in *Literaturnaya gazeta*).

Arbuzov was a surprising person generally. Did you know, for instance, that he and Yuri Trifonov were friends? Arbuzov and Trifonov came together on the common ground of sport – they were both mad football and ice-hockey fans

18.1.4 When both the subject and complement are nouns used with the past or future tense of быть it is not always clear which, if either, should go into the instrumental. For example, in the sentence:

'the answer was a computer'

it would seem that 'the answer' is subject and 'a computer' the complement. But in Russian this would be turned round to say in effect:

'a computer was the answer'

so what is specific, real (i.e. 'a computer') is the subject and is put in the nominative case, while what is the broader concept (i.e. 'the answer') goes into the instrumental case:

отве́том был компью́тер

Note: although the grammar of the two languages is inverted, the word order of the elements is the same.

In order to decide which noun should go into the instrumental as complement you have to work out what the real subject is. To do this it helps to substitute 'was', 'will be', *etc.* with another verb or phrase such as 'serve as', 'provide'. It does not make sense to say 'the answer served as a computer' or 'the answer provided a computer', but 'a computer served as the answer' or 'a computer provided the answer' shows up the 'real' subject.

18.1.5 An infinitive or a phrase starting with an infinitive may form the subject:

вста́ть ра́но **бы́ло оши́бкой** to get up early was a mistake

18.2 Instrumental after verbs of becoming, etc.

18.2.1 Other verbs which are followed by a complement in the instrumental case include:

вы́глядеть (*impf.* only)	to look like
каза́ться/показа́ться	to seem
называ́ться/назва́ться	to be called
ока́зываться/оказа́ться	to turn out to be
остава́ться/оста́ться	to remain
служи́ть/послужи́ть	to serve as
станови́ться/стать	to become
счита́ться (*impf.* only)	to be considered
чу́вствовать/почу́вствовать себя́	to feel
явля́ться/яви́ться	to be

команди́р диви́зии **вы́глядел уста́лым старико́м**
the divisional commander looked like a tired old man

наш оте́ц иногда́ **ка́жется** совсе́м **ребёнком**
our father sometimes seems absolutely (like) a child

тако́й рома́н **называ́ется детекти́вом**
a novel like that is called a detective story

инжене́р **оказа́лся экспе́ртом** по совреме́нному иску́сству
the engineer turned out to be an expert in modern art

его́ жена́ всегда́ **оста́нется** мое́й **подру́гой**
his wife will always remain my friend

о́стров **служи́л убе́жищем**	the island served as a refuge
его́ сестра́ хо́чет **стать врачо́м**	his sister wants to become a doctor
она́ **счита́ется специали́стом**	she is considered a specialist

их реше́ние перее́хать в То́мск **яви́лось неожи́данностью**
their decision to move to Tomsk was a surprise

учи́ться ру́сскому языку́ **оказа́лось** пе́рвым **ша́гом** к блестя́щей карье́ре
studying Russian turned out to be the first step towards a brilliant career

Note: whilst the use of the instrumental for the complement is the norm with verbs such as those given above, the nominative is also found:
'. . . И в са́мом де́ле, пре́жде они́ про́сто бы́ли болва́ны, а тепе́рь они́ вдруг ста́ли нигили́сты' (Turgenev).
And indeed, they were simply fools at that time, but now they have suddenly become Nihilists.

18.2.2 The complement may be an adjective in the nominative or instrumental long form, or in the short form. The nominative is normally considered to express permanent, inherent characteristics, the short form temporary or limited ones, and the instrumental is more literary. This is, however, a general guide, not a firm rule (see notes on short-form adjective pp. 35–6, 38–9). Like nouns, adjectives may appear in the nominative where the instrumental might be expected:

'И вот она́ сперва́ до́лго пла́кала, а пото́м ста́ла зла́я' (Bulgakov).
And so at first she cried for a long time and then got angry.

18.3 Э́то

When э́то is used in identifying a person or persons already mentioned as performing some action (as in: 'Somebody knocked on my door. *It* was my brother'); or in identifying or characterizing some thing or object (as in: 'She found something in the cupboard. *It* was my book'), then that person or thing is expressed by the noun in the nominative: it forms the subject in Russian and the verb agrees with it:

кто́-то стуча́л в дверь. Э́то **был мой брат**
someone was knocking at the door. It was my brother

она́ нашла́ что́-то в шкафу́. Э́то **была́** моя́ **ша́пка**
she found something in the cupboard. It was my fur hat

18.4 Adjectives and participles as complements

18.4.1 When used as a complement to an intransitive verb, an adjective or participle may be put in the nominative or the instrumental case:

'И возвраща́ется профе́ссор домо́й уже́ совсе́м больно́й (*nom.*)' (Bulgakov).
And the professor returns home already quite ill.

'Арка́дий пе́рвый (*nom.*) вы́шел на крыльцо́' (Turgenev).
Arkady came out onto the porch first.

'Па́вел Петро́вич сошёл в гости́ную уже́ гото́вый (*nom.*) к бо́ю' (Turgenev).
Pavel Petrovich came down into the drawing room already prepared to do battle.

'Пе́рвым (*inst.*) заме́тил след отби́вшегося тигрёнка бригади́р Маркел Сиволобов' (Eremin).
Team-leader Markel Sivolobov noticed the stray tiger-cub's track first.

'Первой (*inst.*), си́льно кла́няясь вперёд и вы́тянув ру́ки, дви́галась Да́рья' (V. Rasputin).
Darya moved first, bending sharply forward and stretching out her arms.

'Уйти́ из э́той борьбы́ побеждённым (*inst.*), когда́ зна́ешь, что пра́вда с тобо́й, – э́то сли́шком тяжело́; э́то нельзя́ допусти́ть, потому́ что э́то – коне́ц' (Gladkov).
To leave this struggle defeated when you know that right is on your side is too much; it must not be allowed to happen because that would be the end.

'Я бу́ду спать кре́пко и у́тром просыпа́ться весёлым (*inst.*)' (Kazakov).
I'll sleep soundly and wake up cheerful in the morning.

18.4.2 When used as a complement to a transitive verb, an adjective or participle is normally put in the instrumental case, but the accusative is also possible:

'Я никогда́ не ви́дел её тако́й краси́вой' (*inst.*) (Kazakov).
I never saw her so beautiful.

'Каза́к мой был о́чень удивлён, когда́ уви́дел меня́ совсе́м оде́того (*acc.*)' (Lermontov).
My Cossack was amazed when he saw me fully dressed.

- Note the use of the instrumental case to express similarity:
'Он сбро́сил с себя́ шине́ль, и так ве́село, таки́м молоде́ньким ма́льчиком посмотре́л на отца́, что тот опя́ть о́бнял его́' (Turgenev).
He flung off his overcoat and looked at his father so happily, so like a young boy, that (the old man) again embraced him.

Жемчу́жины наро́дной му́дрости

вре́мя – де́ньги	time is money

EXERCISES

(i) *Translate into English:*

1 Он был пре́жде полковы́м до́ктором.
2 Це́лью па́ртии бы́ло установле́ние социали́зма.
3 'А́нна Серге́евна была́ дово́льно стра́нное существо́' (Turgenev).
4 'База́ров был вели́кий охо́тник до же́нщин и до же́нской красоты́' (Turgenev).
5 'Она́ не чу́вствовала себя́ оскорблённой' (Turgenev).
6 'На обра́тном пути́ у них обыкнове́нно завя́зывался спор, и Арка́дий обыкнове́нно остава́лся побеждённым, хотя́ говори́л бо́льше своего́ това́рища' (Turgenev).
7 'Кот вскочи́л живо́й и бо́дрый' (Bulgakov).
8 'Нау́тро он просыпа́ется молчали́вым, но соверше́нно бо́дрым' (Bulgakov).
9 'Мальчи́шка говори́л пло́хо и ма́ло, рос ди́ким, боязли́вым' (Rasputin).
10 'И́збы стоя́ли чёрные . . . Роса́ уже́ па́ла, трава́ была́ мо́крой' (Kazakov).
11 'Далеко́ впереди́ на друго́й стороне́ реки́ я́ркой то́чкой горе́л костёр' (Kazakov).
12 'Полови́на Москвы́ и Петербу́рга была́ родня́ и прия́тели Степа́на Арка́дьича. Он роди́лся в среде́ тех люде́й, кото́рые бы́ли и ста́ли си́льными ми́ра сего́. Одна́ треть госуда́рственных люде́й бы́ли прия́телями его́ отца́ . . . ; друга́я треть бы́ли с ним на «ты»; а тре́тья – бы́ли хоро́шие знако́мые . . . ' (Tolstoy).

(ii) *Translate into Russian:*

1 Don't be a fool!
2 I want to be rich.
3 He was a real friend.
4 He served as a secretary of the commission.
5 An example of this was his new novel.
6 The aim of the expedition was to build an observation post.
7 Your visit will be a real pleasure for us.
8 Her sister will remain my friend for ever.
9 He will become a great scientist.
10 The commander looked like a little boy.
11 The whole square and all the buildings looked old and dirty.
12 Suddenly I saw someone in the street. It was a Russian soldier.

19 VERB CONSTRUCTIONS

There follows a listing of common Russian verbs according to the grammatical constructions (case, preposition) they require; for various reasons these are not always the ones expected by native speakers of English:

19.1 Verbs taking the accusative

19.1.1 Straight accusative

возглавля́ть/возгла́вить 'to head'
кто возглавля́ет э́ту организа́цию?   who heads this organization?

завоёвывать/завоева́ть 'to gain'
на́ши това́ры завоева́ли хоро́шую репута́цию
our goods have won a good reputation

консульти́ровать/проконсульти́ровать 'to advise'
я хочу́ проконсульти́ровать всех чле́нов коллекти́ва
I want to have a word with all members of the collective

напомина́ть/напо́мнить 'to remind, bring to mind'
она́ напомина́ла мне мою́ сестру́   she reminded me of my sister

обма́нывать/обману́ть 'to deceive'
они́ обма́нывали стару́шку да́же при мне
they were deceiving the old woman even with me present

посеща́ть/посети́ть 'to visit'
обяза́тельно посети́те музе́й!   you must visit the museum

предупрежда́ть/предупреди́ть 'to warn'
мы предупреди́ли его́ жену́ о поведе́нии куха́рки
we warned his wife about the cook's behaviour

пресле́довать (*impf.* only) 'to pursue; persecute'
пресле́довали во́лка весь день   they pursued the wolf all day

проси́ть/попроси́ть 'to ask, request'
он попроси́л де́вушку не кури́ть   he asked the girl not to smoke

спра́шивать/спроси́ть 'to ask, enquire'
мы спроси́ли проводника́, где на́ши места́
we asked the conductor where our seats were

употребля́ть/употреби́ть 'to use'
он употребля́ет то́лько са́мые дороги́е кра́ски
he uses only the most expensive colours

19.1.2 в + accusative

ве́рить/пове́рить 'to believe in'
он уже́ не ве́рил в па́ртию, то́лько в себя́
he no longer believed in the Party, only in himself

поступа́ть/поступи́ть 'to enter (some institution)'
как то́лько он поступи́л в университе́т, начала́сь война́
as soon as he entered university the war began

превраща́ться/преврати́ться 'to turn into, be transformed'
здесь сырьё превраща́ется в гото́вую проду́кцию
here raw materials are transformed into finished products

19.1.3 за + accusative

благодари́ть/поблагодари́ть 'to thank'
благодарю́ за внима́ние   thank you for listening
мы поблагодари́ли де́вушку за то, что она́ помогла́ нам
we thanked the girl for helping us

боро́ться/поборо́ться 'to struggle'
кома́нда бо́рется за пе́рвенство ли́ги
the team is struggling for championship of the league
па́ртия бо́рется за то, чего́ хотя́т все поря́дочные лю́ди
the party is fighting for what all decent people want

бра́ться/взя́ться 'to take up, get down to, undertake'
я обяза́тельно возьму́сь за ремо́нт кварти́ры по́сле пра́здника
I'll definitely get down to decorating the flat after the holiday

отвеча́ть (*impf.* only) 'to be responsible, answer for'
кто отвеча́ет за то, что случи́лось вчера́?
who's responsible for what happened yesterday?

плати́ть/заплати́ть 'to pay'
    подойдя́ к око́шечку, он заплати́л за биле́т
    having gone up to the window he paid for the ticket

19.1.4 на + accusative

влия́ть/повлия́ть 'to influence'
    нельзя́ сказа́ть, что он си́льно повлия́л на её выступле́ние
    we cannot say that he had much influence on her performance

возде́йствовать (*impf.* and *pf.*) 'to affect, act on'
    на́до возде́йствовать на него́ други́м спо́собом
    we'll have to act on him some other way

возража́ть/возрази́ть 'to retort, object'
    ты име́ешь пра́во возража́ть на кри́тику
    you have the right to object to the criticism

гляде́ть/погляде́ть 'to gaze'
    он всё вре́мя гляде́л на же́нщину в си́нем
    he kept staring at the woman in blue

жа́ловаться/пожа́ловаться 'to complain'
    она́ постоя́нно жа́луется на сосе́дей
    she's constantly complaining about the neighbours

наде́яться/понаде́яться 'to hope for; to rely on'
    все наде́ются на повыше́ние зарпла́ты   everyone's hoping for a pay rise
    бесполе́зно наде́яться на уси́лия одни́х фе́рмеров
    it's useless to rely on the efforts of the farmers alone

напада́ть/напа́сть 'to attack'
    во́лки напа́ли на ове́ц   wolves have attacked the sheep

обижа́ться/оби́деться 'to take offence'
    не обижа́йся на меня́   don't be offended by me

опира́ться/опере́ться 'to lean on, look to for support'
    опира́ясь на подде́ржку друзе́й, он реши́л жени́ться
    relying on his friends' support he decided to get married

опа́здывать/опозда́ть 'to be late'
    почему́ вы опозда́ли на ле́кцию?   why were you late for the lecture?

отвечáть/отвéтить 'to answer, respond'
    онá никогдá не отвечáла на анонúмные пúсьма
    she never replied to anonymous letters

откликáться/отклúкнуться 'to respond to'
    Мáша всегдá откликáется на нáши прóсьбы
    Masha always responds to our requests

полагáться/положúться 'to rely on, count on'
    мы полагáемся на то, что вы нам помóжете
    we're relying on your helping us

походúть (*impf.* only) 'to resemble'
    он óчень похóдит на моегó дя́дю   he's very like my uncle

претендовáть (*impf.* only) 'to claim, have pretensions to'
    полúтики обы́чно претендýют на респектáбельность
    politicians usually claim respectability

решáться/решúться 'to resolve'
    он неохóтно решúлся на э́тот шаг   he decided on this step unwillingly

садúться/сесть 'to get on (transport)'
    онá сéла на двáдцать седьмóй автóбус
    she got onto a number twenty-seven bus

сердúться/рассердúться 'to be angry'
    онá почемý-то всегдá сердúлась на негó
    for some reason she always got angry with him

смотрéть/посмотрéть 'to look'
    посмотрúте на лицó ведýщего!   look at the presenter's face

ссылáться/сослáться 'to refer to'
    водúтель извинúлся, ссылáясь на плохóе состоя́ние дорóг
    the driver apologized, referring to the poor condition of the roads

трáтить/потрáтить 'to spend'
    почемý ты трáтишь дéньги на такýю ерундý?
    why are you spending money on rubbish like that?

19.1.5 o + accusative

ударя́ться/уда́риться 'to knock against'
    войдя́ в ко́мнату, он уда́рился о табуре́тку
    on entering the room he banged into a stool

19.2 Verbs taking *either* the accusative (definite, concrete) *or* the genitive (indefinite, abstract)

ждать (*impf.* only) 'to wait'

мы ждём тролле́йбус	we're waiting for the trolleybus
мы ждём тролле́йбус *or:* тролле́йбуса	we're waiting for a trolleybus

ожида́ть (*impf.* only) 'to expect'

она́ ожида́ет письмо́ от Ва́си	she's expecting a letter from Vasya
она́ ожида́ет пи́сем от друзе́й	she's expecting letters from friends
она́ ожида́ет по́мощи от нас	she's expecting help from us
она́ ожида́ет ребёнка	she's expecting a child

иска́ть (*impf.* only) 'to look for, seek'

мы и́щем соба́ку	we're looking for the dog
мы и́щем защи́ты	we're looking for protection

проси́ть/попроси́ть 'to ask for'
    кто попроси́л у меня́ ключ от шка́фа?
    who asked me for the cupboard key?

    кто попроси́л у неё разреше́ния откры́ть шкаф?
    who asked her for permission to open the cupboard?

тре́бовать/потре́бовать 'to demand, require'

они́ тре́буют свои́ де́ньги	they're demanding their money
он тре́бует от нас бо́льших уси́лий	he requires greater efforts from us

19.3 Verbs taking the genitive

19.3.1 Straight genitive

боя́ться (*impf.* only) 'to fear, be afraid of'

я бою́сь его́ прие́зда	I fear his arrival
он бои́тся свое́й жены́	he's afraid of his wife

держа́ться (*impf.* only) 'to keep to, stick to'

он всё де́ржится ста́рых взгля́дов	he still keeps to his old views

избега́ть/избежа́ть *or* **избе́гнуть** 'to avoid'
мне удало́сь избежа́ть встре́чи с ни́ми
I managed to avoid a meeting with them

каса́ться/косну́ться 'to concern, touch'
э́то каса́ется на́шей рабо́ты   this concerns our work
дискуссия косну́лась собы́тий в бы́вшей Югосла́вии
the discussion touched on events in the former Jugoslavia

лиша́ться/лиши́ться 'to be deprived of'
по́сле вы́боров он лиши́лся вла́сти   he lost power after the election

опаса́ться (*impf.* only) 'to be apprehensive of'
на́до опаса́ться Со́ни, когда́ она́ в тако́м плохо́м настрое́нии
it's best to steer clear of Sonya when she's in such a bad temper

пуга́ться/испуга́ться 'to be frightened of'
мы все испуга́лись гро́ма   we were all scared of the thunder

стыди́ться/постыди́ться 'to be ashamed of'
постыди́лись бы вы своего́ поведе́ния
you should be ashamed of your behaviour

хвата́ть/хвати́ть 'to be enough, suffice'
тебе́ хвата́ет эне́ргии на э́то?
have you got enough energy for this?

19.3.2 без + genitive

обходи́ться/обойти́сь 'to do without'
мы обойдёмся без него́   we'll manage without him

19.3.3 из + genitive

состоя́ть (*impf.* only) 'to consist of'
план состои́т из не́скольких часте́й   the plan consists of several parts

19.3.4 от + genitive

боле́ть/заболе́ть 'to be, fall ill'
все мы заболе́ли от тако́й жары́   we all fell ill from the heat

возде́рживаться/воздержа́ться 'to refrain from'
мне прихо́дится возде́рживаться от жи́рной пи́щи
I've got to keep off fatty food

зави́сеть (*impf.* only) 'to depend'
    всё зави́сит от него́   it all depends on him
    всё зависит от того́, что она́ ска́жет   it all depends on what she says

освобожда́ться/освободи́ться 'to free oneself'
    мы освободи́лись от всех э́тих нену́жных дел
    we are free of all that useless bureaucracy

отвыка́ть/отвы́кнуть 'to become unaccustomed to'
    она́ давно́ отвы́кла от тако́й ро́скоши
    she hasn't been used to such luxury for a long time

отка́зываться/отказа́ться 'to refuse'
    не на́до бы́ло отка́зываться от того́, что нам предлага́ли
    we shouldn't have refused what they were offering us

отлича́ться/отличи́ться 'to differ, be distinguished'
    её кварти́ра си́льно отлича́ется от на́шей
    her flat is very different from ours

отстава́ть/отста́ть 'to lag behind; to stop pestering'
    отста́нь от меня́!   leave me alone!
    мы уже́ не отстаём от энерге́тиков
    we're no longer lagging behind the power workers

пря́тать/спря́тать 'to hide'
    он пря́чет все свои́ де́ньги от нас   he hides all his money from us

скрыва́ть/скрыть 'to conceal'
    он скрыва́ет от нас все свои́ мечты́
    he conceals all his pipedreams from us

спаса́ть/спасти́ 'to save, rescue'
    она́ спасла́ его́ от алкоголи́зма   she saved him from alcoholism

тре́бовать/потре́бовать 'to demand'
    больши́е уси́лия тре́буются от всех уча́стников
    big efforts are required from all participants

19.3.5 про́тив + genitive

возража́ть/возрази́ть 'to object, retort'
    кто-то до́лжен возрази́ть про́тив э́того реше́ния
    someone's got to object to this decision

восстава́ть/восста́ть 'to rise up against'
народ восста́л про́тив реше́ния прави́тельства
the populace rose up against the government's decision

протестова́ть (*impf.* and *pf.*) 'to protest'
почему́ лю́ди протесту́ют про́тив нало́гов
why do people protest against taxes?

19.3.6 c + genitive

начина́ть/нача́ть 'to begin'

с чего́ нача́ть?	what shall we start with?
дава́й начнём с са́мого нача́ла	let's begin at the very beginning

19.4 Verbs taking the dative

19.4.1 Straight dative

ве́рить/пове́рить 'to believe'

тру́дно бы́ло пове́рить ему́	it was difficult to believe him
не верь тому́, что тебе́ говоря́т мужчи́ны!	don't believe what men tell you

вреди́ть/повреди́ть 'to harm'
я ча́сто ем проду́кты, кото́рые вредя́т моему́ здоро́вью
I often eat food that harms my health

грози́ть/погрози́ть 'to threaten'

он погрози́л нам кулако́м	he threatened us with his fist

доверя́ть/дове́рить 'to trust'

они́ доверя́ют врача́м во всём	they trust the doctors in all things
мы доверили деньги Бори́су	we entrusted the money to Boris

зави́довать/позави́довать 'to envy'

как я зави́довал тебе́!	how I envied you!
она́ зави́дует успе́ху бра́та	she envies her brother his success

запреща́ть/запрети́ть 'to prohibit, forbid'
категори́чески запреща́ю вам уходи́ть без меня́
I forbid you categorically to leave without me

изменя́ть/измени́ть 'to betray'
счита́ется до сих пор, что они́ измени́ли Ро́дине
it is thought to this day that they betrayed the Motherland

меша́ть/помеша́ть 'to interfere, prevent, stop'
не меша́й мне чита́ть! don't stop me reading

моли́ться/помоли́ться 'to pray'
они́ всё мо́лятся Бо́гу о сча́стье
they keep praying to God for happiness

мстить/отомсти́ть 'to avenge'
она́ отомсти́ла ему́ за сестру́
she took revenge on him for her sister

надоеда́ть/надое́сть 'to bore'
как он надое́л мне со свои́ми расска́зами! how fed up I am with his stories

нра́виться/понра́виться 'to please'
Со́не ужа́сно понра́вился Нью Йорк
Sonya liked New York tremendously

отка́зывать/отказа́ть 'to refuse'
Ма́ша отказа́ла ему́ в деньга́х Masha refused him money

подража́ть (*impf.* only) 'to imitate'
он постоя́нно подража́ет популя́рным певца́м
he's constantly imitating popular singers

подчиня́ться/подчини́ться 'to submit, be subordinated'
никто́ не хоте́л подчиня́ться зако́ну
no one wanted to submit to the law

позволя́ть/позво́лить 'to allow, permit'
как ты позволя́ешь ему́ поступа́ть с тобо́й так жесто́ко?
how can you allow him to treat you so cruelly?

помога́ть/помо́чь 'to help'
помоги́те друзья́м! help your friends

предше́ствовать (*impf.* only) 'to precede'
револю́ция предше́ствовала гражда́нской войне́
the revolution preceded the civil war

препя́тствовать/воспрепя́тствовать 'to hinder, prevent'
долги́ препя́тствовали нам достро́ить гара́ж
debts prevented us from finishing the garage

прика́зывать/приказа́ть 'to order, command'
генера́л приказа́л солда́там стреля́ть
the general ordered the soldiers to fire

принадлежа́ть (*Impf.* only) 'to belong'

машṍна принадлежṍт сосе́ду   the car belongs to our neighbour

проти́виться/воспроти́виться 'to oppose'

сопе́рники недо́лго проти́вились нам

our opponents did not resist us long

противоре́чить (*impf.* only) 'to contradict; run counter to'

иногда́ она́ противоре́чила ма́тери

she sometimes contradicted her mother

э́то реше́ние противоре́чит здра́вому смы́слу

this decision contradicts common sense

разреша́ть/разреши́ть 'to allow, permit'

они́ разреши́ли нам собира́ть цветы́   they allowed us to pick flowers

рекомендова́ть (*impf.* and *pf.*, alternative perfectives **порекомендова́ть, отрекомендова́ть**) 'to recommend'

порекомендова́ли инжене́ру измени́ть констру́кцию

the engineer was recommended to change the design

сове́товать/посове́товать 'to advise'

я сове́тую вам прийти́ пора́ньше   I advise you to get here a bit earlier

соотве́тствовать (*impf.* only) 'to correspond, be equivalent to'

кварти́ра вполне́ соотве́тствует их тре́бованиям

the flat fits their requirements completely

сопротивля́ться (*impf.* only) 'to resist, oppose'

на́ши войска́ упо́рно сопротивля́ются врагу́

our troops are resisting the enemy stubbornly

сочу́вствовать (*impf.* only) 'to sympathize'

кто не сочу́вствует ма́тери больно́го ребёнка?

who can help sympathizing with the mother of a sick child?

спосо́бствовать/поспосо́бствовать 'to assist'

иностра́нный капита́л спосо́бствует разви́тию эконо́мики

foreign capital is assisting the development of the economy

угрожа́ть (*Impf.* only) 'to threaten'

безрабо́тица угрожа́ет мно́гим предприя́тиям

unemployment threatens many factories

удивля́ться/удиви́ться 'to be surprised'

мы удиви́лись тому́, что случи́лось

we were surprised by what happened

учи́ться/научи́ться 'to learn'
> мы давно́ у́чимся э́тому языку́
> we've been learning this language a long time

19.4.2 Accusative for direct object and dative for indirect

дава́ть/дать 'to give'
> кто дал ему́ пра́во звони́ть?   who gave him the right to phone?

обеща́ть/пообеща́ть 'to promise'
> он обеща́л де́тям конфе́ты   he promised the children sweets

подверга́ть/подве́ргнуть 'to subject'
> мы подве́ргли мото́р испыта́нию   we subjected the engine to a test

поруча́ть/поручи́ть 'to entrust, commission'
> она́ поручи́ла им реше́ние   she entrusted the decision to them

посвяща́ть/посвяти́ть 'to dedicate'
> я посвящу́ ей стихи́   I'll dedicate the poem to her
> мы посвяти́ли мно́го вре́мени э́тому де́лу
> we devoted a lot of time to this business

предлага́ть/предложи́ть 'to suggest, offer, propose'
> я предложу́ дире́ктору ваш план
> I'll propose your plan to the headmaster

предпочита́ть/предпоче́сть 'to prefer'
> не́которые предпочита́ют Че́хова Толсто́му
> some prefer Chekhov to Tolstoy

припи́сывать/приписа́ть 'to ascribe'
> мы припи́сываем высо́кий урожа́й ра́нней весне́
> we ascribe the good harvest to the early spring

проща́ть/прости́ть 'to forgive'
> я проща́ю му́жу его́ стра́нное поведе́ние
> I forgive my husband his odd behaviour

уступа́ть/уступи́ть 'to cede, yield'
> они́ уступи́ли нам доро́гу   they gave way for us

19.4.3 к + dative

гото́виться/пригото́виться 'to prepare'
весь ме́сяц он гото́вится к откры́тию вы́ставки
all month he's been preparing for the opening of the exhibition

обраща́ться/обрати́ться 'to turn to, address'
они́ обрати́лись к президе́нту за по́мощью
they turned to the president for help

относи́ться/отнести́сь 'to relate to, treat; to date from'
почему́ вы так пло́хо отно́ситесь к мое́й сестре́?
why do you have such a hostile attitude to my sister?
собо́р отно́сится к оди́ннадцатому ве́ку
the cathedral dates from the eleventh century

прибавля́ть/приба́вить 'to add'
он ничего́ не приба́вил к уже́ ска́занному им
he added nothing to what had been said by him already

прибега́ть/прибе́гнуть 'to resort to'
иногда́ прихо́дится прибега́ть к хи́трости
one sometimes has to resort to cunning

приближа́ться/приблизи́ться 'to approach'
электри́чка приближа́ется к ста́нции
the (suburban) train is approaching the station

привыка́ть/привы́кнуть 'to get used, accustomed to'
я ника́к не привы́кну к тако́му шу́му
I'll never get used to noise like that

прикле́ивать/прикле́ить 'to glue, stick'
прикле́йте афи́шу к стене́!   stick the poster to the wall

прикрепля́ть/прикрепи́ть 'to fix, attach'
прикрепи́те но́мер к две́ри!   fix the number to the door

принадлежа́ть (*impf.* only) 'to belong (to a group), be a member of'
всегда́ счита́лось, что он принадлежи́т к импрессиони́стам
it was always thought that he belonged to the Impressionists

присоединя́ться/присоедини́ться 'to join'
все на́ши студе́нты присоедини́лись к экспеди́ции
all our students joined the expedition

пристава́ть/приста́ть 'to pester, keep coming up to'

    де́ти постоя́нно пристава́ли к посети́телям

    the children kept pestering the visitors

ревнова́ть/(приревнова́ть) 'to be jealous'

    он ревпу́ет меня́ к мои́м многочи́слснным друзья́м

    he is jealous of my numerous friends

стреми́ться (*impf.* only) 'to strive, aspire'

    с са́мого де́тства она́ стреми́лась к вла́сти

    ever since childhood she had been striving for power

19.5 Verbs taking the instrumental

19.5.1 Straight instrumental

боле́ть/заболе́ть 'to be ill'

    он боле́ет гри́ппом   he's got flu

владе́ть (*impf.* only) 'to own, possess, be master of'

    они́ владе́ли тремя́ магази́нами   they used to own three shops

    она́ отли́чно владе́ет францу́зским языко́м

    she has an excellent command of French

вы́глядеть (*impf.* only) 'to look, have the appearance of'

    о́вощи вы́глядят све́жими   the vegetables look fresh

    сего́дня он вы́глядел идио́том   he looked like an idiot today

горди́ться/возгорди́ться 'to be proud of'

    мы о́чень горди́мся свои́м успе́хом   we're very proud of our success

    я горжу́сь тем, что мы вы́играли   I'm proud of our having won

дыша́ть/подыша́ть 'to breathe'

    здесь мы ды́шим све́жим во́здухом   here we breathe fresh air

же́ртвовать/поже́ртвовать 'to sacrifice'

    они́ поже́ртвуют значи́тельными де́нежными су́ммами

    they'll sacrifice significant sums of money

заве́довать (*impf.* only) 'to run, manage'

    он заве́дует фа́брикой   he manages the factory

занима́ться/заня́ться 'to engage in; study'

    я занима́юсь свои́ми дела́ми   I'm minding my own business

    мы занима́емся спо́ртом   we do sport

    она́ занима́ется хи́мией   she does chemistry

заража́ться/зарази́ться 'to catch, be infected by'
    он зарази́тся гри́ппом   he'll catch flu
    мы зарази́лись его́ энтузиа́змом
    we were infected by his enthusiasm

злоупотребля́ть/злоупотреби́ть 'to abuse, overdo'
    мно́гие лю́ди злоупотребля́ют спиртны́ми напи́тками
    a lot of people abuse strong drink

изоби́ловать   (*impf.* only) 'to abound'
    река́ изоби́лует ры́бой   the river abounds in fish

интересова́ться/заинтересова́ться 'to be interested'
    сын заинтересова́лся нау́кой   my son's got interested in science
    (*but:* он заинтересо́ван в прода́же карти́н
    he has an interest in the sale of the pictures)

каза́ться/показа́ться 'to seem' (see also p. 269)
    отве́т показа́лся стра́нным   the answer seemed strange

любова́ться/полюбова́ться 'to admire'
    она́ любу́ется красото́й пейза́жа
    she's admiring the beauty of the landscape

маха́ть/махну́ть 'to wave'
    они́ всегда́ ма́шут нам платко́м
    they always wave to us with a handkerchief
    он махну́л на всё руко́й   he abandoned everything

называ́ться/назва́ться 'to be called'
    го́род называ́лся це́нтром цивилиза́ции
    the town was called the centre of civilization
    (*but:* го́род называ́лся Ленингра́д   the town was called Leningrad)

наслажда́ться/наслади́ться 'to enjoy'
    мы наслажда́емся морски́м во́здухом   we're enjoying the sea air

овладева́ть/овладе́ть 'to take control, master'
    они́ овладе́ли го́родом   they took the town
    стра́нное чу́вство овладе́ло им   a strange feeling took hold of him

ограни́чиваться/ограни́читься 'to confine oneself, be limited'
    он ограни́чивается одно́й сига́рой в день
    he limits himself to one cigar a day
    они́ ограни́чились тем, что постро́или оди́н дом
    they restricted themselves to building one house

остава́ться/оста́ться 'to stay, remain'

    мы оста́лись друзья́ми   we remained friends

отлича́ться/отличи́ться 'to differ'

    его́ да́ча отлича́ется свои́м разме́ром от всех други́х
    his dacha differs in its size from all the others

па́хнуть/запа́хнуть 'to smell, stink'

    от я́мы па́хло се́рой   the hole smelt of sulphur

по́льзоваться/воспо́льзоваться 'to use, exploit; enjoy'

    дава́й воспо́льзуемся слу́чаем   let's make use of the chance
    он воспо́льзовался её трудо́м   he exploited her labour
    она́ по́льзуется популя́рностью среди́ определённой пу́блики
    she enjoys popularity among a particular audience

притворя́ться/протвори́ться 'to pretend'

    он притвори́лся милиционе́ром   he pretended to be a policeman

сла́виться/просла́виться 'to be renowned'

    куро́рт сла́вится мя́гким кли́матом
    the resort is renowned for its gentle climate
    он просла́вился свои́м го́лосом   he became famous for his voice

служи́ть/послужи́ть 'to serve'

    ба́нка служи́ла нам ча́шкой   the jar served us as a cup
    он слу́жит пять лет гла́вным инжене́ром
    he's been working for five years as chief engineer

станови́ться/стать 'to become'

    она́ всю жизнь хоте́ла стать знамени́той актри́сой
    all her life she wanted to become a famous actress

счита́ться (*impf.* only) 'to be considered'

    он счита́ется выдаю́щимся худо́жником
    he is considered to be an outstanding artist

увлека́ться/увле́чься 'to be keen on'

    она́ увлекла́сь му́зыкой   she's become crazy about music

угоща́ть/угости́ть) 'to treat'

    мы угости́ли их борщо́м   we treated them to borshch

удовлетворя́ться/удовлетвори́ться 'to satisfy oneself'

    они́ удовлетвори́лись состоя́нием общежи́тия
    they were satisfied with the condition of the hostel

управля́ть (*impf.* only) 'to control, run'
    она́ управля́ет фина́нсами предприя́тия   she manages the firm's finances

хва́статься/похва́статься 'to boast'
    он хва́стается свои́м бога́тством   he's boasting of his wealth

явля́ться (*impf.* only) 'to be' (see also p. 177)
    он явля́ется мои́м лу́чшим дру́гом   he's my best friend

19.5.2 за + instrumental

гна́ться *and* **гоня́ться** /**погна́ться** 'to pursue, chase'
    все мы го́нимся за сча́стьем   we're all chasing happiness

следи́ть/проследи́ть 'to watch, follow, keep an eye on'
    она́ следи́т за его́ посту́пками   she is watching what he does

сле́довать/после́довать 'to follow'
    сле́дуйте за мной!   follow me
    уро́к сле́дует за переры́вом   the lesson follows the break

смотре́ть/посмотре́ть 'to watch, look after'
    никто́ не смо́трит за старико́м   no one is looking after the old man

уха́живать (*impf.* only) 'to look after; woo'
    ба́бушка уха́живает за детьми́
    grandma's looking after the children
    он уха́живает за бога́той вдово́й   he's courting a wealthy widow

19.5.3 над + instrumental

издева́ться (*impf.* only) 'to mock, play tricks on'
    сержа́нт жесто́ко издева́ется над солда́тами
    the sergeant is making life a misery for the soldiers

преоблада́ть (*impf.* only) 'to predominate'
    здра́вый смысл, наконе́ц, преоблада́ет над предрассу́дками
    common sense is at last prevailing over prejudice

смея́ться/засмея́ться 'to laugh'
    почему́ они́ смею́тся над на́ми?   why are they laughing at us?

19.5.4 перед + instrumental

преклоня́ться/преклони́ться 'to bow down, worship'
молодёжь преклоня́ется пе́ред совреме́нной те́хникой
young people worship modern technology

унижа́ться/уни́зиться 'to degrade oneself'
не́чего унижа́ться всё вре́мя пе́ред ним
there's no need to demean yourself in front of him all the time

19.5.5 с + instrumental

встреча́ться/встре́титься 'to meet (by arrangement)'
за́втра мы встре́тимся с мини́стром   tomorrow we'll meet the minister

здоро́ваться/поздоро́ваться 'to greet, shake hands and say hullo'
он ка́ждый раз здоро́вается со мной   he says hullo to me every time

знако́миться/познако́миться 'to get acquainted'
они́ познако́мились друг с дру́гом в Я́лте
they got to know each other in Yalta

конкури́ровать (*impf.* only) 'to compete'
на́ше предприя́тие конкури́рует с неме́цкой фи́рмой
our factory is competing with a German firm

примиря́ться/примири́ться 'to be reconciled'
мы постепе́нно примири́лись с мы́слью об отъе́зде
we gradually got used to the idea of departure

свя́зываться/связа́ться 'to communicate, be connected'
они́ свя́зываются с на́ми электро́нной по́чтой
they communicate with us by e-mail

соединя́ться/соедини́ться 'to join, combine, unite'
на́ша у́лица соединя́ется с Не́вским проспе́ктом
our street joins Nevsky Prospect

сочета́ться (*impf.* and *pf.*) 'to combine'
э́тот цвет хорошо́ сочета́ется с твои́м костю́мом
this colour goes well with your suit

справля́ться/спра́виться 'to deal with'
онá отли́чно справля́лась со все́ми на́шими проблéмами
she used to cope superbly with all our problems

сра́вниваться/сравни́ться 'to be compared'
э́та систе́ма мо́жет сравни́ться с на́шей   this system can compare with ours

ста́лкиваться/столкну́ться 'to collide'
он столкну́лся с ней в метро́   he bumped into her in the metro

19.6 Verbs taking the prepositional

19.6.1 в + prepositional

нужда́ться (*impf.* only) 'to need'
мы нужда́емся в подде́ржке   we need support

обвиня́ть/обвини́ть 'to accuse'
онá обвини́ла его́ в лицеме́рии   she accused him of hypocrisy

отка́зывать/отказа́ть 'to refuse'
они́ отказа́ли нам в по́мощи   they refused us help

ошиба́ться/ошиби́ться 'to be mistaken'
мы ошиблись в их наме́рениях
we were wrong about their intentions

подозрева́ть/заподо́зрить 'to suspect'
он подозрева́л её в воровстве́   he suspected her of theft

признава́ться/призна́ться 'to admit, confess'
я признаю́сь в обма́не   I admit the deception

разочаро́вываться/разочарова́ться 'to be disappointed'
она разочарова́лась в нём   she was disillusioned in him

сознава́ться/созна́ться 'to confess, plead guilty'
мы должны́ созна́ться в оши́бке   we have to admit our mistake

сомнева́ться/усомни́ться 'to doubt'
никто́ не сомнева́ется в его́ спосо́бностях   no one doubts his abilities

состоя́ть (*impf.* only) 'to consist in'
цель програ́ммы состои́т в разви́тии конта́ктов
the aim of the programme consists in the development of contacts

убежда́ть/убеди́ть 'to convince'
    он убеди́л её в свое́й и́скренности   he convinced her of his sincerity

упрека́ть/упрекну́ть 'to reproach'
    они́ упрекну́ли нас в неосторо́жности
    they reproached us for our carelessness

уча́ствовать (*impf.* only) 'to participate'
    она́ уча́ствует в фестива́ле   she's taking part in the festival

19.6.2 на + prepositional

жени́ться (*impf.* and *pf.*) 'to marry (of a man)'
    он жени́лся на до́чери президе́нта
    he married the president's daughter
(**жени́ться/пожени́ться** 'to marry (of couples)'
    они пожени́лись   they got married)

игра́ть/сыгра́ть 'to play (an instrument)'
    он игра́ет на балала́йке   he plays the balalaika

наста́ивать/настоя́ть 'to insist'
    они́ настоя́ли на повыше́нии зарпла́ты   they insisted on a pay rise

19.6.3 о + prepositional

беспоко́иться/обеспоко́иться 'to worry, be anxious'
    она́ беспоко́ится о его́ здоро́вье   she is worried about his health

забо́титься/озабо́титься *or* **позабо́титься** 'to care, concern oneself'
    они́ забо́тятся о права́х челове́ка
    they are concerned about human rights

напомина́ть/напо́мнить 'to remind'
    мы напо́мнили ему́ о да́те вы́боров
    we reminded him of the date of the elections

19.6.4 о + prepositional, по + prepositional or по + dative

скуча́ть/соску́читься 'to miss, hanker for'
    мы соску́чились о нём, *or* по нём, *or* по нему́ we missed him

EXERCISE

Complete the sentences using the words in brackets with the appropriate preposition if necessary:

Борис Николаевич возглавляет (русская делегация).

Я хотел предупредить (Борис Николаевич) об опасности.

Она просит (я) избегать (контакт) с Николаем.

Я спросила (Нина Петровна), как пользоваться (микрофон).

Какой-то мальчик преследует (моя сестра).

Борис Николаевич отказался платить (покупки) жены.

Маша всегда верит (мой брат), когда он обещает (она), что он не встречается (Таня).

Борис Николаевич поверил (успех) команды.

Нина Петровна постепенно превратилась (энтузиаст) по теннису.

Друзья постоянно жалуются (холодная погода).

Ничто не влияет (его манера) говорить.

Мы все надеемся (победа).

Почему она так рассердилась (Борис Николаевич)?

Они ждут (помощь) от американцев.

Студенты лишаются (свои музыкальные инструменты).

Если боишься (дождь), не выходи на улицу.

Русские машины отличаются (прочность) (все другие иностранные машины).

Не смотри (он) — он обязательно потребует (деньги).

Соседи мешают (Иван Васильевич) спать.

Нина Петровна запретила (свой муж) пить днём.

Александр Павлович поможет (французские туристы) найти гостиницу.

Ключи принадлежат (Лидия Михайловна).

Не рекомендуется (новые студенты) связываться (Николай Александрович).

Советуем (все студенты) следить (свой паспорт).

В школе она училась (испанский язык).

Я отношусь хорошо (все мои соседи).

Наш профессор выглядит совершенно (здоровый).

Брат занимается (автоспорт).

Директор заинтересовался (дополнительный план).

Самолёты служат (самое надёжное средство) эвакуации.

Девушки чаще всего знакомятся (мальчики) в клубе.

Никто не сомневается (искренность) Петра Алексеевича.

Его друзья никогда не отказывают (он) (помощь).

Он никогда́ не отка́зывается (по́мощь) свои́х друзе́й.
Большинство́ молоды́х люде́й уча́ствует (спорти́вные соревнова́ния).
Па́вел Петро́вич наста́ивает (отли́чное поведе́ние).

20 NEGATIVES

20.1 Не 'not'

20.1.1 With the verb **быть**, the following noun or adjective will be in the same case or form as for the positive:

он генера́л	he is a general	**он не генера́л**	he is not a general
э́то молоко́	this is milk	**э́то не молоко́**	this isn't milk
мы дово́льны	we are happy	**мы не дово́льны**	we aren't happy

он был генера́лом he was a general
он не был генера́лом he wasn't a general

пье́са бу́дет смешна́я *or* смешно́й *or* смешна́
the play will be funny
пье́са не бу́дет смешна́я *or* **смешно́й** *or* **смешна́**
the play won't be funny

Жемчу́жины наро́дной му́дрости

> рабо́та не медве́дь, в лес не уйдёт work isn't a bear, it won't go off into the woods

20.1.2 When negated with **не** transitive verbs sometimes require the direct object in the genitive; this is normal when the object is an abstract noun or indefinite:

он потеря́л наде́жду	he has lost hope
он не потеря́л наде́жды	he hasn't lost hope (abstract)
cf. **он не потеря́л соба́ку**	he hasn't lost his dog (concrete)

она́ полу́чит письмо́	she'll get a letter *or* the letter
она́ не полу́чит письма́	she won't get a letter (any letter)
cf. **она́ не полу́чит письмо́**	she won't get the letter (the one we know she was waiting for)

Жемчу́жины наро́дной му́дрости

> игра́ не сто́ит свеч the game is not worth any candles

20.1.3 With intransitive verbs **не** has no effect on the case of dependent nouns or adjectives:

он спит на дива́не	he sleeps on the sofa
он не спит на дива́не	he doesn't sleep on the sofa
она́ рабо́тает весь день в ба́нке	she works in the bank all day
она́ не рабо́тает весь день в ба́нке	she doesn't work all day in the bank

20.2 Нет 'there is no ..., there isn't any, there aren't any'

20.2.1 **нет**, and its past-tense form **не́ было** 'there wasn't any, there weren't any' and future **не бу́дет** 'there won't be any' take the genitive always, either singular or plural:

нет молока́ 'there is no milk	нет пи́сем 'there are no letters'
не́ было молока́ 'there was no milk'	не́ было пи́сем 'there were no letters'
не бу́дет молока́ 'there will be no milk'	не бу́дет пи́сем 'there will be no letters'

Note: **нет**, **не́ было** and **не бу́дет** do *not* change, regardless of whether the noun is *masc., fem.* or *neut., sing.* or *plur.*

Жемчу́жины наро́дной му́дрости

нет ды́ма без огня́	there's no smoke without a fire

- A number of impersonal negative expressions, which may be thought of as variations of **нет** take the genitive, including **не ви́дно** 'cannot be seen', **не слы́шно** 'is inaudible', **не оста́лось** 'there is none left', **не хвата́ет** 'there's not enough:

не ви́дно маяка́ отсю́да	the lighthouse can't be seen from here
не слы́шно бу́дет му́зыки	(we) won't be able to hear the music
не оста́лось ма́сла	there's no butter left
не хвата́ло эне́ргии	there wasn't enough electricity

Note: **нет** is used on its own just to mean 'no'. When used to answer a question containing the verb 'to be', the colloquial form **не́ту** may be used:

– у тебя́ есть ма́рки? – Не́ту	Have you got any stamps? Nope

20.2.2 Used with persons, **нет** + *gen.* does not normally mean that they don't exist, simply that they are out:

его́ нет 'he's not here'	её не́ было 'she wasn't in, she wasn't there'

дире́ктора не бу́дет на заседа́нии
the director won't be at the meeting

20.3 Никто́ 'no one'; ничто́, ничего́ 'nothing'; никако́й 'no' (*adj.*); ниче́й 'no one's'

20.3.1 These negative pronouns and adjectives, like the negative adverbs below, require the negative particle **не** to accompany any verb associating with them, resulting in what looks like a double negative:

никто́ не по́мнит	no one remembers
мы **никого́ не** по́мним	we don't remember anyone
ничто́ не тро́гало его́	nothing moved him
я **ничего́ не** понима́ю	I don't understand anything
никако́й врач **не** помо́жет	no doctor will help
ниче́й биле́т **не** вы́играл	no one's ticket won

Note: никто́ declines like кто (see p. 62); ничто́ like что (see p. 62); никако́й like сухо́й (see p. 32); and ниче́й like чей see (p. 62).

20.3.2 When used with a preposition, the pronoun divides after **ни-**:

мы **ни за кого́ не** пла́тим	we're not paying for anyone
он **ни с кем не** говори́т	he doesn't talk to anyone
я **ни за что не** пойду́	I won't go for anything
она́ **ни о чём не** забо́тится	she doesn't care about anything

она́ **ни при каки́х** усло́виях **не** поёт
she doesn't sing under any circumstances

я **ни за чью** соба́ку **не** отвеча́л
I wasn't responsible for anyone's dog

20.3.3 The nominative form **ничто́** is used only as the subject of transitive verbs:

ничто́ не расстра́ивает её	nothing upsets her

and with short form adjectives:

ничто́ не ве́чно	nothing is permanent

Otherwise, for instance as the subject of intransitive verbs, **ничего́** is used:

ничего́ не случи́лось	nothing happened

почти́ **ничего́ не** оста́нется
almost nothing will remain, there'll be almost nothing left

Note: **никого́ нет** there is nobody, there's no one in, there's no one about
никого́ не бу́дет   there won't be anyone here

ничего́ нет	there is nothing
ничего́ не́ было	there was nothing

Note: **ничего́** has several colloquial meanings: 'all right', 'so-so', 'OK', etc.

ничего́! — it's all right, no harm done

пого́да сего́дня ничего́ — the weather's not too bad today

Note: **ничто́** can be used to mean 'a nonentity'; in this sense it does not divide:

он преврати́лся в ничто́ — he's turned into a nobody

20.4 Ни оди́н 'not a single'

The phrase ни оди́н (ни одна́, etc.; for the declension of оди́н see p. 210) is used for emphasis:

ни одна́ же́нщина не хоте́ла рабо́тать с ним
not a single woman wanted to work with him

я не ви́дела ни одного́ трамва́я — I didn't see a single tram

ни у одного́ из них не́ было биле́та — not one of them had a ticket

20.5 Нигде́ 'nowhere' (position); никуда́ 'nowhere' (direction); никогда́ 'never'; ника́к 'not at all'

These all require **не** with the verb:

мы **нигде́ не** останови́лись — we didn't stop anywhere

она́ **никуда́ не** пое́дет ле́том — she won't go anywhere this summer

он **никогда́ не** улыба́ется — he never smiles

я **ника́к не** могла́ поня́ть, что ему́ ну́жно
I couldn't understand at all what he was after

20.6 Не́кто 'someone', не́что 'something' and their oblique cases

20.6.1 In the nominative case these mean 'somebody' and 'something', respectively, and are *not* negative: не́кто = кто-то, and не́что = что-то.

к нам подошёл **не́кто** в се́ром костю́ме
someone in a grey suit came up to us

во всей э́той исто́рии бы́ло **не́что** стра́нное
there was something strange in this whole story

20.6.2 The oblique cases, however, **не́кого, не́чего**, etc. are negative and are used with the infinitive, *without* не or нет, to make negative assertions of the kind 'there is no one to ask', 'there was nothing to do':

не́кого пригласи́ть	there's no one to invite
не́кому писа́ть	there's no one to write to
не́ с кем идти́	there's no one to go with
не́чего бы́ло де́лать	there was nothing to do
не́чем писа́ть	there's nothing to write with
не́ о чём бу́дет говори́ть	there will be nothing to talk about

Note: the usual accusative of не́что is не́чего (не́чего де́лать 'there is nothing to do', employing the genitive form as the object of a transitive verb in the negative); but when a preposition is required, the accusative не́что is used, dividing as above:

не́ на что сади́ться	there is nothing to sit down on
не́ за что!	don't mention it

Note: не́чего may mean 'there's no need to', 'there is no point in', 'it's useless to':

не́чего спеши́ть	there's no need to hurry
не́чего теря́ть вре́мя здесь	
there's no point in wasting time here	

See also 20.9 below.

20.7 Не́где 'there is nowhere to . . .' (position); не́куда 'there is nowhere to . . .' (direction)

These negative adverbs meaning 'there is nowhere to' are used with the infinitive in the same way as the negative pronouns; не́где refers to a static position, and не́куда to motion or direction:

не́где да́же стоя́ть	there's nowhere even to stand
не́куда бы́ло идти́	there was nowhere to go

20.8 Не́когда 'there's no time to . . .' *or* 'once upon a time'

20.8.1 This negative adverb is also used to introduce an infinitive with the meaning 'there is no time to':

не́когда говори́ть	there's no time to talk
не́когда бу́дет отдохну́ть	there will be no time to relax

20.8.2 But не́когда has a second meaning of 'formerly' 'once upon a time':

не́когда там стоя́ла це́рковь
at one time there was a church there

In this sense не́когда may be used with the past tense of any verb.

20.9 Не́кого, не́чего

With the oblique cases of не́кто, не́что, i.e. не́кого, не́чего, etc., не́где, не́куда and не́когда (meaning 'there is no time to') the 'subject' of the action, the person or object which might perform the action, goes into the dative:

мне не́ с кем говори́ть   there's no one for me to talk to,   I've got no one to talk to

   ему́ не́чего бы́ло де́лать   there was nothing for him to do

   нам не́где сиде́ть   there's nowhere for us to sit

   Никола́ю Петро́вичу не́когда бу́дет ду́мать

   Nikolai Petrovich will have no time to think

Note: this can result in ambiguity, which may be resolved by context and word order:

   ей не́кому писа́ть   there's no one for her to write to

   не́кому ей писа́ть   there is no one to write to her

   не́кому бу́дет помо́чь   there'll be nobody to help

Note: these negative pronouns, adjectives and adverbs can only be used with the infinitive of the verb; no verb, other than бы́ло or бу́дет, can occur in the same phrase.

EXERCISES

(i)   a.   *Translate into English;* b. *put into the past tense;* c. *put into the future:*

   У него́ нет до́ма.
   У нас нет соба́ки.
   У вас нет дете́й?
   У неё нет биле́та.
   У меня́ нет биле́тов.
   У Серге́я нет де́нег.
   У нас нет рабо́ты.
   У Васи́лия Петро́вича нет зубо́в.
   У тебя́ почти́ нет молока́.
   У мое́й жены́ нет самова́ра.
   У мои́х друзе́й нет сомне́ния.
   У ва́ших студе́нтов нет подозре́ний?
   У нас нет пробле́м.

(ii) *Translate into Russian:*

1   He never reads anything.
2   No one likes him.
3   She wasn't going anywhere.
4   He never plays with his brothers.
5   He never plays with anyone.
6   They'll never work in Siberia.
7   The students didn't ever spend anything anywhere.
8   No way can they open the fridge.

9   They aren't interested in this; they aren't interested in anything.
10 We aren't responsible for him; we aren't responsible for anyone.
11 This doesn't relate to them; it doesn't relate to anyone.
12 She isn't guilty of this; she isn't guilty of anything.

(iii) *Translate into Russian and respond according to the model:*

1   She never invites me   She never invites anyone
2   She never writes to me
3   She never visits me
4   She never advises me
5   She never addresses me
6   She never relies on me
7   She never waits for me
8   She never helps me
9   She never talks to me
10 She never shouts at me
11 She never laughs at me
12 She never complains about me
13 She never comes to fetch me
14 She never takes care of me
15 She never approaches me

(iv) *Translate into English:*

'Вдруг я вижу Лилю . . . Она не одна! Рядом с ней стоит парень в шляпе и смотрит на меня . . .

Мы знакомимся. Он крепко жмёт мне руку. В его пожатии уверенность.

– Ты знаешь, Алёша, сегодня у нас с тобой ничего не выйдет. Мы идём сейчас в Большой театр . . . Ты не обижаешься?

– Нет, я не обижаюсь.

– Ты проводишь нас немножко? Тебе ведь всё равно сейчас нечего делать.

– Провожу. Мне действительно нечего делать.

Доходим до Большого театра, останавливаемся. Молчим. Совершенно не о чём говорить' (Kazakov).

'Поблизости не было никого, и некому было крикнуть о помощи' (Kazakov).

'Она никаких идей не имеет ни о воспитании, ни о физиологии, ни о чём.' (Turgenev).

'– Всё это вздор . . . Я не нуждаюсь ни в чьей помощи, – промолвил Павел Петрович' (Turgenev).

'– Феничка! – сказал он. – Любите моего брата! Он такой добрый, хороший человек. Не изменяйте его ни для кого на свете, не слушайте ничьих речей!

Подумайте, что может быть ужаснее, как любить и не быть любимым! Не покидайте никогда моего бедного Николая!' (Turgenev).

(v) *Translate into Russian:*

1   She wasn't interested in any shoes.
2   You never read any good books.
3   I don't want to move to any town.
4   They weren't living in any hotel.
5   The umbrella wasn't standing behind any door.
6   There's nothing to be afraid of.
7   They had no chairs so there was nothing to sit on.
8   There wasn't anyone to discuss the problem with.
9   There won't be anything for her to write about.
10 There's nobody to complain to.
11 There'll be no one for me to show my work to.
12 There's nothing in the fridge and there's nowhere to get any milk.
13 I don't want to sit at home, but there's nowhere to go here.
14 There's no time to think about Russian grammar.
15 There's no point in worrying about it!

21   NUMERALS

21.1 Cardinal numerals

21.1.1 The number '1'

In Russian 'one' has a masculine form **оди́н**, feminine: **одна́**, neuter: **одно́** and even a plural: **одни́**.

sing.	masc.	fem.	neut.	plur.
nom.	оди́н	одна́	одно́	одни́
acc.	оди́н/одного́	одну́	одно́	одни́/одни́х
gen.	одного́	одно́й	одного́	одни́х
dat.	одному́	одно́й	одному́	одни́м
inst.	одни́м	одно́й	одни́м	одни́ми
pr.	об одно́м	об одно́й	об одно́м	об одни́х

21.1.2 The numbers '2', '3', '4'

In Russian 'two' has a masculine and neuter form **два** and a feminine **две**; **три** 'three' and **четы́ре** 'four' are the same for all genders, but all decline:

	'two' *masc. neut.*	fem.	'three' *(all genders)*	'four' *(all genders)*
nom.	два	две	три	четы́ре
acc.	два/двух	две/двух	три/трёх	четы́ре/четырёх
gen.	двух		трёх	четырёх
dat.	двум		трём	четырём
inst.	двумя́		тремя́	четырьмя́
pr.	о двух		о трёх	о четырёх

21.1.3 The numerals **пять** 'five' and above (but not compounds of 'one', 'two', 'three' or 'four').

Numerals from **пять** 'five' to **два́дцать** 'twenty', and from **двадцать пять** 'twenty five' to **три́дцать** 'thirty' decline like singular feminine nouns in -ь (so there is no distinction in declension of these numerals between animate and inanimate):

	'five'	'eight'	'fifteen'	'twenty seven'
nom.	пять	во́семь	пятна́дцать	два́дцать семь
acc.	пять	во́семь	пятна́дцать	два́дцать семь
gen.	пяти́	восьми́	пятна́дцати	двадцати́ семи́
dat.	пяти́	восьми́	пятна́дцати	двадцати́ семи́
inst.	пятью́	восьмью́	пятна́дцатью	двадцатью́ семью́
		or восемью́		
pr.	о пяти́	о восьми́	о пятна́дцати	двадцати́ семи́

Like пять: **шесть** 'six'; **семь** 'seven'; **де́вять** 'nine'; **де́сять** 'ten'; **оди́ннадцать** 'eleven'; **двена́дцать** 'twelve'; **трина́дцать** 'thirteen'; **четы́рнадцать** 'fourteen'; **пятна́дцать** 'fifteen'; **шестна́дцать** 'sixteen'; **семна́дцать** 'seventeen'; **восемна́дцать** 'eighteen'; **девятна́дцать** 'nineteen'; **два́дцать** 'twenty'; **три́дцать** 'thirty'.

Compound numerals ending in 'one', 'two', 'three' or 'four' are made up straightforwardly, e.g. **два́дцать два** *or* **два́дцать две** 'twenty-two'; **три́дцать четы́ре** 'thirty-four';
both numerals decline, e.g. *pr.* **о двадцати́ одно́м** *or* **о двадцати́ одно́й** 'twenty-one'; **о тридцати́ трёх** 'thirty-three', etc.

21.1.4 The numbers 'forty', 'fifty', 'sixty', 'seventy', 'eighty', 'ninety', 'one hundred':

	'forty'	'fifty'	'eighty'
nom.	со́рок	пятьдеся́т	во́семьдесят
acc.	со́рок	пятьдеся́т	во́семьдесят
gen.	сорока́	пяти́десяти	восьми́десяти
dat.	сорока́	пяти́десяти	восьми́десяти
inst.	сорока́	пятью́десятью	восьмью́десятью
pr.	о сорока́	о пяти́десяти	о восьми́десяти

Like со́рок: **девяно́сто** 'ninety' and **сто** 'a hundred' (*gen., dat., instr.* and *pr.* all end in -a: **девяно́ста, ста**.)

Like пятьдеся́т: **шестьдеся́т** 'sixty' and **се́мьдесят** 'seventy' (*gen., dat.* and *pr.* **шести́десяти, семи́десяти;** *inst.* **шестью́десятью, семью́десятью**.)

21.1.5 The numbers '200', '300', '400'

	'two hundred'	'three hundred'	'four hundred'
nom.	две́сти	три́ста	четы́реста
acc.	две́сти	три́ста	четы́реста
gen.	двухсо́т	трёхсо́т	четырёхсо́т
dat.	двумста́м	трёмста́м	четырёмста́м
inst.	двумяста́ми	тремяста́ми	четырьмяста́ми
pr.	о двухста́х	о трёхста́х	о четырёхста́х

21.1.6 The numbers '500', '600', '700', '800', '900'

	'500'	'800'	'900'
nom.	пятьсо́т	восемьсо́т	девятьсо́т
acc.	пятьсо́т	восемьсо́т	девятьсо́т
gen.	пятисо́т	восьмисо́т	девятисо́т
dat.	пятиста́м	восьмиста́м	девятиста́м
inst.	пятьюста́ми	восьмьюста́ми	девятьюста́ми
pr.	о пятиста́х	о восьмиста́х	о девятиста́х

Like пятьсо́т: **шестьсо́т** 'six hundred' and **семьсо́т** 'seven hundred.

21.1.7 The numbers '1,000', '1,000,000', etc.

ты́сяча '1,000', **миллио́н** '1 million', **миллиа́рд** '1000 million', and **триллио́н** '1 million million' decline regularly as nouns.

21.1.8 Compound numerals

Compound numerals consisting of two or more words, '221', '110', '999', etc., should be declined, e.g.

gen.	**двухсо́т два́дцати одного́** *or* **двухсо́т два́дцати одно́й**
	of two hundred and twenty-one
dat.	**к ста десяти́** towards a hundred and ten
inst.	**с девятьюста́ми девяно́ста девятью́** with nine hundred and ninety-nine

Note: adjectives qualifying numerals go into the plural:
ка́ждые семь мину́т   every seven minutes

21.1.9 Trends in declension

With long compound numerals there is a growing tendency to decline only the final element – and the longer the number, the more likely this is to happen. In spoken Russian it is normal and perfectly acceptable to say:

с три́ста два́дцать двумя́ студе́нтами   with 322 students
(instead of с тремяста́ми двадцатью́ двумя́ . . .)
в две́сти шестьдеся́т семи́ слу́чаях   in 267 cases
(instead of в двухста́х шести́десяти семи́ . . .)

Compare the literary norm and the acceptable spoken form:
(Literary)

я ви́дел ты́сячу два́дцать одну́ студе́нтку   I saw 1,021 students
or   я ви́дел ты́сячу два́дцать одного́ студе́нта

(Spoken)

я ви́дел ты́сяча два́дцать одну́ студе́нтку
or   я ви́дел ты́сяча два́дцать одного́ студе́нта

There is also an accepted alternative practice of declining the first and last elements of a long compound numeral:

о двух ты́сячах две́сти пятьдеся́т пяти́ студе́нтах
concerning the 2,255 students

- In practice long compound numerals are rarely declined, a way is usually found to word the idea in such a way as to leave the numeral in its nominative/accusative form. Instead of trying to say 'they performed before 1,750 listeners' Russian prefers a relatively simple, undeclined or barely declined numeral:

в аудито́рии бы́ло ты́сяча семьсо́т пятьдеся́т челове́к
there were 1,750 people in the auditorium

or: пу́блика насчи́тывала ты́сячу семьсо́т пятьдеся́т челове́к
the audience numbered 1,750

21.1.10 Полтора́, полторы́ 'one and a half'

Полтора́ is used with masculine and neuter nouns, полторы́ with feminine. Their declension is unusual:

	masc./neut.	fem.
nom.	полтора́	полторы́
acc.	полтора́	полторы́
gen.	полу́тора	
dat.	полу́тора	
inst.	полу́тора	
pr.	о полу́тора	

• Óба, óбе 'both'

Óба is used with masculine and neuter nouns, óбе with feminine. Óба/óбе decline in both genders:

	masc.	fem.	neut.
nom.	óба	óбе	óба
acc.	óба/обо́их	óбе/обе́их	óба
gen.	обо́их	обе́их	обо́их
dat.	обо́им	обе́им	обо́им
inst.	обо́ими	обе́ими	обо́ими
pr.	об обо́их	об обе́их	об обо́их

21.1.11 Collective numerals

Collective numerals exist for numbers from 'two' to 'ten', the last three being rare: дво́е, тро́е, че́тверо, пя́теро, ше́стеро, се́меро, во́сьмеро, де́вятеро, де́сятеро. Their declension is as follows:

nom.	двóе	чéтверо
acc.	двóе/двóих	чéтверо/четверьíх
gen.	двóих	четверьíх
dat.	двóим	четверьíм
inst.	двóими	четверьíми
prep.	о двóих	о четверьíх

трóе declines like двóе; **пя́теро** to **дéсятеро** decline like чéтверо.

21.1.12 Fractions

Половина 'half', **треть** 'a third', **чéтверть** 'quarter' are regular feminine nouns. Other fractions are formed with the feminine ordinal (see pp. 227, 228):

      одна́ пя́тая 'one fifth'   одна́ двадца́тая 'a twentieth'

21.1.13 Indefinite numerals

Мнóго 'much, many'; **немнóго** 'a little, few'; **мáло** 'a little'; **немáло** 'not a few, quite a lot'; **скóлько** 'how much, how many?'; **стóлько** 'so much, so many'; **нéсколько** 'several'. Apart from мáло and немáло these decline; мнóго 'many' and немнóго 'a few' have alternative nominative forms normally referring to people:

nom.	мнóго *or* мнóгие	скóлько
acc.	мнóго or мнóгие/мнóгих	скóлько/скóльких
gen.	мнóгих	скóльких
dat.	мнóгим	скóльким
inst.	мнóгими	скóлькими
pr.	о мнóгих	о скóльких

немнóгие declines like мнóгие; стóлько and нéсколько decline like скóлько (see also p. 225).

21.2 Use of numerals

21.2.1 **Оди́н** agrees with the noun it refers to in gender, number and case:

    оди́н дом; óколо одногó дóма; в однóм дóме
    one house; near one house; in one house

    одна́ кни́га; из однóй кни́ги; под однóй кни́гой
    one book; out of one book; under one book

    однó окнó; у одногó окна́; над одни́м окнóм
    one window; by one window; over one window

одни́ часы́; по одни́м часа́м; на одни́х часа́х
one clock (*or* watch); according to one clock; on one clock

он купи́л **одну́ кни́гу**   he bought one book

Note: она́ познако́милась с **одни́м** из студе́нтов 'she got to know one of the students'

21.2.2 With the numerals **два/две, три, четы́ре, о́ба/о́бе** *or* **полтора́/ полторы́** in the nominative or inanimate accusative, nouns dependent on them are in the genitive singular:

там **сиде́ли две студе́нтки**   there sat two female students
там **стоя́ло** *or* **стоя́ли три авто́буса**
there stood three buses
у них **четы́ре ко́мнаты**   they have four rooms
я ви́жу **два окна́**   I can see two windows
она́ купи́ла **три биле́та**   she's bought three tickets
полторы́ то́нны войдёт в **о́ба ваго́на**
1½ tons will fit into both wagons

Note: with 'two' or more (except 'twenty-one', 'thirty-one', 'forty-one', etc.) as the subject of the sentence the verb may be in the singular (neuter form in the past tense) *or* the plural.

21.2.3 The animate accusative forms **двух, трёх** and **четырёх** are followed by the animate accusative plural (= genitive plural) of the noun:

я ви́жу **двух студе́нтов** и **трёх студе́нток**
I see two male and three female students
он зна́ет **э́тих четырёх учени́ц**   he knows these four schoolgirls

Note: animals, fish, birds may be treated as animate *or* inanimate:
ма́льчик пойма́л двух ры́бок *or* **две ры́бки**
the little boy caught two little fish

21.2.4 With the numeral in all other cases the noun follows in the same case in the plural:

(*gen.*) **она́ убира́ет ко́мнату двух студе́нтов**
she cleans the two students' room
(*dat.*) **он писа́л двум студе́нтам**   he wrote to the two students
(*inst.*) **она́ познако́милась с четырьмя́ актёрами**
she got to know four actors
(*pr.*) **они́ узна́ли о трёх кварти́рах**   they heard about three apartments

Жемчу́жины наро́дной му́дрости

за двумя́ за́йцами пого́нишься — ни одного́ не пойма́ешь	chase after two hares and you won't catch one

- With words like часы́ (meaning 'clock', 'watch') which exist only in the plural, the nominative forms два/две, три, четы́ре, which must be followed by the genitive singular, cannot be used. The collective numerals дво́е, тро́е and че́тверо (see pp. 221–3) which are followed by the genitive plural are used instead:

дво́е часо́в 'two clocks'	тро́е сане́й 'three sledges'

- In the other oblique cases the problem of the plural-only nouns disappears, since the appropriate plural case of the noun, not the genitive singular, is required:

цена́ двух часо́в	the price of two watches
на трёх саня́х	on three sledges

21.2.5 The numerals пять 'five' and above (but not compounds of 'one', 'two', 'three' and 'four').

With the numerals пять, шесть, etc. in the nominative or accusative case the noun follows in the genitive plural:

(*nom.*)	там стоя́ло *or* стоя́ли пять домо́в	there stood five house
	там сидя́т два́дцать студе́нток	there sit twenty female students
(*acc.*)	мы ви́дели пять домо́в	we saw five houses
	мы ви́дели пять студе́нтов	we saw five students
	я ви́дел три́дцать птиц	I saw thirty birds

Note: This means that for these numbers above four the accusative construction is the same as the nominative even if the noun is animate.

Жемчу́жины наро́дной му́дрости

у медве́дя де́вять пе́сен, и все про мёд	the bear has nine songs and they're all about honey

21.2.6 With the numerals пять 'five' and above in all other cases the noun follows in the same case in the plural:

(*gen.*)	она́ встре́тила роди́телей пяти́ студе́нтов	she met the five students' parents
(*dat.*)	он писа́л двена́дцати студе́нткам	he wrote to twelve female students
(*inst.*)	она́ познако́милась с двадцатью́ студе́нтами	she got to know twenty students
(*pr.*)	она́ говори́т о десяти́ студе́нтах	she's talking about the ten students

21.2.7 The numbers 'forty', 'fifty', 'sixty', 'seventy', 'eighty', 'ninety', 'one hundred'. The case of the noun with these numerals will be the same as for пять, etc. – genitive plural when the numeral is nominative or accusative, otherwise the same case in the plural as the numeral itself:

(*nom.*)	со́рок тра́кторов стоя́ли в по́ле	forty tractors stood in the field
(*acc.*)	мы нашли́ пятьдеся́т грибо́в	we found fifty mushrooms
(*gen.*)	что оста́лось от пяти́десяти ба́нок?	what's left from the fifty tins?
(*dat.*)	я писа́л шести́десяти чле́нам кружка́	I wrote to sixty members of the club
(*inst.*)	он горди́тся семью́десятью лошадьми́	he is proud of the seventy horses
(*pr.*)	поду́май о девяно́ста шахтёрах!	think of the ninety miners

21.2.8 The compound numerals

With the **compounds of 'one'** ('twenty-one', 'thirty-one', 'forty-one', etc., *but* not 'eleven') the noun is in the same case as оди́н:

(*nom.)* два́дцать оди́н студе́нт сиди́т в столо́вой
twenty-one students are sitting in the canteen

три́дцать одна́ студе́нтка занима́лась в библиоте́ке
thirty-one female students were working in the library

со́рок одно́ сло́во непоня́тно в э́том письме́
forty-one words are incomprehensible in this letter

Note: with a compound of 'one' as subject the verb must be in the singular.

(*acc.*)	я купи́л два́дцать оди́н дом	I bought twenty-one houses
	я встре́тил три́дцать одного́ студе́нта	I met thirty-one students
	он написа́л со́рок одну́ кни́гу	he's written forty-one books

(*gen.*) на стола́х пяти́десяти одного́ слу́жащего стои́т та же фотогра́фия
the same photograph stands on the desks of fifty-one employees

в ко́мнатах пяти́десяти одно́й студе́нтки батаре́и не рабо́тают
the radiators don't work in the rooms of fifty-one female students

(*dat.*) он посла́л календа́рь шести́десяти одному́ учрежде́нию
he sent a calendar to sixty-one departments

мы обеща́ли пода́рки семи́десяти одно́й де́вочке
we promised a present to seventy-one little girls

(*inst.*) она́ познако́милась с восьмью́десятью одни́м ученико́м
she got to know eighty-one pupils

(*pr.*) они́ изуча́ют усло́вия в девяно́ста одно́м го́роде
they are studying conditions in ninety-one towns

21.2.9 Compounds of 'two', 'three', 'four' ('twenty-two', 'twenty-three', 'twenty-four', 'thirty two', 'thirty-three', etc.)

With the numeral in the nominative or accusative case the noun is in the genitive singular:

(*nom.*) два́дцать два студе́нта сиде́ли на траве́
twenty-two students were sitting on the grass

двáдцать две студéнтки сидéли в библиотéке
twenty-two female students were sitting in the library

(*acc.*)   мы замéтили трúдцать три студéнта и сóрок четы́ре студéнтки
we noticed thirty-three male and forty-four female students

Note: with the compound numeral in the accusative case the number is followed by
the noun in the genitive singular, even if the noun is animate:

я вúдел двáдцать два студéнта   I saw twenty-two students

[*cf.*   я вúдел двух студéнтов   I saw two students]

- With the numeral in all other cases the noun follows in the same case in
  the plural:

(*gen.*)   средú восьмúдесяти трёх газéт   among eighty-three newspapers
(*dat.*)   по сорокá двум ýлицам   along forty-two streets
(*inst.*)   с двадцатью́ двумя́ студéнтами   with twenty-two students
(*pr.*)   о пятúдесяти четырёх городáх   concerning fifty-four towns
в шестúдесяти трёх слýчаях   in sixty-three cases

21.2.10 Compounds of 'five', 'six', 'seven', 'eight' and 'nine' ('twenty-five', 'twenty-six', 'twenty-seven', 'twenty-eight', 'twenty-nine', etc.) behave
in the same way as the basic numerals 'five', 'six', etc., namely:
with the numeral in the nominative *or* accusative the noun follows in the
genitive plural:

там бы́ло двáдцать семь студéнтов и трúдцать вóсемь студéнток
there were twenty-seven male and thirty-eight female students

мы вúдели двáдцать семь студéнтов и трúдцать вóсемь студéнток
we saw twenty-seven male and thirty-eight female students

Thus, where constructions with cardinal numerals are concerned, the
problem of the animate accusative affects only 'one', 'two', 'three', 'four' and
the compounds of 'one'; all other accusatives are treated as inanimate.

- With the numeral in all other cases the noun follows in the same case in
  the plural:

(*gen.*)   óколо двадцатú пятú дéвушек   about twenty-five girls
(*dat.*)   к тридцатú восьмú грáдусам   towards thirty-eight degrees
(*inst.*)   со стá девятью́ студéнтами   with 109 students
(*pr.*)   на сорокá шестú стýльях   on forty-six chairs

21.2.11 The Numbers '100'–'999'
The appropriate case of 100 to 900 can precede other single- or two-digit
numbers; the rules for numerals over 'five' apply equally to numbers from
100 to 999:

девятьсо́т со́рок одна́ де́вушка	941 girls
восемьсо́т шестьдеся́т два студе́нта	862 students
от пятисо́т двадцати́ пяти́ де́вушек	from 525 girls
бо́льше четырёхсот десяти́ ма́льчиков	more than 410 boys
к двумста́м тридцати́ восьми́ гра́дусам	
towards 238 degrees	
они́ изуча́ют усло́вия в трёхста́х девяно́ста одно́м го́роде	
they are studying conditions in 391 towns	

21.2.12 The numbers '1,000', '1,000,000', etc.

ты́сяча '1,000', миллио́н '1 million', миллиа́рд '1,000 million', and триллио́н '1 million million' are nouns and are invariably followed by the noun they refer to in the genitive plural (whatever the case of the numeral):

ты́сяча студе́нтов пе́ли	a thousand students were singing
миллио́н рубле́й лежа́л на окне́	
a million rubles were lying on the window-sill	
мы пе́ли вме́сте с ты́сячей студе́нтов	
we were singing together with a thousand students	
он мечта́ет о миллио́не рубле́й	he's longing for a million rubles

- But when these words are followed by lesser numerals, the case of the last one determines the case of the noun:

ты́сяча оди́н студе́нт	a 1,001 students
в ты́сяче двухста́х семна́дцати города́х	
in 1,217 towns	
cf. в ты́сяче городо́в	in 1,000 towns

Note: there is an alternative instrumental of ты́сяча, which is followed by the noun in the instrumental:

с ты́сячью студе́нтами	with 1,000 students
cf. с ты́сячей студе́нтов	

21.2.13 Approximation

To express approximation with the numeral the simplest way is to add an adverb, приблизи́тельно *or* приме́рно 'approximately':

приблизи́тельно ты́сяча коро́в	approximately 1,000 cows
приблизи́тельно в пятиста́х дома́х	in about 500 houses
мы отпра́вили приме́рно два́дцать откры́ток	
we sent off about twenty postcards	

- The neatest way with the numeral as subject (nominative) or direct object (normally accusative) is to **invert** the order of the numeral and the noun:

ме́тров пять шёлка ушло́ на э́тот хала́т	
about five metres of silk went on this dressing gown	
они́ заме́тили волко́в де́сять	they noticed about ten wolves

- Another way with the numeral as subject or direct object is to use the preposition **о́коло** (which takes the genitive):
  о́коло четырёх ме́тров шёлка ушло́ на э́ту пижа́му
  about four metres of silk went on these pyjamas
  они́ заме́тили о́коло пятна́дцати волко́в
  they noticed about fifteen wolves

- **Деся́ток** 'ten of', **со́тня** 'a hundred of' are often used for approximation; the plural деся́тки and со́тни correspond to English 'dozens' and 'hundreds' when used loosely and are followed by the genitive plural:
  мы нашли́ деся́тки грибо́в   we found dozens of mushrooms
  они́ познако́мились с со́тнями де́вушек
  they got to know hundreds of girls

21.2.14 Adjectives with numerals
With one exception adjectives agree with the noun in numeral constructions:
  там был оди́н ру́сский студе́нт
  there was one Russian student there

  мы встре́тили одну́ ру́сскую студе́нтку
  we met one Russian female student

  там сиде́ли пять ру́сских студе́нтов
  there were five Russian students sitting there

  он писа́л пяти́ ру́сским студе́нткам
  he used to write to five Russian female students

  она́ пи́шет об усло́виях в семи́десяти трёх ру́сских города́х
  she's writing about conditions in seventy-three Russian towns

- The only complication is more apparent, than real, and concerns **два**, **три**, **четы́ре** and their compounds in the nominative or nominative-accusative (inanimate) case: with the noun after 'two', 'three' or 'four' in the genitive singular, the adjective goes into the genitive plural if masculine or neuter, and the nominative plural (*or*, sometimes, genitive plural) if feminine:
  два ру́сских студе́нта   two Russian students
  две ру́сские студе́нтки   two Russian female students
  три ру́сских го́рода   three Russian towns
  четы́ре удо́бных кре́сла   four comfy armchairs

(It may help to remember that the use of the genitive singular after два/две, три, четы́ре derives from the old *dual* declension, a kind of limited plural, used originally for 'two' of something, but extended by usage to 'three' and 'four'. Nouns had dual forms similar to the genitive singular and preserved a semblance of their earlier declension by adopting the genitive singular after 'two', 'three' and 'four' in the nominative, while adjectives lost all trace of their dual forms.)

Note: the numeral itself if qualified by an adjective is treated as a plural noun:

пе́рвые два го́да   the first two years

'она́ несла́ во́ду на коромы́сле – два но́вых ведра́, по́лные до краёв'
(D. Eremin).

she was carrying water on a yoke – two new buckets, full to the brim

- With numerals in the oblique cases adjective and noun appear in the same case in the plural:

  из трёх ру́сских городо́в   out of three Russian towns
  в трёх ру́сских города́х   in three Russian towns

21.2.15 Verbs – singular or plural?

With a numeral construction ending with оди́н, одна́ or одно́ as subject the verb will be in the singular:

у нас на фа́брике рабо́тает две́сти со́рок одна́ же́нщина
241women work in our factory

Otherwise the verb may be 3rd person singular (neuter in the past tense) or plural. The more the subject may be considered to be acting as a group or single whole, the more likely the verb is to be singular; the more diverse the action, the more likely the verb is to be plural:

в ко́мнате собрало́сь два́дцать пять студе́нтов
twenty-five students had assembled in the room

все два́дцать пять студе́нтов разъе́хались по дома́м
all twenty-five students had gone home

If the verb precedes the subject (i.e. if the word order has the verb next to the numeral: verb|numeral|plural noun) the singular verb seems to be preferred:

у нас на фа́брике **рабо́тает две́сти со́рок во́семь же́нщин**
248 women work in our factory

If the subject precedes the verb so that a plural noun is next to the verb, the plural of the verb is more likely:

две́сти со́рок во́семь же́нщин рабо́тают у нас на фа́брике

21.3 Use of collective numerals

21.3.1 **Дво́е, тро́е, че́тверо** are followed by the genitive plural, so are used instead of два, три, четы́ре in the nominative and inanimate nominative-accusative cases with nouns that have no genitive singular (i.e. which are

plural-only): **двóе часóв** 'two clocks'; **трóе сýток** 'three days (and nights)';
чéтверо санéй 'four sledges'. In the oblique cases of plural-only nouns the
appropriate case of два, три, четы́ре (*not* двóе, трóе, чéтверо) is used:

> чéтверо санéй, *but:* **на четырёх саня́х** 'on four sledges'

Note: The collective numerals do not combine with двáдцать, три́дцать, *etc.* to form
compound numerals, so that it is not possible in Russian to say grammatically 'twenty-
two watches', 'thirty-four sledges', etc., in the nominative or inanimate nominative-
accusative case (not that you are very likely to want to). If it were necessary you
would have to establish first that you were interested in watches and then use the
official-sounding word штýка 'item' (from the German Stück, via Polish) with the
actual numeral:

> **фи́рма дáрит сотрýдникам часы́: нужны́ двáдцать две штýки**
> the firm is giving its employees watches: it needs twenty-two

Also: **двáдцать однá штýка**   twenty-one (watches, or whatever the context
                                implies)

> **закáз на двáдцать пять штук**   an order for twenty-five (items, units)

If the sentence can be paraphrased to put the numeral into an oblique case
where the genitive singular is not required, the problem disappears:

> **на тридцати́ четырёх саня́х**   on thirty-four sledges

With objects that normally come in pairs there are alternatives:

мне нужны́ сапоги́	I need boots
or (more pedantic) **мне нужнá пáра сапóг**	I need a pair of boots
or (even fussier) **мне нужнá однá пáра сапóг**	I need one pair of boots

More than one pair can be specified:

мне нужны́ две пáры сапóг	I need two pairs of boots
мне нужны́ пять пар тýфель	I need five pairs of shoes
три пáры перчáток *or* **трóе перчáток**	three pairs of gloves

Note: **брю́ки** 'trousers' and **джи́нсы** 'jeans' are considered single items:

одни́ брю́ки	one pair of trousers
пáра брюк	two pairs of trousers

21.3.2 The collective numerals are used with **pronouns** denoting people
(male, female or mixed company): **мы двóе** 'we two', **нас двóе** 'there are two
of us'

> **нас бы́ло чéтверо, а их бы́ло пя́теро**
> there were four of us, but five of them
> **кóмната на трои́х**   a room for three

Note: related adverbial forms: **вдвоём** 'in a pair'; **втроём** 'the three together';
вчетверóм 'as a foursome'.

> **мы пошли́ вдвоём**   the two of us set off together

21.3.3   Collective numerals are used with **nouns** denoting **male** persons (especially if they end in -a or -я, e.g. **мужчи́на** 'man'), adjectival nouns denoting people (e.g. **учёный** 'scientist'), **лицо́** when it means 'person' and **де́ти** 'children':

дво́е студе́нтов 'two students'	ше́стеро мужчи́н 'six men'
че́тверо больны́х 'four patients'	се́меро дете́й 'seven children'

тро́е неизве́стных лиц   three persons unknown

Note: there is a tendency towards replacing дво́е with два:

два студе́нта 'two students' is just as good as **дво́е студе́нтов**

21.3.4   When used of people the collective numerals have an animate genitive-accusative:

они́ вы́растили семеры́х дете́й   they brought up seven children

21.3.5   Collective numerals are rarely used with nouns denoting female persons or people of high rank:

два профе́ссора 'two professors' (rather than: дво́е профессоро́в)
три генера́ла 'three generals' (rather than: тро́е генера́лов)

But: **дво́е суде́й** 'two judges' (rather than два судьи́, probably because судья́ ends in -я)

21.4 Челове́к and лю́ди with numerals

The normal plural of челове́к is лю́ди, but with cardinal numerals the oblique plural cases of челове́к are used:

встре́тить пять челове́к	to meet five people
у пяти́ челове́к биле́т есть	five people have tickets
дать э́то пяти́ челове́кам	to give this to five people
речь шла о пяти́ челове́ках	it was a question of five people

With adjectives, however, the corresponding cases of лю́ди are usual:

я уви́дел пять незнако́мых люде́й   I saw five strangers

(although it is also possible to say: я уви́дел пять незнако́мых челове́к)

- With челове́к and лю́ди on their own the cardinal numeral is preferred to the collective numeral, but with adjectives the collective numeral may be used:

четы́ре челове́ка	четы́ре незнако́мых челове́ка
(че́тверо люде́й)	че́тверо незнако́мых люде́й
пять челове́к	пять незнако́мых люде́й
(пя́теро люде́й)	пя́теро незнако́мых люде́й
я уви́дел пять незнако́мых люде́й	
я уви́дел пятеры́х незнако́мых люде́й	

EXERCISES

(i) *Decline the Russian for:* '365 days', '1001 nights'

(ii) a. *Give the Russian for:* 2 towns; 13 towns; 23 towns; 45 towns; 76 towns; 135 towns; 1,450 towns

  b. *With each of the above form phrases with the prepositions:*

  из (+ *gen.*); к (+ *dat.*); над (+ *inst.*); в (+ *pr.*)

(iii) *Complete the sentence:* Они приняли . . . *with the Russian for:*

  'one male student'; 'thirty-one female students'; 'fifteen male students'; 'twenty-four female students'; 'sixty-seven male students'; 'a hundred and fifty-three students'; 'one thousand, one hundred and ten students'.

(iv) *Insert the correct form of* русский *in all the numeral constructions in* (ii) *and* (iii) *above.*

(v) *Translate and comment on the use of the italicized numerals in the passage:*

  ' – Кто из вас перед праздником приходил ко мне домой отвечать урок – встаньте!

Обрюзглый человек в рясе, с тяжёлым крестом на шее, угрожающе посмотрел на учеников. Маленькие глазки точно прокалывали всех *шестерых*, поднявшихся со скамеек, – *четырёх* мальчиков и *двух* девочек. Дети боязливо посматривали на человека в рясе.

– Вы садитесь, – махнул поп в сторону девочек. Те быстро сели, облегчённо вздохнув.

Глазки отца Василия сосредоточились на *четырёх* фигурах.

– Идите-ка сюда, голубчики!

Отец Василий поднялся, отодвинул стул и подошёл вплотную к сбившимся в кучу ребятам:

– Кто из вас, подлецов, курит?

Все *четверо* тихо ответили:

– Мы не курим, батюшка' (N. Ostrovsky).

(vi) *Translate into Russian:*

1 I bought two cheap watches.
2 On three sledges eight people were travelling.
3 I met five very strange people there.
4 Seven men were sitting in the room. One was a doctor. That means there were six patients.

21.5 Use of indefinite quantifiers

21.5.1 **мно́го** 'much, many'; **немно́го** 'a little, few'; **ма́ло** 'a little'; **нема́ло** 'not a few, quite a lot'; **ско́лько** 'how much, how many'; **сто́лько** 'so much, so many'; **не́сколько** 'several'. Nouns following these indefinite Quantifiers go into the genitive – singular or plural depending on the sense: **мно́го шу́ма** 'a lot of noise', **мно́го птиц** 'a lot of birds', **ско́лько ма́сла** 'how much butter', **сто́лько** друзе́й 'so many friends'

- **мно́го, немно́го, ма́ло, нема́ло** are used with **людей**: **мно́го людей** 'many people', **немно́го** людей 'a few people', **ма́ло людей** 'few, not many people'

- **ско́лько, сто́лько** and **не́сколько** are used with **челове́к**:
  не́сколько челове́к   several people

21.5.2 **мно́го** and **немно́го** have alternative adjectival forms **мно́гие** and **немно́гие** for use with plural nouns; there is no difference between:
  мно́го людей *and* **мно́гие лю́ди**   many people

But in the oblique cases the adjectival forms come into their own:
  во мно́гих слу́чаях   in many cases

  то́лько у немно́гих домо́в оста́лась кры́ша
  only a few houses had a roof left

  мы говори́ли со мно́гими интере́сными людьми́
  we talked to many interesting people

- There is a neuter singular form **мно́гое** which is used as an indefinite pronoun:
  мно́гое ста́ло поня́тно   much has become clear
  она́ помога́ет ему́ во мно́гом   she helps him in many ways

21.5.3 **ско́лько, сто́лько** and **не́сколько** also have a plural adjectival declension which is used in the oblique cases:
  со ско́лькими студе́нтами вы говори́ли? – с не́сколькими
  how many students did you talk to? – several
  у сто́льких детей нет ту́фель   so many children don't have shoes

Note: the animate accusative of **ско́лько, сто́лько** and **не́сколько** is not normally used:
  я уви́дел не́сколько слоно́в (rather than: . . . не́скольких . . .)
  I saw several elephants

21.5.4 Óба, óбе 'both'

Like два/две, if óба/óбе is the subject it is followed by the noun in the genitive singular:

óба студéнта, óбе студéнтки	both students

The same goes for the accusative of inanimate nouns:

онá нашлá óбе рýчки и óба карандашá
she found both pens and both pencils

If an adjective is included in the phrase it goes into the genitive plural:

óба нóвых преподавáтеля – жéнщины	both new teachers are women

As with два/две, in the oblique cases dependent nouns and adjectives follow in the same plural case:

мы узнáли обóих студéнтов/обéих студéнток
we recognized both students

в обóих недáвних слýчаях	in both recent cases

21.6 Use of fractions

21.6.1 Полторá, полторы́ 'one-and-a-half'

The construction is the same as for два/две: in the nominative полторá/полторы́ takes the genitive singular of the noun and genitive plural of the adjective (the animate accusative is unlikely – one-and-a-half *and* animate?):

полторá мéтра	one-and-a-half metres
полторы́ буты́лки	one-and-a-half bottles
полторы́ морски́х ми́ли	one-and-a-half nautical miles
óколо полýтора килогрáммов	about one-and-a-half kilogrammes

21.6.2 Половина 'half', треть 'a third', чéтверть 'quarter' are followed by the noun, and adjective, or the pronoun in the genitive:

половина винá	half the wine
половина нóвого винá	half of the new wine
на половине карти́н	on half of the pictures
на половине стáрых карти́н	on half the old pictures
половина нас	half of us
в половине слýчаев	in half the cases
треть всех больны́х	a third of all the patients
бóльше чéтверти студéнтов	more than a quarter of the students

21.6.3 Other fractions are expressed by the feminine form of the ordinal numeral: пя́тая 'a fifth', шестáя 'a sixth', двадцáтая 'a twentieth', etc.:

одна́ шеста́я всех милиционе́ров	one-sixth of all policemen
семь восьмы́х буты́лки	seven-eighths of a bottle
две пя́тых одного́ гру́за	two-fifths of one load

21.6.4 Whole numbers with fractions; genitive singular after 'two', 'three' or 'four' in the nominative or inanimate accusative; genitive plural for 'five' onwards:

два с полови́ной часа́	two and a half hours
пять с полови́ной тонн	five and a half tonnes
три и семь восьмы́х оборо́та	three and seven-eighths revolutions
шесть и две пя́тых ли́тров	six and two-fifths litres

21.7 Decimals

Note how the following are written as well as said:

0,1	ноль це́лых и одна́ деся́тая *or* ноль и одна́ деся́тая	
	or одна́ деся́тая	= 0·1
0,2	ноль (це́лых) и две деся́тых *or* две деся́тых	= 0·2
0,5	ноль (це́лых) и пять деся́тых *or* пять деся́тых	= 0·5
0,03	ноль (це́лых) и три со́тых	= 0·03
0,035	ноль (це́лых) и три́дцать пять ты́сячных	= 0·035
1,25	одна́ це́лая (и) два́дцать пять со́тых	= 1·25
2,75	две це́лых и се́мьдесят пять со́тых	= 2·75
23,5	два́дцать три и пять деся́тых *or* два́дцать три и пять	= 23·5

EXERCISES

(i) *Translate into Russian:*

1 There was wine in both bottles.
2 I decided to write to both grandmothers.
3 They spent one and a half years in Russia.
4 How many Russian towns have you been in?
5 In many towns conditions were better than I expected.
6 How many metres did you buy? Three and three-fifths.

(ii) *Write out the following as decimals:*

0,3   0,75   0,125   1,35   2,4   3,25   10,53   17,7   25,86   50,175

21.8 Ordinal numerals

Ordinal numerals, such as **пе́рвый** 'first', **второ́й** 'second', **тре́тий** 'third', **двадца́тый** 'twentieth', **пятидеся́тый** 'fiftieth', **со́тый** 'hundredth', **двухсо́тый** 'two-hundredth', etc., decline like adjectives (see pp. 29, 32). In compound ordinal numerals only the last element declines:

> **пе́рвый, пе́рвая, пе́рвое; пе́рвые**, etc. first
> **двадца́тый, двадца́тая, двадца́тое; двадца́тые**, etc. twentieth

but: **два́дцать пе́рвый, два́дцать пе́рвая**, etc. twenty-first
> **два́дцать пе́рвый** год the twenty-first year
> **два́дцать пе́рвая** неде́ля the twenty-first week

Note: for the declension of **тре́тий**, see ли́сий p. 30

Note: **пе́рвый эта́ж** 'the ground floor'; **на второ́м этаже́** 'on the first floor', etc.

Note: **сто оди́ннадцатый авто́бус** 'a number 111 bus'; **два́дцать седьмо́й тролле́йбус** 'a number twenty-seven trolleybus', etc.

EXERCISES

(i) *Translate into English:*

> с пе́рвого взгля́да
> о́коло пя́того столба́
> в тре́тьем ряду́
> для ка́ждого деся́того ребёнка
> пе́ред седьмы́м до́мом
> на три́ста во́семьдесят шесто́й страни́це

(ii) *Translate into Russian:*

1   In the sixth shop.
2   Under the second table.
3   On the ninth floor.
4   In a number thirty-one tram.
5   After the third game.
6   Under every fifth armchair.
7   In the eighteenth house.
8   On page 275.
9   Instead of the twelfth lesson.
10 In the reign of Ivan IV.

---

22 MEASUREMENT

Measurement of height, weight, area, etc. may be conveyed in various ways:

22.1 Measurements with numerals

The word identifying the kind of measurement (высота́ 'height', вес 'weight', пло́щадь 'area') appears in the **instrumental** followed nowadays by the numeral in the **nominative** *or* (less often and in the more technical contexts) by **в** + *acc.* of the numeral; the case of nouns after numerals in the nominative has been covered (see pp. 214–16):

> он пойма́л ры́бу длино́й оди́н метр и ве́сом четы́ре килогра́мма
> he caught a fish a metre long (one metre in length) and weighing four kilogrammes (four kilogrammes in weight)
> они́ купи́ли занаве́ски ширино́й пять ме́тров и длино́й два ме́тра
> they bought curtains (measuring) five metres wide and two metres long (five metres in width and two metres in length)
> тури́ст несёт рюкза́к ве́сом два́дцать пять килогра́ммов
> the hiker is carrying a rucksack weighing twenty-five kilogrammes (twenty-five kilogrammes in weight)
> дом продаётся с уча́стком пло́щадью полтора́ гекта́ра
> the house is being sold with a plot of land measuring one-and-a-half hectares (one-and-a-half hectares in area)
> маши́на оснащена́ дви́гателем мо́щностью две́сти лошади́ных сил
> or . . . дви́гателем мо́щностью в две́сти лошади́ных сил
> the car is equipped with a two-hundred-horsepower engine (two hundred horsepower in power)

22.2 Compound adjectives

Sometimes a compound adjective can be used consisting of the numeral in the genitive and the adjectival form of the unit of measurement:

> пятиле́тний план   five-year plan
> семидесятипятиле́тняя годовщи́на   seventy-fifth anniversary
> восьмидесятивосьмимиллиметро́вая пу́шка
> eighty-eight millimetre cannon
> двухко́мнатная кварти́ра   a two-room flat

22.3 Size

'Size' of clothing is разме́р; the actual size is conveyed by the ordinal numeral (see p. 228):

тридцать седьмо́й разме́р   size thirty-seven
ту́фли со́рок шесто́го разме́ра   size forty-six shoes

22.4 Temperature

Temperature is given in degrees Celsius:

на у́лице **восемна́дцать гра́дусов тепла́**   it's plus eighteen outside
но́чью бы́ло **пятна́дцать гра́дусов моро́за**
or: но́чью бы́ло **ми́нус пятна́дцать**   it was minus fifteen last night

22.5 Rate

Rate is expressed by **в** + *acc.*:

они́ встреча́ются **раз в год**   they meet once a year
ве́тер **во́семь ме́тров в секу́нду**   wind speed eight metres per second
мы е́хали **со ско́ростью шестьдеся́т киломе́тров в час**
we were travelling at a speed of sixty kilometres an hour

22.6 Dimensions

Dimensions are expressed by **на** + *acc.*:

я живу́ в ко́мнате **три ме́тра на два с полови́ной**
I live in a room three metres by two and a half

EXERCISE

Translate into English:

река́ ширино́й оди́н киломе́тр
зо́лото сто́имостью сто миллио́нов до́лларов
ба́шня высото́й три́дцать ме́тров
трансформа́тор ве́сом три то́нны
кварти́ра пло́щадью девятна́дцать квадра́тных ме́тров
на берегу́ о́зера глубино́й полтора́ киломе́тра
пятиэта́жный дом
тридцатипроце́нтная ски́дка
десятито́нный груз
в сапога́х пятьдеся́т второ́го разме́ра
руба́шка со́рок тре́тьего разме́ра
Сего́дня два́дцать два гра́дуса моро́за.
Вчера́ бы́ло почти́ два́дцать пять гра́дусов.
Он бре́ется раз в неде́лю.
Она́ е́хала со ско́ростью се́мьдесят пять миль в час.
Коме́та пролета́ет раз в четы́ре ты́сячи пятьсо́т лет.
На́ша ку́рица откла́дывает два яйца́ в день.
Брат моло́же меня́ на четы́ре го́да.
Конте́йнер разме́рами де́сять ме́тров на четы́ре на четы́ре.
Де́ньги бы́ли на́йдены в коро́бке де́вять сантиме́тров на во́семь
на пять.

23   EXPRESSIONS OF TIME

23.1 Duration

23.1.1 Simple duration of an action is expressed by the straight accusative case of the period of time without a preposition:

я сижу́ здесь весь день	I sit here all day
	or I've been sitting here all day
он жил **год** в Москве́	he lived in Moscow (for) a year
они́ и́щут её **всю неде́лю**	they've been looking for her all week
он рабо́тал там **два го́да**	he worked there for two years
она́ ждала́ его́ **три часа́**	she waited for him for three hours
он бу́дет учи́ться у них **пять лет**	he's going to study at their place for five years

23.1.2 Emphasis on the duration of an action may be made with the expression **на протяже́нии** with the genitive case of the period of time:

на протяже́нии сле́дующих шести́ лет он путеше́ствовал в Йндии
for the (duration of the) next six years he was travelling in India

23.1.3 Duration of an intended stay is expressed by the preposition **на** + *acc.*:

она́ приезжа́ет **на год** учи́ться	she's coming for a year to study
они́ уе́дут **на неде́лю**	they'll go away for a week
они́ собира́ются к нам **на Но́вый год**	they're coming to us for the New Year
он прие́хал **на ме́сяц**	he came for a month

23.1.4 Time taken to complete an action is expressed by the prepositions **в** + *acc. or* the rather more emphatic **за** + *acc.*:

мы собра́ли все кни́ги **в оди́н день**	we collected all the books in one day
они́ постро́или гара́ж **за неде́лю**	they built the garage in a week

он нарису́ет тебе́ портре́т **за два часа́**
he'll draw you a portrait in two hours

23.1.5 The limits of a period of time, 'from' . . . 'until' . . ., are expressed by the prepositions **с** + *gen.* and **до** + *gen.*:

с утра́ до ве́чера   from morning to evening

с шести́ часо́в утра́ до полови́ны шесто́го ве́чера
from six in the morning to half past five in the evening

с понедéльника до четвергá
from Monday till (but not including)Thursday

But the limits 'from' . . . 'up to (and including)' . . . are expressed by the prepositions **с** + *gen.* and **по** + *acc.*:

с понедéльника по четвéрг
from Monday to Thursday (inclusive)
с мáя по сентя́брь
from May to September (inclusive)

23.1.6 On the borders between duration of an action and an imprecise indication as to when an action takes place, to express '(sometime) during' a part of the day or season of the year, the straight instrumental case may be used:

мы узнáли у́тром о её успéхе
we learnt of her success in the morning

они́ выхóдят на рабóту рáнним у́тром, а прихóдят пóздней нóчью
they go out to work early in the morning and come back late at night

днём прихóдится занимáться
(we) have to work in the afternoon

лéтом они́ никудá не уезжáют, а óсенью вылетáют в Áфрику
they don't go anywhere in the summer, but fly off to Africa in the autumn

23.1.7 Otherwise 'during' is expressed by **во врéмя** + *gen.* or **в течéние** + *gen.*:

во врéмя войны́ during the war
в течéние мáтча in the course of the match

23.2 Time 'when'

Russian, like English, uses different prepositions with different time spans to indicate the time an action occurred – 'at (five thirty)', 'on (Friday)', 'in (May)'.
There is no satisfactory explanation; they do not correspond to English usage, they just happened. Working 'upwards' we have:

в + *acc.*	**в э́ту секу́нду**	at that second
	в тот момéнт	at that moment
	в час	at one
	в чéтверть шестóго	at quarter past five
в + *pr.*	**в половúне шестóго**	at half past five
в + *acc.*	**в два часá**	at two o'clock

	в по́лночь	at midnight
	в сре́ду	on Wednesday
	в тот день	on that day
на + *pr.*	на э́той неде́ле	this week
в + *pr.*	в апре́ле	in April
	в про́шлом ме́сяце	last month
	в двухты́сячном году́	in the year two thousand
	в э́том году́	this year
в + *acc.*	в восьмидеся́тые го́ды	in the eighties
	в го́ды перестро́йки	in the years of *perestroika*
в + *pr.*	в двадца́том ве́ке	in the twentieth century
в + *acc.*	в сре́дние века́	in the Middle Ages
в + *pr.*	в сле́дующем столе́тии	in the next century
	в тре́тьем тысячеле́тии	in the third millennium
	в про́шлом	in the past
	в бу́дущем	in the future
в + *acc.*	в настоя́щее вре́мя	at present
	во ве́ки веко́в	henceforth and for evermore
	в пе́рвый раз в жи́зни	for the first time in (my) life
	во второ́й раз вообще́	for the second time ever

23.3 Dates

23.3.1 Ordinal numerals are used to denote the **year**:
   ты́сяча девятьсо́т шестьдеся́т пя́тый год   the year 1965
   (This may be written: 1965-ый год *or* 1965г.)

23.3.2 'In' a given year is expressed by **в** + *pr.*:
   в ты́сяча девятьсо́т шестьдеся́т пя́том году́ in 1965
   (This may be written: в 1965-ом году́ *or* в 1965г.)

23.3.3 If a **month** is given, the year follows in the genitive:
   в октябре́ ты́сяча девятьсо́т семна́дцатого го́да   in October 1917
   (в октябре́ 1917-го го́да *or* в октябре́ 1917г.)

23.3.4 A **date in the month** is expressed by the ordinal numeral in the neuter (the noun число 'number, date' is understood):
   сего́дня **второ́е апре́ля**   today is the second of April

23.3.5 'On' a given date is expressed by the ordinal numeral in the genitive case:
   два́дцать второ́го апре́ля   on the 22nd of April

'on the 2nd of April 1965' is, therefore:

второго апре́ля ты́сяча девятьсо́т шестьдеся́т пя́того го́да
(*or* 2-го апре́ля 1965-го го́да *or* 2-го апре́ля 1965г *or* 2 апре́ля 1965г.)

два́дцать пя́того февраля́ ты́сяча девятьсо́т се́мьдесят четвёртого го́да
on 25 February 1974

When the day of the week is included this gives a mixture of в + *acc.* and *gen.*:

в пя́тницу, пе́рвого ма́рта ты́сяча девятьсо́т девяно́сто шесто́го го́да
on Friday 1 March 1996
в суббо́ту, двадца́того ию́ня ты́сяча девятьсо́т во́семьдесят седьмо́го го́да
on Saturday 20 June 1987

Note: Just as the singular forms of год may be abbreviated to г., the plural forms of год, such as годо́в, may be abbreviated to гг.:

собы́тия 1555–1556гг.   the events of 1555–1556

Note: when the genitive plural for 'years' is required after a cardinal or indefinite numeral лет, the genitive plural of ле́то, is used: пятьдеся́т лет 'fifty years'.

я живу́ здесь не́сколько лет   I've lived here several years

After ordinal numerals, however, годо́в is used:

по́сле пе́рвого и второ́го годо́в   after the first and second years

23.3.6 Decades

Ordinal numerals are used to express decades:

семидеся́тые го́ды   the seventies
рефо́рмы пятидеся́тых годо́в   the reforms of the 50s
(*or* рефо́рмы 50-ых годов *or* рефо́рмы 50гг.)

23.3.7 'In' a decade may be expressed by в with either the accusative *or* prepositional case:

в пятидеся́тые го́ды *or* в пятидеся́тых года́х 'in the fifties'

The accusative is more likely in relation to a series of events viewed as a process taking place throughout the decade, while the prepositional relates more often to a single event or isolated events occurring within the period:

'В 50-70-е го́ды уже́ появи́лся ряд иссле́дований сове́тских и
югосла́вских исто́риков, где рассма́тривается отноше́ние ру́сского
о́бщества к собы́тиям на Балка́нах в ука́занный пери́од' (V. M. Khevrolina).

In the period from the fifties to the seventies a number of studies came out by Soviet and Yugoslav scholars in which the attitude of Russian society to events in the Balkans is examined.

'Уже́ в 20-х года́х появи́лись пе́рвые рабо́ты по исто́рии бе́лой ру́сской эмигра́ции' (L. K. Shkarenkov).

By the 1920s the first works on the history of the White Russian emigration had already come out.

23.4 Note on the calendar

Before the 1917 Revolution the Julian calendar was used in Russia, while in Western Europe and America dates were reckoned by the Gregorian calendar which was twelve days ahead of the Julian in the nineteenth century and thirteen days ahead in the twentieth. So 1 January by the Julian calendar is 14 January according to the Gregorian. Russia has generally used the Gregorian calendar since 1917, but the Orthodox Church and some other denominations in Russia continue to celebrate festivals according to the Julian calendar. Confusion can be caused for historians when, for example, Western sources refer to an event as occurring on 30 October 1905, while contemporary Russian sources were recording it as happening on 17 October. Dates given according to the Julian calendar are referred to as ста́рого сти́ля (ст. ст.) 'Old Style' (*or* OS) whereas the Gregorian calendar is referred to when necessary as но́вого сти́ля (н. ст.) 'New Style' (NS).

'BC' in Russian is **до на́шей э́ры**, abbreviated to **до н.э.**; 'AD' is **на́шей э́ры**, abbreviated to **н.э.**

23.5 Time according to the clock

23.5.1 Answering the question: **кото́рый час?** 'what is the time?' time is expressed as follows:

час но́чи	1 a.m.
два часа́ но́чи	2 a.m.
три часа́ но́чи (*or* три часа́ утра́)	3 a.m.
четы́ре часа́ утра́ (*or* четы́ре часа́ но́чи)	4 a.m.
пять часо́в утра́	5 a.m.
шесть часо́в утра́	6 a.m.
семь часо́в утра́	7 a.m.
во́семь часо́в утра́	8 a.m.
де́вять часо́в утра́	9 a.m.
де́сять часо́в утра́	10 a.m.
оди́ннадцать часо́в утра́	11 a.m.
двена́дцать часо́в дня *or* по́лдень	12 p.m.
час дня *or* трина́дцать часо́в	1 p.m.
два часа́ дня *or* четы́рнадцать часо́в	2 p.m.
три часа́ дня *or* пятна́дцать часо́в	3 p.m.
четы́ре часа́ дня *or* шестна́дцать часо́в	4 p.m
пять часо́в дня (*or* ве́чера) *or* семна́дцать часо́в	5 p.m.
шесть часо́в ве́чера *or* восемна́дцать часо́в	6 p.m.
семь часо́в ве́чера *or* девятна́дцать часо́в	7 p.m.
во́семь часо́в ве́чера *or* два́дцать часо́в	8 p.m.
де́вять часо́в ве́чера *or* два́дцать оди́н час	9 p.m.
де́сять часо́в ве́чера *or* два́дцать два часа́	10 p.m.
оди́ннадцать часо́в ве́чера *or* два́дцать три часа́	11 p.m.
двена́дцать часо́в но́чи *or* ноль часо́в *or* по́лночь	12 a.m.

23.5.2 'At' a given hour, answering the question: **в котором часу?** 'at what time?' is expressed by **в** and the accusative case:

в час	at one o'clock	**в три часа**	at three o'clock
в шесть часов	at six o'clock	**в полночь**	at midnight
в три часа дня	at three in the afternoon		

23.5.3 The ordinal numeral is used to express the time between one hour and the next:

первый час	between 12 and 1 o'clock
второй час	between 1 and 2 o'clock
третий час	between 2 and 3 o'clock, and so on ...
это случилось во втором часу ночи	it happened between one and two a.m. *or* sometime after one a.m.

23.5.4 Precise time **in minutes** up to the half hour is expressed as so many minutes of an ordinal hour, so that 'five past one' or 'at five past one' is 'five minutes of the second (hour)': **пять минут второго** (*or obsolete*: **в пять минут второго**). So too:

десять минут третьего	ten past two *or* at ten past two
(*Obsolete:* **в десять минут третьего**	at ten past two)
двадцать пять минут десятого	(at) twenty-five past nine
я приду десять минут второго	I'll arrive at ten past one

23.5.5 **Четверть** 'quarter' is used for the quarter hour:

четверть шестого	a quarter past five

'At' quarter past the hour is expressed by **в** + *acc.*:

в четверть третьего	at a quarter past two

23.5.6 **Половина** 'half' is used for the half hour:

половина второго	half past one

'At' half past the hour is expressed by **в** + *pr.*:

в половине шестого	at half past five

Colloquially половина is abbreviated to **пол** which may be written separately or joined to the ordinal:

пол шестого *or* **полшестого**	half five
в пол шестого *or* **в полшестого**	at half five

23.5.7 **After the half hour** time is expressed by **без** and the genitive case of the number of minutes left to the hour:

без двадцати пяти минут час	twenty-five to one *or* at twenty-five to one

без трёх минýт пять	three minutes to five *or* at three minutes to five
без чéтверти семь	a quarter to seven *or* at a quarter to seven

23.5.8 Time may also be expressed using cardinal numbers as in the English construction 'two fifteen', 'at three forty', etc.:

два пятнáдцать	2.15;	в два пятнáдцать	at 2.15
три сóрок	3.40;	в три сóрок	at 3.40

and, using the 24-hour clock:

ноль часóв сóрок пять минýт	12.45 a.m.
в четы́рнадцать три́дцать пять	at 14.35

23.5.9 Time of predicted or successive action is expressed by the preposition **чéрез** with the accusative:

он приéдет **чéрез час**	he'll arrive in an hour's time
она вы́шла зáмуж **чéрез год**	she married a year later

23.6 Time by, before, until and after

23.6.1 Time by which is expressed by the preposition **к** + *dat.*:

он приéдет **к чáсу**	he'll be here by one
они́ сдéлают ремóнт **к вéчеру**	they'll finish decorating by evening
к концý недéли мы бы́ли свобóдны	by the end of the week we were free

23.6.2 Time (just) before which is expressed by the preposition **пéред** + *inst.*:

пéред Нóвым гóдом	just before the New Year
пéред войнóй в Чечнé	before the war in Chechnya
пéред начáлом спектáкля всё бы́ло ти́хо	
everything was quiet before the start of the show	

(for the conjunction перед тем, как 'before' see p. 247)

23.6.3 A period of time leading up to something is expressed by the preposition **за** + *acc.* followed by **до** + *gen.*:

за час до начáла концéрта	an hour before the start of the concert
за недéлю до откры́тия магази́на	a week before the opening of the shop

23.6.4 Time until or before which expressed by the preposition **до** + *gen.*:

до войны́	before the war
до седьмóго я бýду в Одéссе	until the seventh I shall be in Odessa

до строи́тельства мостá мы не éздили в Уэ́льс
before construction of the bridge we didn't go to Wales

(for the conjunction до того, как 'before' see p. 246–7)

23.6.5 Time after which is expressed by the preposition **после** + *gen.*:

после уро́ка де́ти ста́ли петь   after the lesson the children began to sing
после револю́ции жить ста́ло тяжеле́е
after the revolution life became harder

(for the conjunction по́сле того́, как 'after' see pp. 244, 248)

23.7 Periodicity

Regularly repeated actions may be expressed by *either* the use of the adjective **ка́ждый** 'every' in the accusative case *or* the preposition **по** + *dat. plur.*:

мы помога́ем ей **ка́ждую суббо́ту**	we help her every Saturday
мы помога́ем ей **по суббо́там**	we help her on Saturdays
мы помога́ем ей **ка́ждые три дня**	we help her every three days

Note: the adjectives **ежедне́вный, еженеде́льный, ежеме́сячный, ежего́дный** – daily, weekly, monthly, annual may form adverbs:

ежедне́вно	every day	**еженеде́льно**	every week;
ежеме́сячно	every month	**ежего́дно**	every year, annually.

Жемчу́жины наро́дной му́дрости

растёт не по дням, а по часа́м	grows not daily, but hourly (awfully fast)

Note: **во́время** 'in time': они́ прие́хали во́время 'they arrived in time'
во вре́мя + *gen.* 'during': во вре́мя ма́тча 'during the match'
в тече́ние + *gen.* 'in the course of': в тече́ние го́да 'in the course of the year'
на протяже́нии + *gen.* 'throughout, for the duration of':
на протяже́нии уро́ка 'for the duration of the lesson'
в э́то вре́мя 'at this time':
в э́то вре́мя он жил в Твери́ 'at this time he lived in Tver'
при + *pr.* 'in the time of, during the reign of':
при Ста́лине 'in Stalin's time, in the Stalin era'
при перехо́де к ры́нку 'on transition to a market economy'

EXERCISES

(i)   a.   *Give the following dates in Russian:*
    21/1/1939;   15/2/1942;   3/3/1955;   30/5/1967;   10/VI/1976;
    12/VII/1974;   17/9/1980;   24/X/1988;   2/XI/1991;   1/XII/1999.

    b.   *Give the Russian for 'on' these dates.*

(ii) a. *Give the following times in Russian:*

1   One o'clock in the morning.
2   Ten past four in the morning.
3   Quarter past six in the morning.
4   Half past seven in the morning.
5   Twenty to eight in the morning.
6   Quarter past twelve in the afternoon.
7   Twelve minutes past one in the afternoon.
8   Twenty past three in the afternoon.
9   Twenty-three minutes to seven in the evening.
10 Twenty-five past ten at night.

b. *Give the Russian for 'at' these times.*

(iii) *Read out and write out the times of the TV programmes listed below:*

6.00	Телеу́тро.
9.00, 12.00, 15.00, 18.00, 23.55	Но́вости
9.15	'Но́вая же́ртва'. Сериа́л
10.05	По́ле чуде́с
11.00	Челове́к и зако́н
11.30	Угада́й мело́дию
12.10	В эфи́ре телерадиокомпа́ния 'Мир'
12.55	'Бегу́щий челове́к'. Х/ф [=худо́жественный фильм 'feature film']
14.40	'Про бегемо́та, кото́рый боя́лся приви́вок'
15.30	'Ры́царь Отва́жное Се́рдце'. Мультсериа́л
15.45	Марафо́н-15
16.00	Звёздный час
16.40	'Эле́н и ребя́та'. Молодёжный сериа́л
17.10	Джем
17.35	Вокру́г све́та
18.20	'Но́вая же́ртва'. Сериа́л
19.10	Час пик
19.35	Угада́й мело́дию
20.00	'Ёсли . . .' Веду́щий В. По́знер
20.45	Споко́йной но́чи, малыши́!
21.00	Вре́мя
21.40	'Жесто́кость'. Х/ф
22.45	Матадо́р. 'Карнава́л в Вене́ции'
23.40	Ку́бок ми́ра 'Ма́стер-ра́лли-96'
0.05	'Счастли́вые дни'. Х/ф

(iv) *Translate into English:*

'Рефо́рма календаря́ была́ произведена́ в 46г. до н.э. при Ю́лии Це́заре. В 1582г. па́па ри́мский Григо́рий XIII произвёл но́вую рефо́рму, пропусти́в 10 дней. Ра́зница ме́жду григориа́нским и юлиа́нским календаря́ми возраста́ет: в 17 в. - 10 дней, в 18 в. - 11 дней; в 19 в. - 12 дней; в 20 в. - 13 дней. В СССР григориа́нский календа́рь (но́вый стиль) был введён с 14 февраля́ (1 февраля́ ста́рого сти́ля) 1918г., т.е. по́сле 31 января́ ст. ст. ста́ли счита́ть 14 февраля́ н. ст.' (Энциклопеди́ческий слова́рь в двух тома́х, 1963).

24 CONJUNCTIONS

Conjunctions link two or more parts of a sentence.

24.1 Co-ordinating conjunctions

Co-ordinating conjunctions join two or more clauses of equal or comparable weight within a single compound sentence.

24.1.1 They may do this through simple aggregation:
она́ расска́зывала, и мы все слу́шали   she told the story and we all listened
пу́блика придёт, и тогда́ начнётся спекта́кль
the public will come and then the show will start

Note: и . . . , и . . . is used for 'both . . . and . . .' – either individual words or parts of sentences, or whole clauses:
фильм бу́дет пока́зываться и днём, и ве́чером
the film will be shown both in the afternoon and in the evening

Жемчу́жины наро́дной му́дрости

и о́вцы це́лы, и во́лки сы́ты	both the sheep are safe and the wolves are sated (both sides are happy)

Note: и is used, of course, not only as a conjunction to link whole sentences or parts of sentences – individual words or phrases. It may also be used for emphasis with the sense of 'too' or 'even':
я и не ду́мал, что они́ приду́т сего́дня
It didn't even occur to me that they'd come today

им и там ду́шно   there, too, they feel stuffy

Жемчу́жины наро́дной му́дрости

бу́дет и на на́шей у́лице пра́здник	there will be a festival in our street, too (our turn will come)

24.1.2 Co-ordination may also be expressed through (mild) antithesis:
она́ расска́зывала, а он не слу́шал
she was telling a story, and (but, while) he wasn't listening
я ру́сская, а она́ америка́нка
I'm Russian, and/but she's an American

Жемчу́жины наро́дной му́дрости

> му́дрость в голове́, а не в бороде́ wisdom is in the head, (and, but) not in the beard

24.1.3 or through (sharp) contrast or contradiction:

нам нра́вится го́род, **но** рабо́та сли́шком тяжёлая
we like the town, but the work is too hard

он хоте́л перее́хать в Петербу́рг, **но** она́ реши́ла оста́ться
he wanted to move to St Petersburg, but she decided to stay

мы собира́лись на мо́ре, **но** дождь пошёл
we were going to go to the seaside but it started to rain

24.1.4 or through stating alternatives:

он, должно́ быть, оста́вил дверь откры́той, **и́ли** мо́жет быть кто-то нашёл ключ
he must have left the door open, or maybe someone found the key

ты бу́дешь спать на дива́не, а я на полу́, **и́ли** я бу́ду спать на дива́не, а ты на полу́
you'll sleep on the sofa and I on the floor, or I'll sleep on the sofa and you on the floor

я должна́ верну́ть кни́гу, **а то** меня́ оштрафу́ют
I've got to return the book or else they'll fine me

24.1.5 For clear-cut alternatives: 'either ... , or ...' use **и́ли** ... , **и́ли** ... – both for individual words or parts of sentences and whole clauses:

я прие́ду и́ли на авто́бусе, и́ли на электри́чке
I'll come either by bus or by train

и́ли я прие́ду на авто́бусе, и́ли ты прие́дешь за мной на маши́не
either I'll come by bus or you'll come and fetch me by car

Note: instead of и́ли ... , и́ли ... the slightly colloquial **ли́бо** ... , **ли́бо** ... may be used:

мы пое́дем ли́бо с ним, ли́бо без него́
we'll go either with him or without him

24.1.6 The corresponding negative is **ни** ... , **ни** ... :

ни то, ни друго́е   neither one thing, nor the other

он не игра́ет ни на гита́ре, ни на скри́пке
he doesn't play either the guitar or the violin (plays neither . . ., nor . . .)

Note: **ни** is used not only as a conjunction; it may be used for emphasis:
я не ви́жу ни одно́й пти́цы   I can't see a single bird
он ни ра́зу не писа́л нам   he didn't write to us (even) once

Note: you may come across **да** used as a conjunction particularly in archaic sayings and proverbs with a range of meanings from 'and' to 'but':
щи да ка́ша – пи́ща на́ша   cabbage soup and gruel is our food

рад бы в рай, да грехи́ не пуска́ют
I'd be glad to go to heaven, but my sins don't let me

In ecclesiastical Russian да may be met with the meaning of 'so that':
не суди́те, да не суди́мы бу́дете
judge not that you be not judged

EXERCISES

(i) *Translate into English:*

'И воспомина́ния разгора́лись всё сильне́е. Доноси́лись ли в вече́рней тишине́ в его́ кабине́т голоса́ дете́й, приготовля́вших уро́ки, слы́шал ли он рома́нс и́ли орга́н в рестора́не, и́ли завыва́ла в ками́не мете́ль, как вдруг воскреса́ло в па́мяти всё: и то, что бы́ло на молу́, и ра́ннее у́тро с тума́ном в гора́х, и парохо́д из Феодо́сии, и поцелу́и. Он до́лго ходи́л по ко́мнате и вспомина́л, и улыба́лся, и пото́м воспомина́ния переходи́ли в мечты́, и проше́дшее в воображе́нии меша́лось с тем, что бу́дет' (Chekhov).

(ii) *Translate into Russian:*

1   I play the violin but she plays the guitar.
2   I speak French well, but he doesn't speak it at all.
3   Boris studied physics but went over to Chinese.
4   Everything was wonderful: both the sun shone and the birds sang.
5   She remembered nothing: neither the snow nor the mountains.

24.2 Subordinating conjunctions

Subordinating conjunctions introduce subordinate clauses which amplify the meaning of the main clause of a sentence.

24.2.1 They may do this in terms of time:

    она́ нашла́ ключ, **когда́** он ушёл   she found the key when he'd left

    она́ нашла́ ключ, **по́сле того́ как** он ушёл
    she found the key after he'd gone

    как то́лько он вы́йдет, я скажу́ ему́ пра́вду
    as soon as he comes out I'll tell him the truth

    пре́жде чем я соглашу́сь пойти́ с ним, ему́ придётся подстри́чься
    before I agree to go with him he'll have to have a haircut

    он пил чай, **до того́ как** она́ верну́лась
    he drank tea until she returned

    пока́ он пил чай, она́ чита́ла вечёрку
    while he was drinking his tea she read the evening paper

    мы оста́немся здесь, **пока** он **не** уйдёт
    we'll stay here until he goes away ('while he doesn't' = 'until he does')

    на́ши друзья́ не рабо́тают, **с тех пор как** они́ живу́т на мо́ре
    our friends haven't worked since they've been living at the seaside

    по ме́ре того́ как станови́лось теплее́, распуска́лись цветы́
    as it became warmer flowers came out

24.2.2 or of place:

    мы жи́ли в до́ме, **где** она́ писа́ла пе́рвый рома́н
    we were living in the house where she wrote her first novel

    она́ ча́сто хо́дит в теа́тр, **куда́** оте́ц води́л её в де́тстве
    she often goes to the theatre where her father took her in childhood

Жемчу́жины наро́дной му́дрости

> не всегда́ там ку́рочка куда́хчет, где яйцо́ снесла́   the hen doesn't always cluck
>   where it has laid its egg

24.2.3 or of cause:

    они́ опозда́ли, **потому́ что** закры́ли мост
    they were late because the bridge had been closed

    мы пошли́ в рестора́н, **так как** сего́дня день рожде́ния Бори́са
    we went to the restaurant since it's Boris's birthday today

его до́лго допра́шивали **в связи́ с тем, что** он жил в го́роде без пропи́ски
they were interrogating him for a long time in connection with the fact that he
had been living in the town without a residence permit

нас не впусти́ли **из-за того́, что** мы бы́ли оде́ты неприли́чно
they wouldn't let us in on account of the fact that we were improperly dressed

мы заболе́ли **оттого́, что** ле́то бы́ло тако́е холо́дное
we fell ill because the summer was so cold

ввиду́ того́, что у неё нет дете́й, ей отказа́ли в посо́бии
in view of the fact that she has no children she was refused benefit
or: in view of her not having any children . . .

популя́рность президе́нта вы́росла, **благодаря́ тому́, что** ре́зко упа́ла
инфля́ция
the president's popularity grew due to the fact that inflation fell sharply
or: . . . thanks to inflation falling sharply

всле́дствие того́, что цена́ на нефть вы́росла на два́дцать проце́нтов,
тра́нспорт стал значи́тельно доро́же
as a consequence of the price of oil rising by 20 per cent, transport has
become significantly more expensive

24.2.4 or of purpose:

они́ откры́ли воро́та, **что́бы** коро́вы могли́ вы́йти в по́ле
they opened the gates so that the cows could go out into the field

бы́ли вы́ставлены карти́ны **для того́, что́бы** пу́блика сама́ вы́брала лу́чшие
the pictures were exhibited for the public to choose the best ones itself

24.2.5 or of consequence:

ключ упа́л о́коло стола́, **так что** мы нашли́ его́ сра́зу
the key fell near the table so we found it at once

они́ пришли́ **так** ра́но, **что** мы ещё не вста́ли
they arrived so early we hadn't yet got up

24.2.6 or of concession:

мы пошли́ в теа́тр, **хотя́** у нас не́ было биле́тов
we went to the theatre though we did not have tickets

он добра́лся до до́ма, **несмотря́ на то, что** слома́л но́гу
he managed to get home despite having broken his leg

24.2.7 or of comparison:

он шёл бы́стро, **как бу́дто** кто-то пресле́довал его́
he was walking fast as if someone was pursuing him

Note: If the subject of the main clause and the subordinate clause is the same it is sometimes possible to replace the subordinate clause with an infinitive; this applies only to conjunctions meaning 'before' and those containing что́бы:

пре́жде чем зайти́ ко мне, он позвони́л
before dropping in to see me he rang up

пе́ред тем как гуля́ть в па́рке, он всегда́ надева́ет сапоги́
before going for a walk in the park he always puts on his boots

мы подошли́ бли́же к экра́ну, **для того́ что́бы** лу́чше ви́деть
we moved closer to the screen in order to see better

она́ слу́шает му́зыку, **вме́сто того́ что́бы** гото́виться к уро́ку
she listens to music instead of getting ready for the lesson

Remember: the conjunction must not be confused with the preposition; in English the same word may be used for both:

(Preposition)   до за́втрака   before breakfast
                 по́сле за́втрака   after breakfast
(Conjunction)   он пошёл гуля́ть, **до того́ как** они́ поза́втракали
                 he had a walk before they had breakfast
                 (*or,* if the subjects are the same:)
                 до того́ как поза́втракать, он пошёл гуля́ть
                 before having breakfast he went for a walk

24.2.8

The conjunctions of time require further explanation. In the last example, the use of **до того́ как** suggests that there was no connection between the two events; he didn't do one as a necessary prerequisite to doing the second. So, too, **пока́ не**:

до того́ как постро́или мост, нам на́до бы́ло е́здить че́рез Каза́нь
or: **пока́ не** постро́или мост, нам на́до бы́ло е́здить че́рез Каза́нь
before (*or* until) they built the bridge we had to go via Kazan
(such actions may be separated by time or several other events)

до того́ как она́ поступи́ла в университе́т, она́ рабо́тала в ра́зных места́х
or: **до того́ как** поступи́ть в университе́т, она́ рабо́тала в ра́зных места́х
or: **пока́** она́ **не** поступи́ла в университе́т, она́ рабо́тала в ра́зных места́х
before she went to university she had worked in various places

пока́ не откро́ют библиоте́ку, придётся нам стоя́ть здесь под дождём
until they open the library we'll have to stand here in the rain

- But if the two actions are seen as logically connected, one as a necessary preliminary to the next, the intention to carry out the second already present, **пре́жде чем** is preferred:

  пре́жде чем поза́втракать, он пошёл погуля́ть
  before he had breakfast he went for a walk

  он пошёл погуля́ть, **пре́жде чем** они́ поза́втракали
  he went out for a walk before they had breakfast

- For immediately preceding action in infinitive constructions only you may use **пе́ред тем как**:

  пе́ред тем как откры́ть письмо́, она́ вы́пила табле́тку
  before she opened the letter she took a pill

- For continuous action, 'up to the point when' use **пока́ не**:

  о́вощи сле́дует вари́ть то́лько до тех пор, **пока́** они́ **не** ста́нут мя́гкими
  vegetables should be cooked only until they go soft

Жемчу́жины наро́дной му́дрости

пока́ гром не гря́нет, мужи́к не перекре́стится   until there is a clap of thunder the peasant won't cross himself

Compare: до того́ как она́ вы́шла за́муж, она́ всё вре́мя чита́ла рома́ны
до того́ как вы́йти за́муж, она́ всё вре́мя чита́ла рома́ны
пока́ она́ не вы́шла за́муж, она́ всё вре́мя чита́ла рома́ны

and

пе́ред тем как вы́йти за́муж, она́ продала́ свою́ маши́ну
пре́жде чем она́ вы́шла за́муж, она́ продала́ свою́ маши́ну
пре́жде чем вы́йти за́муж, она́ продала́ свою́ маши́ну

and

до тех пор, пока́ она не вы́шла за́муж, она́ жила́ у тёти.

Some further examples:

пока́ шёл дождь, мы мы́ли посу́ду
while it was raining we did the washing up

пока́ он поднима́лся по ле́стнице, он услы́шал стук в дверь
while (*or* as) he was going upstairs he heard a knock at the door

пока́ они́ е́ли, она́ гото́вила для них ко́мнату
while they were eating she was getting the room ready for them

после того как пробили часы, медленно открылась дверь
after the clock struck the door slowly opened

после того как посмотрим спектакль, мы пойдём к Борису
after we see the show we'll go to Boris's

после того как уехал брат, нам стало скучно
after my brother went away we became bored

с тех пор, как уехал брат, нам стало скучно
since my brother went away we've become bored

с тех пор, как мы работаем здесь, мы ни разу не курили
 since we've been working here we haven't smoked once

с тех пор, как я начал учить русский язык, я стал крепко спать
ever since I began studying Russian I've begun sleeping well

с того дня, как он увидел её, он уже спать не может
he hasn't been able to sleep since the day he saw her

с того момента, как мы познакомились, ты ни разу не рассказывала мне о себе
from the moment we got to know each other you haven't told me about yourself once

как только прибежала собака, появился и Миша
the moment the dog ran in Misha, too, appeared

как только мы кончили работу, нас попросили перекрасить обе стены
as soon as we finished work they asked us to repaint both walls

едва пошёл дождь, как выключили электричество
it had just started raining when they turned off the electricity
(едва is only used nowadays for effect – poetic, etc.)

по мере того как становится теплее, её настроение улучшается
as it gets warmer her mood improves

она худела и худела, **по мере того как** её муж покупал всё больше цветов
she kept getting thinner as her husband kept buying more flowers

бедные студенты всё больше грустят, **по мере того как** триместр подходит к концу
the poor students grieve more and more as the term approaches its end

24.2.9 Some conjunctions are characteristic of bureaucratic Russian (the alternative for normal speech is given in brackets):

в то вре́мя как он лежа́л в больни́це, она́ смотре́ла за фе́рмой
(**пока́** он лежа́л в больни́це, . . .)
while he was in hospital, she looked after the farm

он рабо́тает в конто́ре, **в то вре́мя как** она́ во́дит тролле́йбус
(он рабо́тает в конто́ре, **а** она́ во́дит тролле́йбус)
he works in an office while she drives a trolleybus

у нас то́лько дво́е дете́й, **в то вре́мя как** у них це́лых пя́теро
(у нас то́лько дво́е дете́й, **а** у них це́лых пя́теро)
we have only two children while they have five of them

мы живём в ста́рой кварти́ре, **ме́жду тем как** у сы́на но́вая
(мы живём в ста́рой кварти́ре, **а** у сы́на но́вая)
we live in an old flat whereas our son has a new one

брат худо́жник, **тогда́ как** я учи́тель
(брат худо́жник, **а** я учи́тель)
my brother is an artist while I'm a teacher

Note: the subordinate clause is always separated from the main clause by a comma

Жемчу́жины наро́дной му́дрости

когда́ я ем, я глух и нем	when I eat I'm deaf and dumb

- To convey the idea of one subject perceiving another performing an action, Russian uses the conjunction **как** to introduce a subordinate clause:

  он ви́дел, **как** она́ танцева́ла   he saw her dancing
  я слы́шу, **как** лес шуми́т   I can hear the forest roaring

- The commonest conjunction of all is **что** in the meaning of 'that' – which is often omitted in English, but which cannot be omitted in Russian:

  она́ зна́ет, **что** он музыка́нт   she knows (that) he's a musician
  я не по́нял, **что** вы уже́ знако́мы   I didn't realize you already knew each other
  вы, наве́рное, ду́маете, **что** он ге́ний
  you probably think he's a genius

EXERCISES

(i) *Translate into English:*

Пока́ мы не найдём ключи́, им придётся стоя́ть на у́лице.
Пока́ мы и́щем ключи́, они́ мо́гут почита́ть газе́ты.
Пока́ он не заме́тил её, она́ ничего́ не сказа́ла.
Она́ споко́йно ждала́, пока́ он не заме́тит её.
Пока́ она́ спала́, он прочита́л все её пи́сьма.
Пе́ред тем как закры́ть окно́, она́ услы́шала чей-то знако́мый го́лос.
Прошёл це́лый год, пре́жде чем он получи́л изве́стие о ней.
Пока́ ты не найдёшь биле́ты, мы никуда́ не пое́дем.
Мы жда́ли конца́ войны́, что́бы верну́ться домо́й.
С тех пор как мы живём здесь, никто́ не проезжа́л ми́мо до́ма.
Она́ рабо́тает, в то вре́мя как он допи́сывает рома́н.
По ме́ре того́ как развива́лась эконо́мика, атмосфе́ра в стране́ меня́лась.

(ii) *Complete the sentences:*

. . . она́ откры́ла письмо́, пришла́ подру́га.
. . . вы́йти за́муж, она́ купи́ла пистоле́т.
. . . она́ наде́ла пальто́, она́ посмотре́ла на себя́ в зе́ркало.
. . . он пое́хал домо́й, он вы́ключил компью́тер.
Он заказа́л себе́ такси́, . . . нам пришло́сь добра́ться на авто́бусе.
Они́ заме́тили разби́тое стекло́, . . . зайти́ в дом.
. . . жизнь станови́лась веселе́е, лю́ди ста́ли забыва́ть про́шлое.
. . . верну́лась жена́, ему́ пришло́сь бро́сить кури́ть.

25   THE AWKWARD SQUAD: WORDS KNOWN TO CAUSE DIFFICULTY

25.1 'Also'

There are two words given in most dictionaries for 'also': то́же *or* та́кже. То́же is the more general, while та́кже has the meaning of 'besides, additionally':

| Бори́с врач; На́дя то́же врач | Boris is a doctor; Nadya is, too |
| Бори́с врач; он та́кже пиани́ст | Boris is a doctor; he's also a pianist |

In practice the distinction is not always observed.

Other words may be met with the meaning of 'also':

| и она́ музыка́нт | she, too, is a musician |
| мы говори́ли ещё о му́зыке | we talked also about music |

EXERCISE

Translate into Russian:

1   Boris speaks French; they, too, speak French.
2   They speak Russian; they speak French, too.
3   We also thought the film was very strange.
4   But we thought it was also very beautiful.
5   Why didn't he come, too?

25.2 'Any'

25.2.1   There is no equivalent of 'any' as an indefinite article in Russian:

| вы ви́дели птиц? | did you see any birds? |
| мы не нашли́ грибо́в | we didn't find any mushrooms |

But for emphasis in negative constructions the adjective **никако́й** (**никака́я, никако́е; никаки́е,** etc. see p. 204) may be used:

она́ никогда́ не встреча́ла **никаки́х ру́сских**
she had never met any Russians

я не говори́л **ни о каки́х програ́ммах**
I wasn't talking about any programmes

25.2.2 'Any' as an adjective is translated by **любóй** (**любáя, любóе; любы́е,** etc.):

в любóм слу́чае	in any case
любóй америкáнец вам скáжет	any American will tell you

он интересовáлся **любы́ми необы́чными обстоя́тельствами**
he was interested in any unusual circumstances

EXERCISE

Translate into Russian:

1   Did you buy any wine?
2   There isn't any milk.
3   I couldn't see any flowers.
4   He doesn't live in any big town.
5   Can you see any Americans?

25.3 'Ask'

'Ask' in English means *either* 'ask a question' *or* 'ask for something'.

25.3.1 'To ask (a question)' in Russian is **спрáшивать/спроси́ть**; it denotes an enquiry:

онá спрáшивает, что он дéлает	she asks what he is doing
спроси́ егó, где банк	ask him where the bank is
где ключи́, спрáшивается?	where are the keys, I'd like to know?

он спроси́л меня́, знáешь ли ты Бори́са
he asked me if you knew Boris

почему́ ты не спрóсишь её, у неё ли твой словáрь?
why don't you ask her if she has your dictionary?

Note: the person asked is in the accusative.

Note: a question like those above introduced by the statement that someone asked it is called an 'indirect question'; in English the tense of the verb in the indirect question depends on the tense of the verb 'to ask', e.g.:

'I asked (past tense) where he was' (past tense) whereas the direct question (the question as actually spoken: 'where is he?') was in the present. In Russian, the tense of the direct question is preserved in the indirect question: **я спроси́л, где он** '(literally) I asked where is he'. Similarly:

мы спроси́ли их, где они́ живу́т	we asked them where they lived
мы спроси́ли их, где они́ жи́ли	we asked them where they used to live

он спра́шивал, когда́ вы ко́нчите сочине́ние
he was asking when you were going to finish the essay

она́ хоте́ла знать, пойдёте ли вы в теа́тр за́втра
she wanted to know if you were going to the theatre tomorrow

Note: when introducing indirect questions the Russian for 'if' or 'whether' is ли which is placed as the second element in the clause:

ма́ма спроси́ла, **лю́бишь ли ты** блины́
mum asked if you liked pancakes

я не зна́ю, **чита́ла ли ты** *А́нну Каре́нину*
I don't know whether you've read 'Anna Karenina'

Интере́сно, **у него́ ли** мой видеомагнитофо́н
I wonder if he has my video recorder

25.3.2 'To ask (for something)' is **проси́ть/попроси́ть**; it denotes a request:

он про́сит у неё ключ	he asks her for the key
они́ попроси́ли у меня́ слова́рь	they asked me for the dictionary
попроси́ у врача́ сове́та!	ask the doctor for advice

Note: The person asked is in the genitive after the preposition у; the thing asked for is in either the accusative (concrete) or the genitive (abstract):

он проси́л журна́л	he was asking for the magazine
он проси́л по́мощи	he was asking for help

25.3.3 'To ask (someone to do something)' is also **проси́ть/попроси́ть**:

я попроси́ла его́ откры́ть окно́	I asked him to open the window
попро́сим их показа́ть нам доро́гу	let's ask them to show us the way

Note: The person asked is in the accusative followed by an infinitive.

Note: instead of the infinitive it is also possible to use an 'indirect command' introduced by чтобы:

я попроси́л, чтобы он откры́л окно́   I asked that he open the window
The infinitive construction is easier and commoner.

EXERCISE

Translate into Russian:

1 Ask them what they were doing.
2 Tanya asked Misha to send her a postcard.
3 He asked her how she made pancakes.

4   Have you asked them when they're arriving?
5   Have you asked them for the sugar?
6   Have you asked them to sell you their car?
7   I asked them if they knew when the film began.
8   I'll ask her for her photograph.
9   I wonder if they'll find their dog.
10 Why don't you ask her? She's sure to know.
11 Don't ask me how to get there. Ask him to help you.
12 I don't know why she asked me for a hammer.
13 They are always asking us for advice about money.
14 Where's the station, I'd like to know.
15 The cashier asked us for another 5,000 roubles.
16 I was afraid to ask him where she was.

25.4 'Can', 'may', 'can't'

Russian distinguishes between various kinds of ability:

25.4.1 'to be able' in the straightforward sense of having the physical ability or the opportunity to do something is **мочь/смочь**; for conjugation, see p. 85):

я могу́ идти́ с тобо́й сего́дня на конце́рт
I can go to the concert with you today

там **вы смо́жете купи́ть** всё, что ну́жно для пое́здки
there you'll be able to buy everything you need for the trip

The impersonal **возмо́жно** 'it is possible' has the same meaning of physical ability or opportunity:
здесь **возмо́жно найти́** редча́йшие цветы́
here one can find the rarest flowers

Note: both мочь and возмо́жно may be negated; note that невозмо́жно is written as one word and is synonymous with нельзя́ meaning impossibility (see p. 265):
я не могу́ идти́ с тобо́й сего́дня в теа́тр
I can't go to the theatre with you today

здесь **невозмо́жно найти́** ни одного́ цветка́
it's impossible to find a single flower here

25.4.2 'to be able' in the sense of 'may', of being allowed to do something, is also conveyed by **мочь**, but in this case the impersonal equivalent is **мо́жно**:

мы мо́жем купа́ться то́лько по́сле десяти́ часо́в
we may swim only after ten o'clock

им мо́жно е́здить в США без ви́зы   they can travel to the USA without a visa

когда́ пойма́ют ти́гра, мо́жно бу́дет войти́ в парк
when they catch the tiger it'll be possible to enter the park

Note: мочь may be negated, but the corresponding negative to мо́жно is нельзя́ (see also p. 265):

мы не мо́жем входи́ть без разреше́ния режиссёра
we can't go in without the director's permission

нельзя́ сиде́ть на ле́стнице   you are not allowed to sit on the stairs

25.4.3 'to be able' in the sense of knowing how to do something is уме́ть (perfective суме́ть):

она́ уме́ет говори́ть и по-испа́нски, и по-италья́нски
she can speak both Spanish and Italian

я не уме́ю ката́ться на конька́х   I can't skate

мы суме́ли раскры́ть та́йну их после́днего путеше́ствия
we managed to solve the mystery of their last journey

EXERCISE

Translate into Russian and explain your choice of words:

1   We can see the sea from here.
2   You won't be able to catch the tiger without professional assistance.
3   It isn't possible to buy skates in this shop.
4   Why can't you understand what they say?
5   Can you draw when it's so cold?
6   Can you draw?
7   She will be able to meet you at the station.
8   It'll be impossible to see one another in the crowd.
9   It was possible to get into the theatre without a ticket.
10 Do you know how to translate this word?

25.5 'Completely', 'absolutely', 'totally'

Dictionaries give совершённо, совсём, вполнé *and/or* пóлностью for these words; they are largely interchangeable, but совсём is associated with mainly negative connotations:

вполнé возмóжно 'perfectly possible' *but* совсём невозмóжно 'completely impossible'

онá говорúт совершённо свобóдно	she speaks completely fluently
он совсём сумасшéдший	he's completely mad
мы пóлностью соглáсны с нúми	we're completely in agreement with them

---

EXERCISE

Translate into Russian:

1 He wrote the article completely seriously.
2 We didn't expect the snow at all.
3 It was a completely original plan.
4 It was a totally stupid idea.
5 The house was totally empty.

25.6 'Each other', 'one another'

25.6.1 This is sometimes conveyed by a reflexive verb:

онú целýются всё врéмя	they're always kissing each other
мы подружúлись	we made friends with each other

25.6.2 Referring to animate beings 'each other' is normally translated by the appropriate form of the phrase друг дрýга; in this phrase only the second element changes, even if the subject refers to more than two; note that any preposition required comes after the first друг:

мы лю́бим **друг дрýга**	we love each other
мы помогáем **друг дрýгу**	we help each other
мы дýмали **друг о дрýге**	we thought about each other

все нáши друзья́ согласúлись **друг с дрýгом**
all our friends agreed with one another

25.6.3 Referring to inanimate objects 'each other' is normally translated by a combination of the numeral одúн and the adjective другóй, both of which must agree in gender and number with the object, одúн (*or* однá, однó *or* однú) remaining in the nominative while the case of другóй depends on the grammatical construction:

карти́ны висе́ли **одна́ над друго́й**
the pictures were hanging one above the other

EXERCISE

Translate into Russian:

1 Why don't you help each other?
2 We found one another by the fountain.
3 They write to each other often.
4 They understand each other very well.
5 We can never agree with each other.
6 The books are lying on top of one another.
7 We're putting the plates on top of each other.
8 They are always writing articles about each other.
9 They can't go anywhere without one another.
10 You don't seem to talk to each other much.

25.7 'Have'

25.7.1 'To have' in the sense of 'to own, possess' is normally expressed by the preposition **у** + *gen.*, eg: **у нас маши́на** 'we have a car'; маши́на 'car' is the subject in this construction and is therefore in the nominative with есть the present tense of the verb 'to be' often understood. In the past and future tenses the appropriate form of the verb 'to be' corresponds to the subject, while the person or organization doing the 'owning' is in the genitive after the preposition **у**:

у нас была́ маши́на	we had a car
у Бори́са был ста́рый мотоци́кл	Boris had an old motorbike
у всех де́вушек бы́ли бе́лые ту́фли	all the girls had white shoes
у не́мцев бу́дет инфля́ция	the Germans will have inflation

у прави́тельства бу́дут но́вые зда́ния
the government will have new buildings

25.7.2 To negate this construction the forms **нет** (for the present tense), **не́ бы́ло** (for the past) and **не бу́дет** (future), all followed by the genitive, are used, eg:

у нас нет маши́ны	we don't have a car
ни у кого́ нет маши́ны	no one has a car
у нас не́ бы́ло маши́ны	we didn't have a car

у Бори́са не́ бы́ло ста́рого мотоци́кла
Boris didn't have an old motorbike

у де́вушек не́ бы́ло никаки́х бе́лых ту́фель
the girls didn't have any white shoes

у прави́тельства не бу́дет но́вых зда́ний
the government won't have any new buildings

у не́мцев не бу́дет инфля́ции
the Germans won't have any inflation

Note: **у** has other meanings, eg: **у нас** can mean 'at our place', 'in our house', 'in our country'.

25.7.3 The verb **име́ть** 'to have' is used not so much in the sense of physical possession as in the abstract sense of 'having by association, implying, being a source of', eg:

вы име́ете пра́во молча́ть	you have the right to be silent
что она́ име́ла в виду́?	what did she have in mind? what did she mean?

э́то реше́ние име́ло громáдное значе́ние
this decision had enormous significance

де́ло име́ет отноше́ние к финáнсовому положе́нию
the case has a relationship to the financial situation

EXERCISE

Translate into Russian:

1 Vladimir will have a new car.
2 No one will have a new car.
3 Natasha had three daughters.
4 Natasha didn't have any daughters.
5 Who had my camera?
6 Noone has your camera.
7 They have no hope.
8 What does he mean?
9 The government will have financial problems.
10 She didn't have the right to tell you.

25.8 'If'

Remember that there are two varieties of 'if':

25.8.1 The conditional clause with **éсли** was described on pp. 147, 148:

я уйду́, е́сли он прие́дет	I'll go out if he arrives
я бы ушёл, е́сли бы он прие́хал	I'd have gone out if he'd arrived

25.8.2 The indirect question with 'if' meaning 'whether' requires the particle **ли** (*not* е́сли); this creates a subordinate clause like those illustrated on p. 253, except that **ли** normally comes second in the clause:

я спроси́ла, прие́хал ли он	I asked if (= whether) he'd arrived
мы не зна́ем, до́ма ли Бори́с	we don't know if Boris is at home
интере́сно, по́мнят ли они́ Никола́я	I wonder if they remember Nikolai
непоня́тно, у́чатся ли ма́льчики	it's not clear if the boys go to school

Word order can be varied for emphasis; ли stays in second place:

я спроси́ла, он ли прие́хал	I asked if it was he who'd arrived

мы не зна́ем, ва́шу ли маши́ну укра́ли
we don't know if it was your car that was stolen

EXERCISE

Translate into Russian:

1 Let's ask if he knows the way.
2 Do you know if he's going to Moscow?
3 We can find out if she likes the room.
4 They couldn't decide whether to tell her.
5 It wasn't clear if they'd found the dog.

25.9 'Keep'

25.9.1 'To keep' in the literal sense of 'to preserve, hold' is translated according to context in a number of ways, not always obvious:

мы **оста́вили себе́** ста́рые газе́ты	we kept the old newspapers
он **храни́т** де́ньги в ба́нке	he keeps his money in the bank
храня́т о́вощи в подва́ле	vegetables are kept in the basement
ключи́ **у ма́тери**	his mother keeps the keys
где **лежа́т** ва́ши ту́фли?	where do you keep your shoes?
or: где вы **храни́те** ва́ши ту́фли?	where do you keep your shoes?

or:	куда вы **складываете** ваши туфли?	where do you keep your shoes?
	туфли у него **всегда** чистые	he keeps his shoes clean
	наша машина **стоит** в гараже	we keep our car in the garage
	они **держат** коров	they keep cows
	они **разводят** лошадей	they keep (breed) horses
	канадские войска **сохранили** мир	Canadian forces kept the peace
	(миротворческие силы ООН	UN peacekeeping forces)

25.9.2 'To keep (doing something)' in the sense of 'to continue' is translated either by the verb продолжать/продолжить or by an adverb:

	он **продолжал** читать	he kept on reading
or	он **всё** читал	he kept on reading

	она **всё** спрашивает, когда мы поедем	
or	она **постоянно** спрашивает, когда мы поедем	
	she keeps asking when we're going	

25.9.3 other idiomatic uses of 'to keep' have to be paraphrased:

он не закрыл магазин	he kept the shop open
она заставила ждать толпу	she kept the crowd waiting
он всегда чистит свою машину	he keeps his car clean
каша даёт мне энергию	porridge keeps me going

EXERCISE

Translate into Russian:

1   They'll keep the money.
2   They keep rabbits.
3   They keep smiling.
4   She kept hoping he'd return.
5   She always kept the butter in the fridge.

25.10 'Leave'

25.10.1 'To leave' a place or a person is *either* покидать/покинуть *or* оставлять/оставить which take the accusative:

он **покинул** город рано утром	he left town early in the morning

она **оставила** его, когда он начал пить
she left him when he started drinking

25.10.2 Alternatively one of the verbs of motion such as **уходить/уйти** or

уезжа́ть/уе́хать can be used; these may require a preposition to complete the sense:

> **я уйду́ от тебя́**, е́сли ты бу́дешь вести́ себя́ так
> I'll leave if you go on behaving like that

> **они́ уе́хали из Ло́ндона** по́здно ве́чером
> they left London late in the evening

Colloquially **броса́ть/бро́сить**, literally: 'to throw, chuck', may be used in this sense:

он бро́сил жену́	he left his wife
она́ бро́сила рабо́ту	she left her job

25.10.3   'To leave' something behind, or 'to leave' someone alone is **оставля́ть/оста́вить**:

> он ча́сто **оставля́ет очки́** в ва́нной
> he often leaves his glasses in the bathroom

оста́вь меня́ в поко́е!	leave me in peace

EXERCISE

Translate into Russian:

1   He left the letter on the table.
2   We're leaving Moscow in the autumn.
3   Don't leave me here; I'm frightened.
4   Close the door when you leave.
5   Why did he leave her?

25.11 'For a long time', 'for long'

25.11.1 **Давно́** has two meanings: 'for a long time' [and still going on at the time]:

мы давно́ живём здесь	we've lived here a long time [and still do]
мы давно́ жи́ли там	we had lived there a long time [and still did]

and: 'a long time ago':

мы познако́мились давно́	we got to know each other long ago
мы жи́ли там давно́	we lived there a long time ago

25.11.2 Дóлго means 'for a long time [but not any more]':

мы дóлго жи́ли там	we lived there for a long time
	[but no longer do]
	or we had lived there a long time
	[but no longer did]
я не бу́ду дóлго ждать	I won't wait long

EXERCISE

Translate into Russian:

1 Have you lived there for long?
2 He didn't work in Siberia for long.
3 Had she been standing there for long when you saw her?
4 I always read the paper for a long time after breakfast.
5 She met him long ago, but then didn't see him for a long time.

25.12 'Must' (necessity, obligation)

Several ways of expressing necessity are possible in Russian:

25.12.1 дóлжен is a short-form adjective (*fem.* **должнá**, *neut.* **должнó**; *plur.* **должны́**). It is possibly the commonest word for 'must'. As a short-form adjective it agrees with the subject in gender and number; think of it meaning 'obliged':

онá должнá встать рáно сегóдня   she's got to get up early today

студéнты должны́ читáть мáссу книг
students have to read a lot of books

The appropriate forms of the past and future tenses of быть 'to be' can be added to convey past and future obligation:

он дóлжен был встать рáно сегóдня   he had to get up early today

вы должны́ бу́дете читáть мáссу книг   you'll have to read a lot of books

25.12.2 нáдо is the other common way of expressing necessity. It is an indeclinable, impersonal word meaning 'it is necessary', so the person who has to do something goes into the dative in Russian ('it is necessary *for him* to do it'):

ему́ на́до отве́тить на все вопро́сы   he must answer all the questions
всем тури́стам на́до получи́ть ви́зу   all tourists have to get a visa

The third person singular ('it' forms) of the past and future tenses of быть are used with на́до to convey past and future necessity:

ему́ на́до бы́ло отве́тить на все вопро́сы
he had to answer all the questions

всем тури́стам на́до бу́дет показа́ть паспорта́
all the tourists will have to show their passports

Note: there is in theory a discernible difference in usage between до́лжен and на́до. До́лжен implies a moral obligation to do something, while на́до states an absolute necessity; in practice they are often synonymous.

25.12.3 There are several other words to express obligation and necessity: an alternative to до́лжен, and used in the same way, is **обя́зан**:

на́ши друзья́ обя́заны бу́дут приня́ть ме́ры про́тив свои́х сосе́дей
our friends will be obliged to take measures against their neighbours

Note: this word is particularly useful in the negative to convey the meaning 'don't have to', 'not obliged to', when it may be followed by either the imperfective or perfective infinitive, depending on context (до́лжен and the other words expressing obligation when negated mean 'mustn't' and are followed by the imperfective; see below):

мы не обя́заны плати́ть (*or* заплати́ть) за горя́чую во́ду
we don't have to pay for the hot water

25.12.4 An official tone is conveyed by **вы́нужден**:

фи́рма вы́нуждена бу́дет тре́бовать компенса́ции
the company will be obliged to seek compensation

25.12.5 **ну́жно** is used impersonally like на́до:

мне ну́жно бу́дет самому́ заплати́ть за биле́т
I'll have to pay for the ticket myself ('It'll be necessary for me to . . .')

• **Ну́жно** is the neuter short form of the adjective ну́жный 'necessary', which can be used as a normal adjective:

ну́жные рефо́рмы не́ были введены́ во́время
the necessary reforms were not introduced in time

нам ужа́сно нужна́ э́та кни́га
We need this book terribly ('this book is terribly necessary to us')

25.12.6 **необходи́мо** is used in the same way as ну́жно, with the meaning of 'essential':

необходи́мо зара́нее **посмотре́ть** расписа́ние
it is essential to look at the timetable beforehand

здесь бы́ли все **усло́вия, необходи́мые для** хоро́шего урожа́я
there were all the conditions here necessary for a good crop

25.12.7 Impersonal usage of the verb **приходи́ться/прийти́сь** conveys a distinctly undesirable quality to the obligation:

ей прихо́дится всё де́лать само́й	she has to do everything herself
им придётся перепеча́тать текст	they'll have to retype the text

Никола́ю Бори́совичу пришло́сь сходи́ть к врачу́
Nikolai Borisovich had to go to see the doctor

25.12.8 **сле́довать** is used impersonally with the meaning 'ought':

мне сле́дует купи́ть ему́ пода́рок	I ought to buy him a present

сле́довало бы нам всем по́мнить их подви́г
we should all have remembered their feat

EXERCISE

Translate into Russian; indicate alternatives and explain your choice of aspect:

1   We had to switch on the light; it had already got quite dark.
2   You ought to answer letters in time; then you'll get your money.
3   I've got to pay for the medicine.
4   I don't have to pay for the medicine.
5   You must write to Nikolai Petrovich; he wants to know your plans.
6   His firm was forced to take measures against him.
7   We'll have to show our passports in the hotel.
8   Galina Borisovna had to buy a new car.
9   Ivan Borisovich didn't have to buy a new shirt.
10 Lev Nikolaevich had to write about the terrible conditions in Moscow.

25.13 'Mustn't', 'shouldn't'

25.13.1 Negation of до́лжен, на́до, ну́жно and сле́дует is straightforward in that the subsequent infinitive is invariably imperfective; compare:

за́втра **я до́лжен (должна́) приня́ть** лека́рство
I must take the medicine tomorrow

за́втра я не до́лжен (должна́) принима́ть лека́рство
I mustn't take any medicine tomorrow

на́до ему́ сказа́ть	he must be told
не на́до ему́ говори́ть	he mustn't be told
нам сле́дует допи́ть молоко́	we should finish the milk
нам не сле́дует допива́ть молоко́	we shouldn't finish the milk

25.13.2 **нельзя́** is used with the imperfective infinitive to convey prohibition or moral obligation not to do something:

нельзя́ ходи́ть   (one) mustn't go ('don't cross the road')

нам не́льзя бы́ло умыва́ться в фонта́не
we weren't allowed to wash our hands in the fountain

Note: нельзя́ with the imperfective may also express impossibility when the action you are referring to is continuous:

нам нельзя́ бы́ло рабо́тать здесь; бы́ло сли́шком хо́лодно
it was impossible for us to work here; it was too cold

With the perfective infinitive нельзя́ conveys only impossibility:

нам нельзя́ бы́ло умы́ться в фонта́не; воды́ не́ было сего́дня
it was impossible for us to wash our hands in the fountain; there was no water today

нельзя́ meaning impossibility may be replaced by не мочь or невозмо́жно (see p. 254)

Note: **нельзя́ не** means literally 'it is impossible not to . . .', and is one way to say 'one is bound to . . .' or 'one cannot but . . .'; its meaning is therefore positive:

нельзя́ не восхити́ться её мастерство́м
one has to admire her skill

The same can be done with **не могу́ не** and the infinitive:

я не могу́ не восхити́ться её мастерство́м
I cannot but admire her skill

EXERCISE

Translate into Russian; indicate alternatives with variation of meaning and explain your choice of aspect for the infinitives:

1 You mustn't look at the answers beforehand.
2 Fyodor Mikhailovich shouldn't have written about the war.
3 It was impossible not to hear the music.
4 We cannot but sympathize with him.
5 One is bound to expect that sort of thing.

25.14 'Must' (inevitability)

To translate 'must' when it means 'it is obvious that' or 'I know for a fact that' the phrase **должно́ быть** 'it must be' has to be inserted, between commas, into the basic statement:

я, должно́ быть, дура́к	I must be a fool
он, должно́ быть, уви́дел нас	he must have seen us

она́ ду́мала, что он, должно́ быть, уе́хал в Росси́ю
she thought he must have gone away to Russia

Note: parenthetic words and phrases such as должно́ быть, мо́жет быть 'perhaps', наприме́р 'for example', ка́жется 'it seems' require commas in Russian.

EXERCISE

Translate into Russian:

1 They must be at home.
2 She must have gone out.
3 The concert must have begun.
4 You must want a car very much.
5 He must be going to the library.

25.15 'Put'

Russian is particular in its use of words for 'to put, place', distinguishing between **ста́вить /поста́вить** 'to put standing' and **класть/положи́ть** 'to put lying'.

25.15.1 **ста́вить/поста́вить** is used for anything which can stand or which has a base:

поста́вь стул в у́гол	put the chair in the corner
он поста́вил па́лку за дверь	he stood the pole behind the door
они́ ста́вят таре́лки на́ стол	they are putting the plates on the table
	(plates are thought of as standing on their base)

25.15.2 **класть/положи́ть** (for conjugation see p. 90) is used for anything which lies flat:

я всегда́ кладу́ ножи́ в я́щик	I always put the knives in the drawer
кто положи́л кни́ги на моё ме́сто?	who put the books on my seat?

EXERCISE

Translate into Russian:

1 Who put the chair by the window?
2 Why are you putting the letters on the plate?
3 Where have you put the flowers?
4 I'll put the newspaper on the table.
5 She always puts the phone on the chair.

25.16 'Quite'

25.16.1 Qualifying an adjective or adverb, the adverb 'quite' meaning 'rather' may be translated by довóльно:

Сóня довóльно высóкая дéвушка   Sonya is quite a tall girl

мы довóльно чáсто éздим во Фрáнцию
we go to France quite often

25.16.2 Qualifying a verb 'quite' meaning 'rather' may be omitted (Russian does not have an equivalent understatement) or augmented by a suitable adverb:

	онá лю́бит стихи́	she quite likes poetry
or:	онá довóльно стрáстно лю́бит стихи́	... quite (passionately)

	Борúс хóчет есть	Boris is quite hungry
or:	Борúс довóльно сúльно хóчет есть	Boris really is quite hungry

25.16.3 Qualifying an adjective or adverb, 'quite' meaning 'completely' may be translated by совершéнно or, particularly if the sense is negative, by совсéм (see 'completely' above):

э́тот мост совершéнно нóвый   this bridge is quite new

их положéние бы́ло сосéм безнадёжно
their situation was quite hopeless

EXERCISE

Translate into Russian:

1 I quite want to go to Siberia.
2 It was quite a new car.
3 The film was quite interesting.
4 She was quite exhausted.
5 We quite like the new flat.

25.17 'Rather'

For 'rather' in the sense of 'quite' – see the previous entry.

For 'rather' in the sense of 'preferably' use **лучше** 'better' or the verb **предпочитáть/ предпочéсть** 'to prefer':

я лýчше пойдý	I'd rather go
or: я предпочёл бы идтú	

онú бы лýчше сидéли там	they'd rather sit there
or: онú предпочитáют сидéть там	

EXERCISE

Translate into Russian:

1 I'd rather be in Moscow.
2 It's rather quiet here.
3 Nina would rather have gone to Yalta.
4 He's rather interested in cars.
5 Would you rather go to the theatre?

25.18 'Remain', 'be left'

The verb normally used is **оставáться/остáться**:

он остаётся дóма сегóдня	he's staying at home today
окнó остáнется откры́тым	the window will remain open
оставáлись тóлько крóшки	only crumbs were left
остáлись тóлько крóшки	only crumbs have been (are) left
ничегó не остáлось	nothing remains, there's nothing left

Note: the imperfective past tense describes a situation that prevailed in the past: он оставался 'he remained, stayed, was left' some time in the past and has now probably moved on; the perfective past tense describes an action in the past that was completed, resulting in an outcome: он остался 'he has remained, stayed, been left' and is evidently still here. The perfective past is thus synonymous with the present он остаётся 'he remains, is left':

осталось (*or:* остаётся) то́лько убра́ть ко́мнату
it remains only to tidy up the room

остава́лось то́лько убра́ть ко́мнату
it remained only to tidy up the room

EXERCISE

Translate into Russian:

1 The door will stay closed
2 The director will remain at work.
3 There was one lesson left.
4 There is one lesson left.
5 It only remained to write one letter.

25.19 'Seem'

Каза́ться/показа́ться 'to seem' cannot, as in English, be combined with the infinitive ('he seems to like the picture', etc.); the way the Russians convey this is to insert **ка́жется** 'it seems' (*or* **каза́лось** 'it seemed') parenthetically into the basic statement:

он, **ка́жется,** рабо́тает   he seems to be working
                            (= 'he, it seems, is working')
ему́, **ка́жется,** понра́вилась карти́на
he seems to have liked the picture

они́, **каза́лось,** не хоте́ли пове́рить его́ слова́м
they didn't seem to want to believe his words

Note: каза́ться may also be followed by adjectives or participles directly, not parenthetically, in the instrumental:

они́ **ка́жутся уста́лыми**   they seem tired
ты **показа́лась** стра́шно **взволно́ванной**
you seemed terribly upset

EXERCISE

Translate into Russian:

1 You seem to work all day.
2 We seem to have worked all day.
3 He seemed to like the picture.
4 She seems to believe him.
5 They don't seem to be listening.
6 He didn't seem to understand the film.
7 We seem to have arrived in Moscow.
8 Why does he always seem so upset?
9 This seems to be the answer.
10 It seemed to be the first page of a novel.

25.20 'Some'

25.20.1 Russian does not always require a word for 'some' where English may:

они́ купи́ли муку́   they bought some flour
дай мне во́ду!   give me some water

привезу́т кирпичи́, е́сли ну́жно бу́дет
they'll bring some bricks if it's necessary

25.20.2 'Some' is sometimes conveyed by putting a direct object in the genitive:

он принёс нам молока́   he brought us some milk

25.20.3 There are, however, two words for 'some' expressing the idea of an indeterminate quantity: **не́сколько** 'some', 'several' or 'a few', and **не́который** 'some', 'certain'.

In the nominative and accusative **не́сколько** is followed by the *gen. plur.*:

оста́лось **не́сколько ва́жных вопро́сов**
several (some) important questions remain

за́втра **мы бу́дем обсужда́ть не́сколько ва́жных вопро́сов**
tomorrow we'll discuss several important questions

A distinct animate accusative is not normally formed (see pp. 214, 225):
мы встре́тили не́сколько же́нщин на доро́ге
we encountered several women on the road

In the other oblique cases не́сколько declines and agrees like a plural adjective (see p. 215):
они пое́хали в Пари́ж с не́сколькими друзья́ми
they went to Paris with a few friends

Note: не́сколько can be used adverbially with the meaning 'rather', like дово́льно:
э́то не́сколько стра́нный вопро́с   that's a rather strange question

25.20.4 **не́который** is an adjective, declining in both singular and plural and agreeing with the noun it qualifies; it has the sense of 'certain, some of':
в не́которой сте́пени   in some degree, to a certain extent
в не́которых слу́чаях   in certain cases
'по́сле не́которого размышле́ния он реши́л, что са́мое лу́чшее – э́то спря́таться в хозя́йкин по́греб' (Chekhov).
After some thought he decided that the best thing was to hide in his landlady's cellar.

The plural не́которые is often used with the preposition из to distinguish 'some of':
не́которые из них уме́ют петь   some of them can sing

о не́которых из на́ших ро́дственников мы ничего́ не зна́ем
we know nothing about some of our relatives

EXERCISE

Translate into Russian:

1   Buy some eggs on the way home.
2   I want some paper.
3   Some people thought we were very clever.
4   Some people were standing on the bridge.
5   Some of my friends are working in Moscow.
6   We saw some girls in the park.
7   We saw some of the girls in the park.
8   She found some flowers on the river bank.
9   He arrived with some letters from Boris.
10 With some letters there were photographs.

25.21 'Sorry'

25.21.1   Apologies in Russian are normally expressed by **извини́!**
(**извини́те!**) from **извиня́ть/извини́ть** *or* **прости́!** (**прости́те!**) from
проща́ть/прости́ть, both meaning 'to excuse, forgive'. They may be used
on their own or with за + *acc.*:

> **извини́ меня́ за беста́ктность!**   forgive my tactlessness

Note: the verb 'to be sorry for, to apologize for' is **извиня́ться/извини́ться** with за +
acc.:

> **он извиня́ется за своё поведе́ние**   he apologizes for his conduct

25.21.2   To express sorrow for someone or something **жаль** is used with the
dative of the person regretting and
either the accusative of the person for whom the sorrow is felt:

> **мне жаль сестру́**   I'm sorry for my sister

or the genitive of the thing about which regret is being expressed:

> **мне жаль бы́ло де́нег**   I was sorry about the money

EXERCISE

Translate into Russian:

1   Sorry for the noise!
2   She forgave him his tactlessness.
3   We were sorry for the girl.
4   She's sorry about the milk.
5   They are sorry for the mess (disorder).

25.22 'Stay'

25.22.1 'To stay' in the sense of 'to spend time' can be simply conveyed by
жить/прожи́ть:

> **я прожи́л две неде́ли у бра́та**   I stayed two weeks at my brother's/cousin's

> **мы бу́дем жить, ка́жется, в гости́нице**
> we'll be staying in a hotel, it seems

Alternatively, the verb **остана́вливаться/останови́ться** 'to stop' may be
used if the context allows:

мы всегда́ остана́вливаемся в гости́нице «Метропо́ль»
we always stay at the Hotel Metropole

она́ останови́лась в «Метропо́ле» she stayed at the "Metropol"
or: 'has stopped' and therefore 'is staying' at the "Metropol"

In the sense of 'to remain' the verb used is **оставáться/остáться**:
он остаётся до́ма сего́дня   he's staying at home today

EXERCISE

Translate into Russian:

1   I'll stay a week at my sister's.
2   We stayed in various hotels in France
3   Do you want to stay here? It looks beautiful.
4   Do you want to stay here while I go and get the key?
5   I'm staying in the library this morning.

25.23 'Stop'

25.23.1   'To stop (someone or something)' in Russian is **остана́вливать/ останови́ть**:

останови́те по́езд!   stop the train

де́ти всегда́ остана́вливают его́ в коридо́ре
the children always stop him in the corridor

- 'To stop' intransitively, with the meaning 'to come to a halt', is conveyed by the reflexive **остана́вливаться/останови́ться**:

по́езд остана́вливается   the train is stopping
они́ останови́лись у фонта́на   they stopped by the fountain

25.23.2   'to stop' (someone doing something) in the sense of 'to prevent, interfere or interrupt' is **меша́ть/помеша́ть** which takes the dative of the person and infinitive of the activity:

де́ти меша́ют мне спать   the children stop me sleeping

25.23.3   'to stop', in the sense of 'to cease (doing something), is *either*: **перестава́ть/ переста́ть**, which may be used with an infinitive:

он перестаёт писа́ть то́лько в по́лночь
he stops writing only at midnight

перестáнь!	stop it!
дождь перестáл	the rain has stopped
онá поёт, не переставáя	she sings without stopping

or: **прекращáть/прекратúть**, which may be used with a noun in the accusative denoting an activity or with an infinitive:

учáстники хотя́т **прекратúть переговóры**
the participants want to stop the talks

мы никогдá не бýдем прекращáть нáши усúлия
we will never cease our efforts

онú прекратúли перепúсываться   they stopped writing to each other

So: **перестáли** *or* **прекратúли разговáривать**   they stopped talking
but: **прекратúли разговóр**   they stopped the conversation

EXERCISE

Translate into Russian:

1 Stop talking.
2 Don't stop the bus.
3 She always stops smoking when she falls in love .
4 Don't stop playing.
5 Don't stop him playing.

25.24 'Succeed'

25.24.1 'To succeed' in the sense of achievement requires use of the impersonal verb удавáться/удáться, i.e. using the verb in the 3rd person singular the dative of whoever is successful: мне удаётся 'I succeed', ей удаётся 'she succeeds', нам удаётся 'we succeed', *etc.* Such constructions will normally include an infinitive:

им всегдá удаётся найтú решéние   they always manage to find a solution
емý не удалóсь открыть окнó   he didn't succeed in opening the window

ты дýмаешь, Елéне удáстся поднять чемодáн?
do you think Elena will manage to lift the suitcase?

25.24.2 'To succeed' in the sense of having time to do something is conveyed by the verb успевáть/успéть which may be followed by an infinitive or by на + *acc*.:

| он успе́л дочита́ть кни́гу | he managed to finish the book |
| она́ успе́ла на авто́бус | she caught the bus |

EXERCISE

Translate into Russian:

1. Did she manage to have breakfast?
2. We usually succeeded in walking through without a ticket.
3. I usually succeed in catching the train.
4. Nikolai will manage to change the programme.
5. They must often succeed in getting through on the phone.

25.25 'Take'

'To take' is used with a range of meanings in various English expressions which do not correspond word for word with Russian, so check with a good dictionary if there is the slightest doubt. The basic meaning is conveyed by **брать/взять** (see pp. 84, 86):

| Они́ **беру́т** биле́ты с собо́й | they're taking the tickets with them |
| Он **взял** кни́гу | he's taken the book |

This verb cannot, however, be used for some other common uses of 'to take':

доро́га занима́ет три часа́	the journey takes three hours
он три часа́ мо́ет маши́ну	he takes three hours to wash his car
его́ маши́на вмеща́ет пять челове́к	his car takes five people
они́ везу́т фру́кты на ры́нок	they're taking the fruit to market
он принима́ет душ	he's taking a shower
я иду́ с ней в теа́тр	I'm taking her to the theatre
он провожа́ет её домо́й	he's taking her home
мы понима́ем его́ слова́ всерьёз	we take his words seriously

EXERCISE

Translate into Russian:

1. I took five hours to buy this bath.
2. I'm taking this bath with me. I'm taking it to London.
3. This bath takes two people.
4. I'll take a bath when I get to London.
5. Then I'll take all my friends to the theatre.

25.26 'Use'

25.26.1 The commonest occurrence of 'to use' in English is probably as the auxiliary verb forming one of the past tenses: 'he used to read *Pravda*', 'I used to go to church', etc. In Russian this is equivalent to the imperfective past and so is not translated literally: он читáл *Прáвду*, я ходи́ла в цéрковь.

25.26.2 'To use' in the literal sense is usually imperfective in meaning (continuous or repeated action) and is most commonly translated in Russian by the verbs:

испóльзовать (*impf.* only) (+ *acc.*)

or: **пóльзоваться/воспóльзоваться** (+ *inst.*)

испóльзовать is neutral in meaning; пóльзоваться/воспóльзоваться has the sense of 'to make use of' or even 'to exploit':

они́ испóльзовали компьютер	they used a computer
он постоя́нно испóльзует её	he is always using her

мы должны́ бы́ли испóльзовать си́лу
we had to use force

он всегдá пóльзуется словарём	he always uses a dictionary
мы пóльзуемся слýчаем	we're taking the opportunity
они́ воспóльзовались лопáтой, чтóбы сломáть дверь	

we used a spade to break the door

25.26.3 less common for 'to use' are:

употребля́ть/употреби́ть (+ *acc.*)

and: **применя́ть/примени́ть** (+ *acc.*)

- употребля́ть/употреби́ть is neutral in meaning but tends to be restricted *either* to certain specific contexts:

рáньше онá употребля́ла наркóтики	previously she used drugs
это слóво почти́ не употребля́ется	this word is hardly ever used

or to situations where the object is used up:

я всегдá употребля́ю расти́тельное мáсло
I always use vegetable oil

- применя́ть/примени́ть has the meaning of 'to use, employ (e.g. a technique)':

в строи́тельстве туннéля применя́ли нóвую технолóгию
new technology was used in the tunnel's construction

25.26.4 Sometimes it is better to paraphrase:

диван служит кроватью   the sofa is used as a bed

можно я позвоню по вашему телефону?
may I use your phone?

EXERCISE

Translate into Russian:

1   Why don't you use a hammer?
2   I'm not allowed to use the computer.
3   He often uses that expression.
4   She will use him for her own purposes.
5   Who's been using my shampoo?

KEY TO
TRANSLATION-INTO-RUSSIAN
EXERCISES

The answers provided are not necessarily the only correct versions possible;
they are the ones which use the forms or constructions under discussion in
that chapter.

p. 33
1 В но́вой шине́ли.
2 Министе́рство Вну́тренних Дел.
3 На све́жем во́здухе.
4 На откры́том мо́ре.
5 На седьмо́м не́бе.
6 Нет серьёзных пробле́м.
7 Ско́лько там ли́шних люде́й?
8 Благодаря́ пре́жнему дире́ктору.
9 За далёкими гора́ми.
10 Под тре́тьим высо́ким де́ревом.
11 На второ́м ме́сте.
12 От голубы́х цвето́в.

p. 42–3
1 Он был бо́лен вчера́, но сего́дня он здоро́в.
2 Моя́ ба́бушка была́ больна́я.
3 Сего́дня о́чень хо́лодно.
4 Джи́нсы дороги́е, потому́ что они́ мо́дные.
5 Ю́бка была́ сли́шком коротка́ для неё.
6 В нача́ле семе́стра аудито́рии бы́ли полны́ студе́нтов.
7 Он не бу́дет дово́лен твое́й рабо́той.
8 Э́то типи́чно для него́.
9 Она́ ужа́сно бледна́ – вы не ду́маете, что она́ голодна́?
10 Росси́я бога́та есте́ственными ресу́рсами.
11 Росси́я – страна́, бога́тая есте́ственными ресу́рсами.
12 Они́ бы́ли о́чень ве́селы сего́дня.

p. 50
1 Э́та ле́кция интере́снее, чем я ожида́л(а).
2 Она́ гора́здо/намно́го моло́же, чем он *or* ... моло́же его́.
3 Чем бо́льше он рабо́тает, тем ме́ньше он узнаёт.

4 Они́ приду́т как мо́жно скоре́е.

5 Я ду́маю *or* мне ка́жется, что здесь холодне́е весно́й, чем зимо́й.

6 Вчера́ на ней была́ бо́лее дли́нная ю́бка.

7 Они́ де́лают лу́чшую ме́бель, чем на всех други́х фа́бриках.

8 Ста́ршее поколе́ние не понима́ет, что для студе́нтов усло́вия трудне́е, чем они́ бы́ли ра́ньше.

9 Ру́сская грамма́тика безусло́вно сложне́е англи́йской (грамма́тики) *or* . . . бо́лее сло́жная, чем англи́йская (грамма́тика).

10 Я счита́ю ру́сскую грамма́тику бо́лее сло́жной, чем я́дерная фи́зика.

p. 53

1 Это са́мый знамени́тый магази́н в Москве́.

2 Его́ фи́льмы бы́ли интере́снее всех.

3 Изо всех писа́телей того́ вре́мени у него́ был са́мый я́ркий тала́нт.

4 Слу́шать э́ту програ́мму – скучне́е всего́.

5 В са́мых холо́дных места́х нет да́же волко́в.

6 Она́ рабо́тала с са́мыми нео́пытными врача́ми.

7 Во всех крупне́йших города́х есть университе́т.

8 Моя́ мать одна́жды дала́ мне поле́знейший сове́т.

9 Они́ рабо́тали в трудне́йших усло́виях.

10 Кто твой ближа́йший друг?

p. 58

Она́ посмотре́ла на него́ . . .

ве́село; неохо́тно; скепти́чески *or* скепти́чно; жа́дно; открове́нно

p. 61 (iv)

1 Я уважа́ю его́, но я беспоко́юсь о его́ сы́не.

2 Где её слова́рь? Я не ви́жу его́.

3 Где его́ кассе́ты? Я не ви́жу их.

4 Мы сде́лаем э́то для него́ и его́ семьи́.

5 Он не мо́жет жить без неё. Он не мо́жет жить без её де́нег.

6 Когда́ они́ привы́кли к нему́, они́ разреши́ли ему́ сиде́ть с ни́ми.

7 Мы ничего́ не зна́ем о них и их пла́нах.

8 Вчера́ ве́чером я разгова́ривал(а) с ней, её му́жем и их детьми́.

p. 61 (vi)

1 Она́ счита́ет себя́ хоро́шей пиани́сткой.

2 Он купи́л себе́ но́вый мотоци́кл.

3 Ты взял/взяла́ фотоаппара́т с собо́й?

4 Как ты себя́ чу́вствуешь?

p. 63

(ii) a. Кого́ ты зна́ешь/вы зна́ете?   Что ты пи́шешь/вы пи́шете?   Кому́ ты пи́шешь/вы пи́шете?   С кем ты е́дешь/вы е́дете в Шотла́ндию? Чем ты интересу́ешься/вы интересу́етесь? О ком они́ говоря́т? О чём они́ говоря́т?

(ii) b. Чей э́то зо́нтик? Чья э́то ко́мната? Чью кни́гу она́ взяла́? Чьё и́мя он забы́л? В чьём до́ме нашли́ её? Чьим роди́телям он писа́л?

p. 65

1 Е́сли вы хоти́те уви́деть что-нибу́дь, спроси́те у ги́да.
2 Ка́жется, я ви́дел(а) что-то в воде́.
3 Она́ нашла́ чьи-то очки́ в авто́бусе.
4 Дождь идёт. Мы должны́ е́хать в чьей-нибу́дь маши́не.
5 Он всегда́ говори́т что-нибу́дь прия́тное мне.
6 Он узна́л об э́том от кого́-то из знако́мых.
7 Ты заме́тил(а)/Вы заме́тили кого́-нибу́дь в коридо́ре?
8 Мы заме́тили кого́-то в коридо́ре.

p. 67

1 Она́ встре́тила его́ бра́та в кни́жном магази́не.
2 Она́ встре́тила своего́ бра́та в кни́жном магази́не.
3 Её брат встре́тил её в её кни́жном магази́не.
4 Её брат встре́тил её в своём кни́жном магази́не.
5 Ты нашёл/нашла́ свою́ *or* твою́ соба́ку? *or*
  Вы нашли́ свою́ *or* ва́шу соба́ку?
6 Они́ нашли́ свою́ соба́ку?
7 Она́ оста́лась до́ма, что́бы зако́нчить свою́ дома́шнюю рабо́ту.
8 Она оста́лась до́ма, что́бы помо́чь своему́ бра́ту с (его́) дома́шней рабо́той.
9 Мы попроси́ли его́ почини́ть на́ше окно́.
10 Мы посове́товали ему́ почини́ть его́ окно́.

p. 70

1 Мы ви́дели бизнесме́на, кото́рый посети́л нас/кото́рый был у нас в гостя́х на про́шлой неде́ле.
2 Мы ви́дели бизнесме́на, кото́рого мы посети́ли/у кото́рого мы бы́ли в гостя́х на про́шлой неде́ле.
3 Мы ви́дели бизнесме́на, жена́ кото́рого откры́ла вы́ставку *or* Мы ви́дели бизнесме́на, чья жена́ откры́ла вы́ставку.
4 Мы ви́дели бизнесме́на, кото́рому мы писа́ли в про́шлом году́.
5 Мы ви́дели бизнесме́на, с кото́рым мы е́здили в Москву́.
6 Мы ви́дели бизнесме́на, о кото́ром мы говори́ли вчера́.
7 Маши́на, кото́рая стои́т под тем де́ревом, принадлежи́т её отцу́.
8 Мы е́здили в Ло́ндон в маши́не, кото́рую её оте́ц купи́л ей.
9 Мне не нра́вится маши́на, в кото́рой нет ра́дио.
10 Кни́ги, кото́рыми интересу́ется мой друг, сли́шком дороги́е.
11 Во всех кни́гах, о кото́рых мы говори́ли, бы́ло мно́го филосо́фии.
12 В газе́тах, кото́рых он ещё не чита́л, есть о́чень интере́сные статьи́.

p. 72

1 Тот, кто откры́л дверь, очеви́дно ви́дел э́того челове́ка.

2 Она́ уе́хала в Оде́ссу с тем, кто живёт на тре́тьем этаже́.
3 То, что она́ сказа́ла, бы́ло чрезвыча́йно интере́сно.
4 Мы ду́мали о том, что она́ сказа́ла.
5 Он слы́шит всё, что они́ де́лают.
6 Меня́ интересу́ет всё, что она́ пи́шет.
7 Все, кто слы́шит э́ту му́зыку, засыпа́ют.
8 Она́ написа́ла всем, кто посла́л ей пода́рок.
9 Э́ти кни́ги принадлежа́т тем, с кем мы ходи́ли в теа́тр.
10 Я никогда́ не обраща́ю внима́ния на тех, кто гро́мко спо́рит.

p. 73
1 Чья соба́ка укуси́ла почтальо́на?
2 Я никогда́ не встреча́л(а) челове́ка, от чьей по́мощи зави́села моя́ судьба́.
3 Чей э́то слова́рь?
4 Же́нщина, чей слова́рь вы нашли́, лю́бит чита́ть иностра́нные кни́ги.
5 Дире́ктор, без чьего́ влия́ния я не получи́л (а) бы рабо́ту, оказа́лся дя́дей мое́й жены́.

p. 92 Я ся́ду, ты ся́дешь . . . они́ ся́дут на дива́н.
Я спасу́, ты спасёшь . . . они́ спасу́т лес.
Я упаду́, ты упадёшь . . . они́ упаду́т в ре́ку.
Я ля́гу, ты ля́жешь . . . они́ ля́гут на доро́гу.
Я начну́, ты начнёшь . . . они́ начну́т петь.
Я возьму́, ты возьмёшь . . . они́ возьму́т э́ти кни́ги.
Я ста́ну, ты ста́нешь . . . они́ ста́нут в о́чередь.
Я поддержу́, ты подде́ржишь . . . они́ подде́ржат ле́стницу.
Я соску́чусь, ты соску́чишься . . . они́ соску́чатся.

p. 93
1 Моё се́рдце принадлежи́т О́льге.
2 Она́ берёт кни́гу из библиоте́ки.
3 Бори́с гребёт на Во́лге.
4 Мы спасём собо́р.
5 Берёзы расту́т на пло́щади.
6 Они́ жгут *or* сжига́ют ста́рые газе́ты.
7 Она́ кладёт ло́жки в я́щик.
8 Почему́ вы даёте ей то́лько одну́ таре́лку?
9 Я жму ему́ ру́ку.
10 Вы мо́жете реши́ть, как хоти́те.

p. 94
1 Кто среди́ вас реша́ет?
2 Кто де́ржит флаг?
3 Они́ всегда́ молча́т.
4 Мы лиша́ем её мя́са и ма́сла.
5 Он бьётся голово́й о сте́ну.

6 Эти кни́ги содержат сочине́ния всех вели́ких поэ́тов.

7 Не́которые из их имён звуча́т стра́нно.

8 Кому́ принадлежи́т та ло́шадь?

9 Почему́ ты не отвеча́ешь?

10 Кто э́то лежи́т посреди́ ко́мнаты?

11 Он никогда́ не сообща́ет мне о вре́мени своего́ прие́зда *or* прибы́тия.

12 Вы слы́шите звон колоколо́в отсю́да?

13 Она́ ду́мает, что он превраща́ется в лягу́шку.

14 Она́ запреща́ет им ходи́ть на стадио́н.

15 Му́зыка конча́ется.

16 Э́то стихотворе́ние выража́ет любо́вь поэ́та к приро́де.

17 Он посвяща́ет э́тот рома́н свое́й жене́.

18 Ма́льчики разбива́ют *or* лома́ют ста́рые воро́та.

19 Почему́ ты кричи́шь? Никто́ никогда́ не отвеча́ет.

20 Она́ всегда́ и́щет свои́ очки́.

p. 106

1 Что ты де́лал(а) сего́дня?

2 Что ты де́лал(а) сего́дня?

3 Что ты де́лал(а) сего́дня?

4 Что ты де́лал(а) *or* сде́лал(а) сего́дня?

5 Она́ нашла́ пода́рок, когда́ она́ вста́ла.

6 Я не заме́тил(а), что я потеря́л(а) свои́ *or* мои́ очки́.

7 Мы три дня кра́сили дом.

8 Она́ три часа́ покупа́ла мя́со *or* она́ ждала́ три часа́, что́бы купи́ть мя́со.

9 Она́ ду́мала, что она́ уже́ забы́ла, как гото́вить борщ.

10 Ты чита́л(а) «Войну́ и мир»? – Да, но я ещё не ко́нчил(а) её *or* дочита́л(а) её до конца́.

11 Она́ два часа́ выбира́ла шля́пу и, наконе́ц, вы́брала жёлтую.

12 Мне всегда́ нра́вилась Я́лта, но на э́тот раз я предпочёл/предпочла́ Со́чи.

13 Э́тот худо́жник не нарисова́л ни одного́ портре́та за пять лет.

14 Мы убира́ли *or* чи́стили ку́хню це́лый час.

15 Он сшил себе́ костю́м за пять часо́в.

16 Постепе́нно они́ вы́работали план, с кото́рым ка́ждый мог согласи́ться.

17 Мы продава́ли я́блоки це́лый день; к ве́черу мы про́дали все.

18 Кто взял мой зо́нтик? Я не могу́ найти́ его́.

19 Кто брал мой зо́нтик? Он сло́ман.

20 Он ме́дленно сел и на́чал чита́ть газе́ту.

21 Что вы собира́етесь де́лать сего́дня у́тром? – Я хочу́ купи́ть шля́пу.

22 Три го́да я не опа́здывал(а) на ле́кцию.

23 Я ни ра́зу не опозда́л(а) на ле́кцию.

24 Он писа́л свое́й ма́ме ка́ждую неде́лю.

25 Он бу́дет писа́ть свое́й ма́ме ка́ждый ме́сяц.

p. 108

1 Ка́ждый день он идёт на рабо́ту пешко́м, а е́дет обра́тно на трамва́е.
2 Я лечу́ за́втра в Петербу́рг; я ча́сто лета́ю туда́ по дела́м.
3 Она́ пла́вала в о́зере, когда́ он бежа́л на ста́нцию.
4 Они́ несли́ свои́ чемода́ны к гости́нице.
5 Я веду́ её на по́чту, а пото́м иду́ в библиоте́ку
   or Я везу́ её на по́чту, а пото́м е́ду в библиоте́ку.

p. 113

1 Когда́ бы я ни заходи́л(а) к Бори́су, он всегда́ рабо́тает в саду́.
2 Когда́ я зайду́ к Бори́су, я спрошу́ его́ о са́де.
3 Когда́ бы я ни е́здил(а) в Ло́ндон, я всегда́ захожу́ в Брита́нский музе́й.
4 Он е́здил вчера́ в Ло́ндон и привёз ей пода́рок.
5 Она́ пробежа́ла ми́мо меня́, когда́ я выходи́л(а) из до́ма.
6 Мы привезли́ ему́ биле́т и повезли́ *or* отвезли́ его́ на стадио́н.
7 Ребёнка нашли́ за дива́ном; он запо́лз туда́ и засну́л.
8 Когда́ он сле́зет с кры́ши, я вы́гоню его́ из па́рка.
9 Э́то превзошло́ все мои́ ожида́ния: тепе́рь мы обойдёмся без маши́ны.
10 А́втор то́нко подошёл к те́ме и то́чно воспроизвёл разгово́рный стиль конца́
    про́шлого ве́ка *or* столе́тия.
11 Что произошло́, когда́ по́езд ушёл?
12 Что произошло́, когда́ по́езд уходи́л?
13 Он ду́мал о ней, когда́ он шёл на ста́нцию.
14 Дождь пошёл, когда́ мы сиде́ли на берегу́ реки́.
15 Когда́ она́ шла на рабо́ту, она́ заме́тила стра́нную пти́цу.

p. 119

1 Газе́та получа́ет мно́го пи́сем от люде́й, рабо́тающих на Да́льнем восто́ке.
2 Газе́та получа́ла мно́го пи́сем от люде́й, рабо́тающих на Да́льнем восто́ке.
3 Газе́та получа́ет мно́го пи́сем от люде́й, рабо́тавших на Да́льнем восто́ке.
4 Газе́та получа́ла мно́го пи́сем от люде́й, рабо́тавших на Да́льнем восто́ке.

p. 128

1 Кварти́ра была́ ку́плена.
2 Грибы́ бы́ли со́браны.
3 Пьеса была́ переведена́ Пастерна́ком.
4 Письмо́ бы́ло полу́чено.
5 Де́ньги бы́ли поте́ряны.
6 Фа́брика была́ постро́ена в про́шлом году́.

p. 132

1 Респу́блика была́ образо́вана по́сле войны́.
2 Она́ была́ гото́ва рабо́тать.
3 Пла́ны бы́ли определённые и я́сные.
4 Це́ли бы́ли определены́ комите́том.
5 Солда́ты, ра́ненные в бою́, лежа́ли на земле́.

6　Ра́неные солда́ты лежа́ли на земле́.
7　Она́ пришла́ с кра́шеными волоса́ми.
8　Она́ пришла́ с волоса́ми, покра́шенными в кра́сный цвет.
9　У нас не́ было да́нных о безрабо́тице.
10　Мы получи́ли да́нные от учёных.

p. 139

1　Мы разгова́ривали, си́дя на траве́.
2　Открыва́я дверь, она́ нашла́ письмо́.
3　Любя́ Бори́са, она́ всегда́ ве́рит ему́.
4　Не замеча́я дождя́, она́ шла на ста́нцию.
5　Он про́сто сиде́л там, не дви́гаясь.

p. 139

1　Откры́в шкаф, он вы́брал кни́гу.
2　Устро́ив дела́, она́ верну́лась в конто́ру.
3　Найдя́ письмо́, Ната́ша побежа́ла на ку́хню.
4　Услы́шав но́вости, он удиви́тся.
5　Не услы́шав звонка́, мы продолжа́ли говори́ть.

p. 139

1　Откры́в окно́, мы уви́дели медве́дя.
2　Око́нчив своё сочине́ние, она́ начала́ петь.
3　Когда́ мы привы́кли к кли́мату, он показа́лся нам норма́льным.
4　Вы́мыв маши́ну, он не захоте́л е́хать че́рез по́ле.
5　Он бежа́л че́рез пло́щадь, не замеча́я дождя́.
6　Придя́ домо́й, мы включи́м ра́дио.
7　Заплати́в за обе́д, мы вы́шли на у́лицу.
8　Когда́ авто́бус придёт, мы спро́сим води́теля.
9　Я чита́л(а) «Войну́ и мир», не говоря́ уже́ о бо́лее коро́тких сочине́ниях.
10　Су́дя по облака́м, я ду́маю, что пойдёт снег.

p. 141 (i)

1　Де́вушка чита́ла газе́ту, лёжа на полу́
　　or (less probably) де́вушка чита́ла газе́ту, лежа́щую на полу́.
2　Я нашёл соба́ку, гуля́я вдоль бе́рега реки́
　　or (less probably) я нашёл соба́ку, гуля́ющую вдоль бе́рега реки́.
3　Како́й студе́нт не засыпа́ет кре́пко, чита́я Толсто́го?
　　or (less probably) како́й студе́нт, чита́ющий Толсто́го, не засыпа́ет кре́пко?
4　Они́ ко́нчили стро́ить кры́шу, защища́ющую руи́ны от дождя́
　　or (less probably) они́ ко́нчили стро́ить кры́шу, защища́я руи́ны от дождя́.
5　Я всегда́ собира́ю газе́ты, оста́вшиеся, когда́ други́е пассажи́ры вы́шли из
　　авто́буса *or* (less probably) я всегда́ собира́ю газе́ты, остава́ясь, когда́
　　други́е пассажи́ры вы́шли из авто́буса.

p. 141 (ii)

1 Так как мы постро́или гара́ж, на́ша маши́на тепе́рь не бу́дет в опа́сности
    or когда́ мы постро́им гара́ж . . .

2 Когда́ (*or* по́сле того́ как) сире́нь отцветёт, мы её сре́жем.

3 Когда́ мы слу́шали но́вости, зазвони́л телефо́н.

p. 146

1 Она́ положи́ла туда́ кни́гу, что́бы они́ могли́ ви́деть её.

2 Я скажу́ ему́, что́бы он знал моё мне́ние.

3 Они́ посыла́ют её в Москву́, что́бы она́ могла́ зако́нчить кни́гу.

4 Я напишу́ им запи́ску, что́бы они́ не забы́ли.

5 Он хо́чет найти́ свою́ соба́ку.

6 Он хо́чет, что́бы мы нашли́ его́ соба́ку.

7 Он хо́чет помо́чь ей.

8 Она́ хо́чет, что́бы он помо́г ей.

9 Студе́нты хотя́т идти́ домо́й.

10 Мы не хоти́м, что́бы студе́нты ушли́ домо́й.

11 Я хоте́л(а), что́бы она́ откры́ла дверь.

12 Я попроси́л(а) её откры́ть дверь.

13 Я предложи́л(а), что́бы она́ откры́ла дверь.

14 Я посове́товал(а) ей откры́ть дверь.

15 Я потре́бовал(а), что́бы она́ откры́ла дверь.

16 Я наста́ивал(а) на том, что́бы она́ откры́ла дверь.

17 Я приказа́л(а) ей откры́ть дверь.

18 Ну́жно бы́ло, что́бы она́ откры́ла дверь.

19 Ва́жно бы́ло, что́бы она́ откры́ла дверь.

20 Она́ должна́ была́ бы *или* Ей сле́довало бы откры́ть дверь.

21 Бори́с всегда́ ожида́л, что мы приглаcи́м его́ в Ви́ндзор.

22 Она́ всегда́ говори́т им, что́бы они́ не шуме́ли.

23 Мы ча́сто ждём не́сколько часо́в, что́бы они́ откры́ли воро́та.

24 Тури́сты иногда́ про́сят её спеть ещё одну́ пе́сню
    or Тури́сты иногда́ про́сят её, что́бы она́ спе́ла ещё одну́ пе́сню.

25 Почему́ они́ всегда́ наста́ивают на том, что́бы мы cиде́ли здесь?

26 О́чень ва́жно, что́бы он встре́тил нас в четве́рг.

27 Я хочу́, что́бы ты услы́шал(а)/вы услы́шали э́то.

28 Она́ не хоте́ла, что́бы мы нашли́ те́ло.

29 Я не по́мню, что́бы он когда́-ли́бо говори́л э́то.

30 Немы́слимо *или* Невозмо́жно, что́бы она́ ушла́ так ра́но.

31 Что́бы ты ни говори́л(а)/вы ни говори́ли, ничего́ не меня́ется.

32 Где бы они́ ни рабо́тали, они́ всегда́ бы́ли сча́стливы.

33 Когда́ бы он ни ду́мал о ней, он всегда́ закрыва́ет глаза́.

34 Куда́ бы ни е́хали мои́ сёстры, они́ всегда́ звоня́т мне.

35 Она́ всегда́ жа́ловалась, что бы он ни носи́л.

36 Как бы тру́дно ни́ было, мы должны́ ко́нчить э́то к шести́ часа́м.

p. 148

1   Éсли шёл дождь, мы обы́чно шли в кино́.
2   Éсли ты хо́чешь/вы хоти́те, мы мо́жем пообе́дать в го́роде.
3   Éсли они́ прие́дут за́втра, мы должны́ бу́дем уйти́.
4   Я покажу́ ей мои́ сла́йды, е́сли бу́дет идти́ дождь.
5   Мы мо́жем нача́ть рабо́ту, е́сли ты гото́в(а)/вы гото́вы.

p. 149

1   Бы́ло бы прия́тно, е́сли бы он говори́л «спаси́бо» иногда́.
2   Он уе́хал бы в Ло́ндон, е́сли бы у него́ бы́ли де́ньги.
3   Он пое́дет в Ло́ндон, е́сли у него́ бу́дут де́ньги.
4   Кварти́ра понра́вилась бы мне бо́льше, е́сли бы она́ была́ на второ́м этаже́.
5   Я ду́маю, что она́ уби́ла бы его́, е́сли бы она́ ви́дела его́.

p. 154

1   Убира́й(те) посте́ль!
2   Убери́т(те) посте́ль!
3   Посыла́й(те) им фотогра́фии!
4   Пошли́(те) им фотогра́фии!
5   Не теря́й(те) докуме́нты/докуме́нтов!
6   Не потеря́й(те) докуме́нты/докуме́нтов!
7   Не забыва́й(те) наде́ть ша́пку!
8   Не забу́дь(те) наде́ть ша́пку!

p. 156

1   Дава́й(те) пое́дем *or* Пое́дем(те) в Москву́.
2   Пуска́й она́ е́дет в Москву́, е́сли хо́чет.
3   Пусть она́ пое́дет в Москву́ за карти́ной.
4   Дава́й(те) помо́жем ему́ найти́ (его́) соба́ку.
5   Пуска́й *or* Пусть они́ и́щут его́ соба́ку.

p. 173–4

1   Они́ пропуска́ли люде́й.
2   Они́ выпуска́ют дете́й.
3   Нас отпуска́ют на́ день.
4   Она́ подпусти́ла их к две́ри.
5   Спу́тники запуска́ют отсю́да.
6   Расписа́ние измени́ли весно́й.
7   В сле́дующий раз мы поменя́ем цвет стен.
8   Он соверше́нно перемени́лся *or* измени́лся с тех пор, как она́ уе́хала.
9   Её лицо́ измени́лось, когда́ он вошёл.
10 Éсли бы то́лько кто-нибу́дь смени́л *or* перемени́л ла́мпочку.
11 Смени́ли бельё сего́дня.
12 Я хочу́ поменя́ть *or* обменя́ть до́ллары на рубли́.
13 Я хочу́ разменя́ть э́ту банкно́ту.
14 Ка́ждый год мы обме́ниваемся студе́нтами.

15 Я ду́маю, что мы по оши́бке поменя́лись *or* обменя́лись зонта́ми.
16 Её обсчита́ли, когда́ она́ спеши́ла.
17 Я обяза́тельно включу́ его́ в спи́сок.
18 Грибы́ не́ были хорошо́ прожа́рены.
19 Дава́й сни́мем карти́ну со стены́.
20 Э́то возбужда́ет моё любопы́тство.
21 Она́ напекла́ ма́ссу блино́в.
22 Мы просмотре́ли его́ оши́бку.
23 Я хочу́ продолжа́ть рабо́тать здесь до пе́нсии *or* , пока́ не получу́ пе́нсию.
24 Они́ ме́дленно отодви́нулись друг от дру́га.
25 Он вы́рвал страни́цу из кни́ги.
26 Она́ увлекла́сь чте́нием те́кста.
27 Его́ обме́рили, когда́ ему́ отреза́ли кусо́к тка́ни.
28 Оста́лось только дописа́ть три после́дних страни́цы.
29 Ты хорошо́ вы́спался?
30 Он всма́тривался в моё лицо́.

p. 180

1 Не будь дурако́м!
2 Я хочу́ быть бога́тым/бога́той.
3 Он был настоя́щий друг.
4 Он служи́л секретарём коми́ссии.
5 Приме́ром э́того была́ его́ но́вая кни́га.
6 Це́лью экспеди́ции бы́ло установи́ть наблюда́тельный пункт.
7 Ваш визи́т бу́дет настоя́щим удово́льствием для нас.
8 Её сестра́ оста́нется мои́м дру́гом/мое́й подру́гой навсегда́.
9 Он бу́дет вели́ким учёным.
10 Команди́р вы́глядел мальчи́шкой.
11 Вся пло́щадь и все зда́ния вы́глядели ста́рыми и гря́зными.
12 Вдруг я уви́дел(а) кого́-то на у́лице: э́то был ру́сский солда́т.

p. 207–8 (ii)

1 Он никогда́ ничего́ не чита́ет.
2 Никто́ не лю́бит его́ *or* Он никому́ не нра́вится.
3 Она́ никуда́ не ходи́ла.
4 Он никогда́ не игра́ет со свои́ми бра́тьями.
5 Он никогда́ не игра́ет ни с кем.
6 Они́ никогда́ не бу́дут рабо́тать в Сиби́ри.
7 Студе́нты никогда́ ничего́ нигде́ не тра́тили.
8 Они́ ника́к не мо́гут откры́ть холоди́льник.
9 Они́ не интересу́ются э́тим; они́ ниче́м не интересу́ются.
10 Мы не отве́тственны за него́; мы ни за кого́ не отве́тственны.
11 Э́то не отно́сится к ним; э́то ни к кому́ не отно́сится.
12 Она́ не винова́та в э́том; она́ ни в чём не винова́та.

p. 208 (iii)

1 Она́ никогда́ не приглаша́ет меня́; она́ никогда́ никого́ не приглаша́ет.
2 Она́ никогда́ не пи́шет мне; она́ никогда́ никому́ не пи́шет.
3 Она́ никогда́ не посеща́ет меня́; она́ никогда́ никого́ не посеща́ет.
4 Она́ никогда́ не сове́тует мне; она́ никогда́ никому́ не сове́тует.
5 Она́ никогда́ не обраща́ется ко мне; она́ никогда́ ни к кому́ не обраща́ется.
6 Она́ никогда́ не полага́ется на меня́; она́ никогда́ ни на кого́ не полага́ется.
7 Она́ никогда́ не ждёт меня́; она́ никогда́ никого́ не ждёт.
8 Она́ никогда́ не помога́ет мне; она́ никогда́ никому́ не помога́ет.
9 Она́ никогда́ не говори́т со мной; она́ никогда́ ни с кем не говори́т.
10 Она́ никогда́ не кричи́т на меня́; она́ никогда́ ни на кого́ не кричи́т.
11 Она́ никогда́ не смеётся надо мной; она́ никогда́ ни над кем не смеётся.
12 Она́ никогда́ не жа́луется на меня́; она́ никогда́ ни на кого́ не жа́луется.
13 Она́ никогда́ не захо́дит за мной; она́ никогда́ ни за кем не захо́дит.
14 Она́ никогда́ не забо́тится обо мне; она́ никогда́ ни о ком не забо́тится.
15 Она́ никогда́ не подхо́дит ко мне; она́ никогда́ ни к кому́ не подхо́дит.

p. 209

1 Она́ не интересова́лась никаки́ми ту́флями.
2 Ты никогда́ не чита́ешь никаки́х хоро́ших книг.
3 Я не хочу́ перее́хать ни в како́й го́род.
4 Они́ ни в како́й гости́нице не жи́ли.
5 Зо́нтик не стоя́л ни за како́й две́рью.
6 Не́чего боя́ться.
7 У них не́ было (никаки́х) сту́льев, так что не́ на чем бы́ло сиде́ть.
8 Не́ с кем бы́ло обсужда́ть пробле́му.
9 Не́ о чем бу́дет писа́ть ей.
10 Не́кому жа́ловаться.
11 Не́кому бу́дет мне показа́ть (мою́ *or* свою́) рабо́ту.
12 Ничего́ нет в холоди́льнике, и не́где купи́ть молоко́.
13 Я не хочу́ сиде́ть до́ма, но здесь не́куда идти́.
14 Не́когда/Нет вре́мени ду́мать о ру́сской грамма́тике.
15 Не́чего расстра́иваться/беспоко́иться/волнова́ться (об э́том).

p. 224

1 Я купи́л две па́ры дешёвых часо́в.
2 Во́семь челове́к е́хали на трёх саня́х.
3 Я встре́тил(а) там пятеры́х *or* пять о́чень стра́нных люде́й.
4 Семь челове́к *or* се́меро люде́й сиде́ли в ко́мнате. Оди́н был врач.
   Зна́чит, бы́ло шесть больны́х *or* ше́стеро больны́х.

p. 227

1 В обе́их буты́лках бы́ло вино́.
2 Я реши́л(а) написа́ть обе́им ба́бушкам.
3 Они́ провели́ полтора́ го́да в Росси́и.
4 В ско́льких города́х вы бы́ли?
5 Во мно́гих города́х усло́вия бы́ли лу́чше, чем я ожида́л(а).
6 Ско́лько ме́тров вы купи́ли? Три и три пя́тых.

p. 228
1 В шестóм магазúне.
2 Под вторы́м столóм.
3 На деся́том этажé.
4 Пóсле трéтьей игры́.
5 На три́дцать пéрвом трамвáе.
6 Под кáждым пя́тым крéслом.
7 В восемнáдцатом дóме.
8 На двéсти сéмьдесят пя́той страни́це.
9 Вмéсто двенáдцатого урóка.
10 При Ивáне четвёртом *or* В цáрствование Ивáна четвёртого.

p. 243
1 Я игрáю на скри́пке, а онá игрáет на гитáре.
2 Я говорю́ хорошó по-францýзски, а он вообщé не говори́т (по-францýзски).
3 Бори́с занимáлся фи́зикой, но перешёл на китáйский язы́к.
4 Всё бы́ло прекрáсно: и сóлнце сия́ло, и пти́цы пéли.
5 Онá ничегó не пóмнила: ни снéга, ни гор.

p. 251 'Also'
1 Бори́с говори́т по-францýзски; они́ тóже говоря́т по-францýзски.
2 Они́ говоря́т по-рýсски; они́ тáкже говоря́т по-францýзски.
3 Мы тóже дýмали, что карти́на óчень стрáнная.
4 Но мы дýмали, что онá тáкже óчень краси́вая.
5 Почемý он тóже не приходи́л?

p. 252 'Any'
1 Ты купи́л(а)/Вы купи́ли винó/винá?
2 Нет молокá.
3 Я не ви́дел(а) цветóв.
4 Он ни в какóм большóм гóроде не живёт.
5 Ты ви́дишь/Вы ви́дите америкáнцев?

p. 253–4 'Ask'
1 Спроси́(те) их, что они́ дéлали.
2 Тáня попроси́ла Ми́шу послáть ей откры́тку.
3 Он спроси́л её, как онá дéлает блины́.
4 Ты спроси́л(а)/Вы спроси́ли их, когдá они́ придýт/приéдут?
5 Ты проси́л/Вы проси́ли у них сáхар/сáхара?
6 Ты проси́л/Вы проси́ли их продáть тебé/вам их маши́ну/автомоби́ль?
7 Я спроси́л(а) их, знáют ли они́, когдá начинáется фильм.
8 Я попрошý у неё её фотокáрточку.
9 Интерéсно, найдýт ли они́ свою́ собáку.
10 Почемý ты не спрáшиваешь/вы не спрáшиваете её? Онá обязáтельно знáет.
11 Не спрáшивай(те) меня́, как добрáться тудá! Попроси́(те) егó помóчь!
12 Я не знáю, почемý онá попроси́ла у меня́ молотóк.

13 Они всё время просят у нас совета о деньгах.
14 Где станция/вокзал, спрашивается?
15 Кассир попросил у нас ещё пять тысяч рублей.
16 Я боялся/боялась спросить его, где она.

p. 255 'Can'

1 Мы можем видеть море отсюда.
2 Ты не сможешь/Вы не сможете поймать тигра без профессиональной помощи.
3 Невозможно купить коньки в этом магазине.
4 Почему ты не можешь/вы не можете понять, что они говорят?
5 Ты можешь/Вы можете рисовать, когда так холодно?
6 Ты умеешь/Вы умеете рисовать?
7 Она сможет встретить тебя/вас на станции/вокзале.
8 Невозможно будет увидеть друг друга в толпе.
9 Можно было пройти в театр без билета.
10 Ты знаешь/Вы знаете, как перевести это слово?

p. 256 'Completely'

1 Он написал статью совершенно серьёзно.
2 Мы совсем не ожидали снега.
3 Это был совершенно оригинальный план.
4 Это была совсем глупая идея.
5 Дом был совершенно/совсем пустой/пустым/пуст.

p. 257 'Each other'

1 Почему вы не помогаете друг другу?
2 Мы нашли друг друга у фонтана.
3 Они пишут друг другу часто.
4 Они понимают друг друга очень хорошо.
5 Мы никогда не можем согласиться друг с другом.
6 Книги лежат одна на другой.
7 Мы ставили тарелки одна на другую.
8 Они всегда пишут статьи друг о друге.
9 Они никуда не могут пойти друг без друга.
10 Вы, кажется, не очень много говорите друг с другом.

p. 258 'Have'

1 У Владимира будет новая машина.
2 Ни у кого не будет новой машины.
3 У Наташи было три дочери.
4 У Наташи не было никаких дочерей.
5 У кого был мой фотоаппарат?
6 Ни у кого не было вашего аппарата.
7 У них нет надежды.
8 Что он имеет в виду?

9 У прави́тельства бу́дут фина́нсовые пробле́мы.
10 У неё не́ было пра́ва сказа́ть вам э́то.

p. 259 'If'

1 Дава́й(те) спро́сим, зна́ет ли он доро́гу.
2 Ты зна́ешь/вы зна́ете, е́дет ли он в Москву́?
3 Мы мо́жем узна́ть, нра́вится ли ей ко́мната.
4 Они́ не могли́ реши́ть, сказа́ть ли ей.
5 Непоня́тно бы́ло, нашли́ ли (они́) соба́ку.

p. 260 'Keep'

1 Они́ оста́вят себе́ де́ньги.
2 Они́ разво́дят кро́ликов.
3 Они́ всё улыба́ются.
4 Она́ всё наде́ялась, что он вернётся.
5 Она́ всегда́ храни́т ма́сло в холоди́льнике.

p. 261 'Leave'

1 Он оста́вил письмо́ на столе́.
2 Мы уезжа́ем из Москвы́ о́сенью.
3 Не оставля́й(те) меня́ здесь (одного́/одну́), я бою́сь.
4 Закро́й(те) дверь, когда́ ты (вы) ухо́дишь (ухо́дите).
5 Почему́ он бро́сил/оста́вил её?

p. 262 'for long'

1 Ты давно́ живёшь/Вы давно́ живёте там ?
2 Он не рабо́тал до́лго в Сиби́ри.
3 Она́ давно́ стоя́ла там, когда́ ты уви́дел(а)/вы уви́дели её.
4 Я всегда́ до́лго чита́ю газе́ту по́сле за́втрака.
5 Она́ встре́тила его́ давно́, но пото́м до́лго не ви́дела его́.

p. 264 'Must'

1 Мы должны́ бы́ли/Нам пришло́сь включи́ть свет, ста́ло уже́ совсе́м темно́.
2 Вы должны́ бу́дете/Вам на́до бу́дет отве́тить на пи́сьма во́-время, тогда́ вы полу́чите свои́ де́ньги.
3 Я до́лжен (должна́)/Мне на́до/Мне ну́жно плати́ть за лека́рство.
4 Мне не на́до плати́ть за лека́рство.
5 Вы должны́/Вам на́до бу́дет написа́ть Нилола́ю Петро́вичу, он хо́чет знать ва́ши пла́ны.
6 Его́ фи́рма была́ вы́нуждена приня́ть ме́ры про́тив него́.
7 Нам придётся/Мы должны́ бу́дем показа́ть на́ши паспорта́ в гости́нице.
8 Гали́на Бори́совна должна́ была́/Гали́на Бори́совна вы́нуждена была́/ Гали́не Бори́совне пришло́сь купи́ть но́вую маши́ну.
9 Ива́ну Бори́совичу не на́до бы́ло покупа́ть но́вую руба́шку.
10 Лев Никола́евич до́лжен был/вы́нужден был/Льву Никола́евичу пришло́сь написа́ть об усло́виях в Москве́.

p. 265 'Mustn't'

1 Вы не должны́ смотре́ть на отве́ты зара́нее.
2 Фёдор Миха́йлович не до́лжен был/Фёдору Миха́йловичу не сле́довало
   писа́ть о войне́.
3 Невозмо́жно бы́ло/Нельзя́ бы́ло не слы́шать му́зыку.
4 Мы не мо́жем не симпатизи́ровать ему́.
5 Э́того сле́дует ожида́ть.

p. 266 'Must' (inevitability)

1 Должно́ быть, они́ до́ма *or* Они́, должно́ быть, до́ма.
2 Должно́ быть, она́ вы́шла.
3 Конце́рт, должно́ быть, начался́.
4 Должно́ быть, вы о́чень хоти́те маши́ну.
5 Он, должно́ быть, идёт в библиоте́ку.

p. 267 'Put'

1 Кто поста́вил стул у окна́?
2 Почему́ ты кладёшь/вы кладёте пи́сьма на таре́лку?
3 Куда́ ты поста́вил(а)/вы поста́вили цветы́?
4 Я положу́ газе́ту на́ стол.
5 Она́ всегда́ ста́вит телефо́н на стул.

p. 268 'Quite'

1 Мне хо́чется е́хать в Сиби́рь.
2 Э́то была́ дово́льно/доста́точно но́вая маши́на *or*
   Э́то был дово́льно/доста́точно но́вый автомоби́ль.
3 Фильм был дово́льно/доста́точно интере́сный/интере́сным/интере́сен.
4 Она́ была́ совсе́м изнеможена́/изнурена́ *or* Она́ совсе́м переутоми́лась.
5 Нам дово́льно нра́вится но́вая кварти́ра.

p. 268 'Rather'

1 Я предпочёл/предпочла́ бы быть в Москве́.
2 Здесь дово́льно ти́хо.
3 Ни́на предпочла́ бы пое́хать в Я́лту.
4 Он немно́жко интересу́ется маши́нами/автомоби́лями.
5 Ты бы предпочёл/предпочла́ *or* Вы бы предпочли́ идти́ в теа́тр?

p. 269 'Remain'

1 Дверь оста́нется закры́той.
2 Дире́ктор оста́нется на рабо́те.
3 Остава́лась одна́ ле́кция.
4 Оста́лась одна́ ле́кция.
5 Остава́лось то́лько написа́ть одно́ письмо́.

p. 270 'Seem'

1 Ты, ка́жется, рабо́таешь/Вы, ка́жется, рабо́таете весь день.
2 Мы, ка́жется, рабо́тали весь день.

3 Каза́лось, ему́ понра́вилась/Ему́, каза́лось, понра́вилась карти́на.
4 Ка́жется, она́ ему́ ве́рит.
5 Они́, ка́жется, не слу́шают.
6 Каза́лось, он не понима́л фильм.
7 Ка́жется, мы прие́хали в Москву́.
8 Почему́ он всегда́ ка́жется таки́м расстро́енным?
9 Ка́жется, э́то отве́т.
10 Каза́лось, э́то была́ пе́рвая страни́ца рома́на.

p. 271 'Some'

1 Купи́ (не́сколько) яи́ц по доро́ге домо́й.
2 Я хочу́ бума́ги.
3 Не́которые счита́ли нас о́чень у́мными.
4 Не́сколько челове́к стоя́ло на мосту́.
5 Не́которые из мои́х друзе́й рабо́тают в Москве́.
6 Мы ви́дели не́сколько де́вушек в па́рке.
7 Мы ви́дели не́которых из де́вушек в па́рке.
8 Она́ нашла́ цветы́ на берегу́ реки́.
9 Он прие́хал с не́сколькими пи́сьмами от Бори́са.
10 В не́которых пи́сьмах бы́ли фотогра́фии.

p. 272 'Sorry'

1 Извини́(те) за шум!
2 Она́ прости́ла его́ за беста́ктность.
3 Нам бы́ло жаль де́вушку.
4 Ей бы́ло жаль молока́.
5 Они́ извиня́ются за беспоря́док.

p. 273 'Stay'

1 Я бу́ду жить неде́лю у мое́й сестры́.
2 Мы остана́вливались в ра́зных гости́ницах во Фра́нции.
3 Ты хо́чешь/Вы хоти́те останови́ться здесь? Ка́жется краси́во.
4 Ты хо́чешь/Вы хоти́те оста́ться здесь, пока́ я схожу́ за ключо́м?
5 Я бу́ду в библиоте́ке сего́дня у́тром.

p. 274 'Stop'

1 Переста́нь(те) разгова́ривать/Прекрати́(те) разгово́ры!
2 Не остана́вливай(те) авто́бус!
3 Она́ всегда́ перестаёт/броса́ет кури́ть, когда́ влюбля́ется.
4 Не прекраща́й(те) игра́ть! *or* Не прекраща́й(те) игру́!
5 Не меша́й(те) ему́ игра́ть!

p. 275 'Succeed'

1 Она́ успе́ла поза́втракать?
2 Нам обы́чно удава́лось пройти́ без биле́та.
3 Я обы́чно успева́ю на по́езд.

4 Никола́ю уда́стся измени́ть програ́мму.
5 Им, должно́ быть, ча́сто удаётся дозвони́ться.

p. 275 'Take'

1 Я пять часо́в покупа́л э́ту ва́нну.
2 Я беру́ э́ту ва́нну с собо́й. Я отвезу́ её в Ло́ндон.
3 Э́та ва́нна вмеща́ет двух челове́к.
4 Я приму́ ва́нну, когда́ я прие́ду в Ло́ндон.
5 Пото́м я пойду́ в теа́тр с друзья́ми.

p. 277 'Use'

1 Почему́ ты не воспо́льзуешься/вы не воспо́льзуетесь молотко́м?
2 Мне не разреша́ют по́льзоваться компью́тером.
3 Он ча́сто употребля́ет э́то выраже́ние.
4 Она́ воспо́льзуется им в свои́х це́лях.
5 Кто по́льзовался мои́м шампу́нем?

SUBJECT INDEX

INDEX OF RUSSIAN WORDS

The index lists only significant entries – the pages where you may find helpful information about the morphology or usage of the word, not where it merely features in an example.